AMERICAN HISTORY

myWorld
INTERACTIVE
Active Journal

SAVVAS
LEARNING COMPANY

ISBN-13: 978-0-328-96024-8
ISBN-10:   0-328-96024-1
14 2021

CONTENTS

CONTENTS

Topic 3
The Revolutionary Era (1750–1783)

Topic 4
A Constitution for the United States (1776–Present)

CONTENTS

Topic 5
The Early Republic (1789–1825)

Topic 6
The Age of Jackson and Westward Expansion
(1824–1860)

CONTENTS

Topic 7
Society and Culture Before the Civil War
(1820–1860)

Topic 8
Sectionalism and Civil War (1820–1865)

CONTENTS

Topic 9
The Reconstruction Era (1865–1877)

Topic 10
Industrial and Economic Growth (1865–1914)

CONTENTS

CONTENTS

Topic 12
Imperialism and World War I (1853–1919)

CONTENTS

Topic 16
A Global Superpower Facing Change (1975–2000)

Topic 17
Meeting New Challenges (1975–Present)

TOPIC 1

The Early Americas and European Exploration Preview

Essential Question How much does geography affect people's lives?

Before you begin this topic, think about the Essential Question by completing the following activities.

1. Name three geographical features and how they might influence human activity.

2. Preview the topic by skimming lesson titles, headings, and graphics. Then, place a check mark next to the human activities that are directly influenced by geography.

__Farming   __Trade   __Singing   __Culture

__Dancing   __Navigation   __Exploration   __Sports

Timeline Skills

As you read, write and/or draw at least three events from the topic. Draw a line from each event to its correct position on the timeline.

500   700

Map Skills

Using the map in your text, label the outline map with the regions listed. Then, draw lines to represent the migration of people into these regions based on the land-bridge theory and the coastal-route theory.

Eastern Woodlands	Great Plains	Southeast	Southwest
Arctic/Subarctic	Northwest Coast	California/Great Basin	

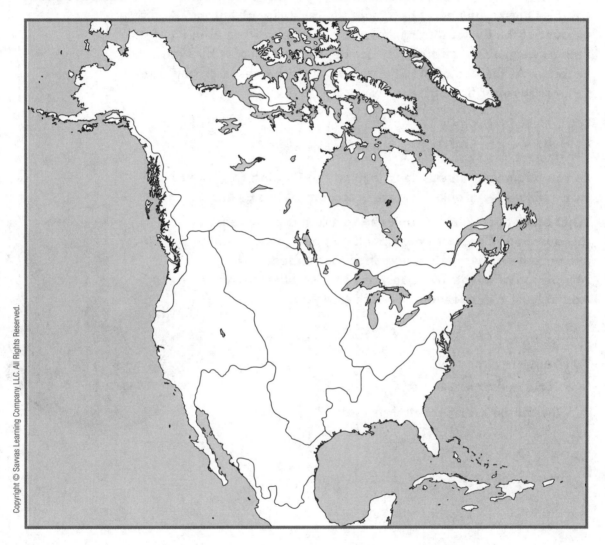

900   1100   1300   1500

Quest

Document-Based Writing Inquiry

The Easter Mutiny

On this Quest, you need to evaluate the reliability of Antonio Pigafetta's account of the Easter Mutiny. You will examine sources from Pigafetta's time as well as an interpretation of one of these sources by a modern historian. At the end of the Quest you will write a research paper that summarizes your findings.

1 Ask Questions (See Student Text, page 6)

As you begin your Quest, keep in mind the Guiding Question:
How reliable is Antonio Pigafetta's account of the Easter Mutiny?

What other questions do you need to ask in order to answer this question? Consider how a person's point of view can influence his or her writing and affect our understanding of a person or event. Two questions are filled in for you. Add at least two questions for each category.

Theme Purpose

Sample questions:

Why did the author write this document?

How did the author intend this document to be used?

Theme Author

Theme Audience

Theme Origin

Theme Bias or Perspective

Theme My Additional Questions

 INTERACTIVE

For extra help with Step 1, review the
21st Century Tutorial: **Ask Questions**.

Quest CONNECTIONS

2 Investigate

As you read about the early Americas and European exploration, collect five connections from the text to help you answer the Guiding Question. Three connections are already chosen for you.

Connect to Mansa Musa

Lesson 3 In-Text Primary Source *Catalan Atlas* (See Student Text, page 34)

Here's a connection! Look at the quote in your text from *Catalan Atlas*. How does this quote verify the information in Mansa Musa's biography?

What other type of primary source might verify Mansa Musa's biography?

Connect to Magellan's Biography

Lesson 4 5 Things to Know About Ferdinand Magellan
(See Student Text, page 43)

Here's another connection! What facts from Magellan's biography help you verify facts in Pigafetta's account?

What questions would you ask Pigafetta about his journey with Magellan if you could talk to him?

Connect to Christopher Columbus

Primary Source Christopher Columbus's Diary (See Student Text, page 47)

Do you believe Columbus's account of his journey?

Do the details he provides give credibility to his account?

It's Your Turn! **Find two more connections. Fill in the title of your connections, then answer the questions. Connections may be images, primary sources, maps, or text.**

Your Choice | Connect to

Location in text

What is the main idea of this connection?

How does this connection help verify related primary sources?

Your Choice | Connect to

Location in text

What is the main idea of this connection?

How does this connection help verify related primary sources?

③ Examine Primary Sources (See Student Text, page 48)

Examine the primary and secondary sources provided online or from your teacher. Fill in the chart to show how these sources provide further information about the Easter Mutiny. The first one is completed for you.

Source	What this source tells me about the Easter Mutiny . . .
Pigafetta's Account of the Easter Mutiny	Members of Magellan's crew rebelled against him but were stopped by Magellan.
Interpretation of a Modern Historian	
The Log of the Pilot of the *Trinidad*	
Report to King Charles from His Secretary Maximillianus Transylvanus	
Report of the Mutiny by a Portuguese Historian	

👆 INTERACTIVE

For extra help with Step 3, review the 21st Century Tutorial: **Analyze Primary and Secondary Sources**.

④ Write Your Essay (See Student Text, page 48)

Now it is time to put together all of the information you have gathered and use it to write your essay.

1. **Prepare to Write** You have collected connections and explored primary and secondary sources. This will help you understand how sources can be used to verify information in other sources. Look through your notes and choose the evidence you will use in your essay. Record your evidence and sources here.

Evidence and Sources

2. **Write a Draft** Using evidence from the clues you found and the documents you explored, write a draft of your response to the Guiding Question: **How reliable is Antonio Pigafetta's account of the Easter Mutiny?** Consider all the evidence and draw your own conclusions. In your essay, be sure to clearly state your view in a strong topic sentence, use logical organization, and support your conclusion with evidence and relevant facts.

3. **Share with a Partner** Exchange your draft with a partner. Tell your partner what you like about his or her draft and suggest any improvements.

4. **Finalize Your Essay** Revise your essay. Incorporate any feedback you received. Correct any grammatical or spelling errors. Use a word-processing program to type a final version.

5. **Reflect on the Quest** Think about your experience completing this topic's Quest. What did you learn about Magellan and his journeys? What did you learn about assessing the reliability of source documents? What questions do you still have about Magellan and his explorations? How will you answer them?

Reflections

Take Notes

Literacy Skills: Summarize Use what you have read to complete the table. Include at least one detail from the text for each subtopic listed. The first one has been completed for you. Then, use the information you have gathered to create a summary statement.

Mayas	Aztecs	Incas
Environment and Modifications • Grew enough corn to feed large cities • Made roads between the coast and the inland city-states	**Environment and Modifications**	**Environment and Modifications**
Government • Each city-state controlled a city and its surrounding area. • City-states battled for land, riches, and trade route access.	**Government**	**Government**
Religion and Culture • Priests performed ceremonies for harvests and battle victories. • Priests studied astronomy and mathematics and made calendars.	**Religion and Culture**	**Religion and Culture**

Summary Statement: How did farming affect early settlers of the Americas?

 INTERACTIVE

For extra help, review the 21st Century Tutorial: **Summarize**.

Practice Vocabulary

Use a Word Bank Choose one word from the word bank to fill in each blank. When you have finished, you will have a short summary of important ideas from the section.

Word Bank

terraces   quipus   causeways   city-state

civilizations   surplus   settlements   glaciers

.... caused sea levels to fall, uncovering

the land bridge between Siberia and present-day Alaska. This allowed

people to spread across the continent. Eventually people began to

farm, which led to permanent ...., In

time, growing a .... of food allowed the

first cities to form. These cities—along with an organized government,

different social classes, complex religion, and record keeping—gave

rise to new .... in the Americas. The first

were the Olmecs in what is now Mexico. They later influenced Mayas,

who developed the ...., a political unit that

controls a city and its surrounding land. Later, Aztecs formed a

civilization to the northwest with ....,

or raised dirt roads. Far to the south, Incas also maintained roads,

which teams of runners used to spread royal orders. They carried

..........................., cords with knots that stood for numbers,

thereby serving as message-recording devices. Incas used engineering in

advanced ways, including creating .... that

allowed them to farm mountainsides.

Take Notes

Literacy Skills: Classify and Categorize Use what you have read to complete the flowchart. Include at least one detail from the text for each subtopic listed. The first one has been started for you.

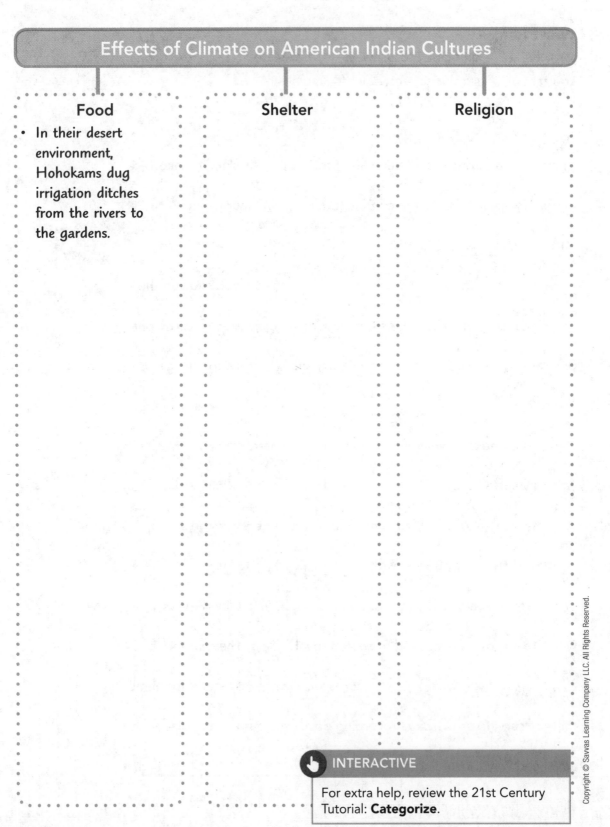

Effects of Climate on American Indian Cultures

Food

- In their desert environment, Hohokams dug irrigation ditches from the rivers to the gardens.

Shelter

Religion

INTERACTIVE

For extra help, review the 21st Century Tutorial: **Categorize**.

Practice Vocabulary

Use a Word Bank Choose one word from the word bank to fill in each blank. When you have finished, you will have a short summary of important ideas from the section.

Word Bank

culture	diffusion	tribe	potlatch	adobe
Pueblo	Iroquois League	clan	culture region	

A .... is the way of life of a group of

people. Most cultures have a distinct style or type of home, clothing,

economy, arts, and government. For example, the Anasazi, called

.... (meaning village) Indians by the Spanish,

built homes with ...., or sundried brick. A

.... is a large area where people share a lifestyle.

A .... is a community of people that shares common

customs, language, and rituals. Through ....,

the process of spreading ideas from one culture to another, skills, such as

farming, were exchanged. For example, you may have been to a potluck, or

a communal meal with food supplied by the people in attendance. A similar

even occurs in American Indian cultures of the Pacific Northwest during a

ceremonial dinner called a .... American Indian

families from this region host these dinners to improve social standing by

sharing food and gifts. An example of governmental unification is with

the Iroquis. A .... is a group of related families.

In the 1500s, the original five nations formed an alliance, known as the

........................, to end the frequent wars with each other.

Quick Activity Matching Game

Draw lines to match each American Indian culture in Column 1 with the corresponding fact about its climate, resources, or lifestyle in Column 2.

Column 1	Column 2
Hohokams	1. built large buildings with walls of stone and adobe
Anasazis	2. played games on ballcourts
Hopewells	3. were nomads who followed the buffalo
Inuits	4. used redwood trees to build houses and canoes
Yoruk	5. made earth mounds for religious ceremonies
Natchez	6. religious leaders prayed to kachinas for good harvests
Iroquois	7. women held political power, owned property, and did most of the farming
Sioux	8. used seal-oil lamps and made waterproof boots from seal skins
Pueblo	9. used calendars with 13 months named after foods they harvested and animals they hunted

Team Challenge! Create a matching game with sets of cards using the name of an American Indian culture on one card and the facts about its climate, resources, or lifestyle on the other. Play your game with a partner.

Take Notes

Literacy Skills: Summarize Use what you have read to complete the flowchart. Include at least one detail from the text for each subtopic listed. The first one has been completed for you. Then, use the information you have gathered to create a summary statement.

Effects of Increased Trade on Renaissance Leaders	Effects of Increased Trade on Renaissance Exploration	Effects of Increased Trade on Renaissance Scholars
• Trade brought new prosperity, which increased rulers' power. • In England and France, kings and queens worked to bring powerful feudal lords under their control. • In Spain and Portugal, Christian monarchs drove out Muslim rulers, who had governed there for centuries.		

Summary Statement: What was the impact of increased trade on the European Renaissance?

INTERACTIVE

For extra help, review the 21st Century Tutorial: **Summarize**.

Practice Vocabulary

Words in Context For each question below, write an answer that shows your understanding of the boldfaced key term.

1. In European **feudalism** in the Middle Ages, how was the role of lord defined in relation to a monarch?

2. What is a technological **innovation** that traveled from the Muslim world to Europe, and what benefit did it bring?

3. What trade routes became known as the **Silk Road**?

4. In what sense was **kinship** central to many ways of life in early Africa?

5. How did the invention of the **astrolabe** help sailors?

6. How did feudal life evolve around the **manor**?

7. During the **Crusades**, who were the Christians fighting against, and why were they fighting?

8. What was the **Renaissance**?

Take Notes

Literacy Skills: Identify Cause and Effect Use what you have read to complete the chart. Draw a line connecting each cause to its effect. The first one has been completed for you.

Cause	Effect
1. King Ferdinand and Queen Isabella financed Columbus's voyage west across the Atlantic to reach the East Indies.	Almost half the world's food crops come from plants that were first grown in the Americas.
2. Portuguese sailors pioneered new routes around Africa toward Asia in the late 1400s.	The monarchy of Spain paid for the cost of new exploration because it wanted the riches that might be discovered.
3. American Indians introduced Europeans to valuable produce.	Within 100 years, the Taino population was almost wiped out by European diseases and harsh conditions imposed by colonizers.
4. Europeans introduced domestic animals from Europe and Africa.	The crew of the *Niña*, *Pinta*, and *Santa Maria* changed course and approached land.
5. A flock of birds flew southwest over Columbus's ships.	American Indians learned to ride horses and to use them to carry heavy loads.

 INTERACTIVE

For extra help, review the 21st Century Tutorial: **Identify Cause and Effect**.

Practice Vocabulary

Word Map Study the word map for the word *colony*. Characteristics are words or phrases that relate to the word in the center of the word map. Non-characteristics are words and phrases not associated with the word. Use the blank word map to explore the meaning of the word *circumnavigate*. Then make word maps of your own for these words: *turning point* and *Columbian Exchange*.

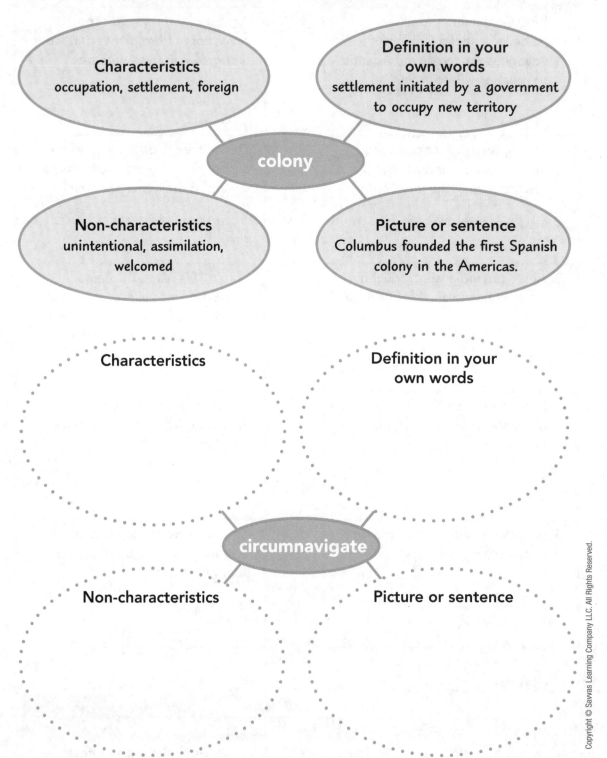

Characteristics
occupation, settlement, foreign

Definition in your own words
settlement initiated by a government to occupy new territory

colony

Non-characteristics
unintentional, assimilation, welcomed

Picture or sentence
Columbus founded the first Spanish colony in the Americas.

Characteristics

Definition in your own words

circumnavigate

Non-characteristics

Picture or sentence

Quick Activity Dinner Party

Plan a dinner party using items from the Columbian Exchange. Make a list of ingredients to include in the dinner. These ingredients must be foods that American Indians introduced to Europeans or that Europeans introduced to American Indians. Make another list of activities and conversation topics to entertain your guests. These must relate to the skills exchanged by Europeans and American Indians, and to the negative and positive impacts of the Columbian Exchange.

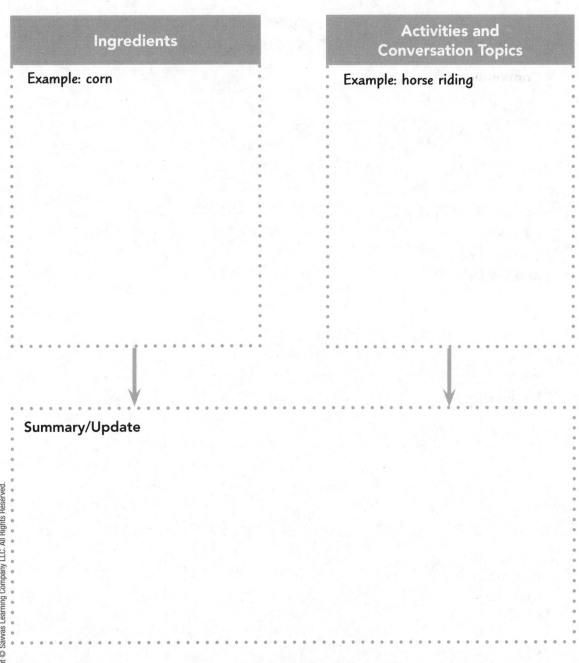

Ingredients	Activities and Conversation Topics
Example: corn	Example: horse riding

Summary/Update

Team Challenge! Write a summary/update about the results of your Columbian Exchange dinner party. Share your summary with a partner.

Writing Workshop Research Paper

As you read, build a response to this question: **How did a travel-related invention or improvement in the 1400s or 1500s affect exploration and trade during this time period?** The prompts below will help walk you through this process.

Lessons 1, 2, 3, and 4 Writing Tasks: Generate Ideas
(See Student Text, pages 13, 24, 38, and 46)

For each lesson, record details about the impact of travel-related inventions on the peoples of North America.

Lesson	Impact of Travel-Related Inventions on . . .
1. Communication	
2. Farming Technology and Trade	
3. Exploration	
4. Voyages of Columbus and Magellan	

Lesson 3 Writing Task: Develop a Clear Thesis (See Student Text, page 38)

Choose a travel-related invention or improvement that you learned about in this topic. You will write about your choice in your research paper. Based on your selection, write an introduction to your research paper in which you clearly state your thesis. Your thesis should address the question: How did a travel-related invention or improvement in the 1400s or 1500s affect exploration and trade during this time period?

Lesson 4 Writing Task: Find and Use Credible Sources
(See Student Text, page 46)

Identify three credible sources of information you could use to write your research paper. You will use this information to conduct research and to cite the evidence you collect from these sources.

Writing Task (See Student Text, page 49)

Using the thesis you wrote, answer the following question in a five-paragraph research paper: How did a travel-related invention or improvement in the 1400s or 1500s affect exploration and trade during this time period? As you write, be sure to support your ideas with evidence and cite sources. Use a word-processing program to produce and publish your research paper.

TOPIC 2

European Colonization of North America Preview

Essential Question Why do people move?

Before you begin this topic, think about the Essential Question by completing the following activities.

1. List three reasons why people in your community, or someone you know, may have moved.

2. Preview the topic by skimming lesson titles, headings, and graphics. Then, place a check mark next to the ideas that may have prompted Europeans to move to the Americas.

___ luxury   ___ glory and gold

___ make money trapping animals   ___ become a monk

___ conquest of land   ___ more say in government

___ study Indian languages   ___ search for a passage to the Far East

___ practice religion freely

Timeline Skills

As you read, write and/or draw at least three events from the topic. Draw a line from each event to its correct position on the timeline.

1500	1550	1600

Map Skills

Using the map in your text, label the outline map with the places listed.
Then, color the water blue and use other colors to shade the regions of
Spanish, French, and British territories.

Middle Plantation

Charles Town

Roanoke River

Baltimore

St. Augustine

Quebec

Savannah River

Philadelphia

New Amsterdam

Mississippi River

Plymouth

New Orleans

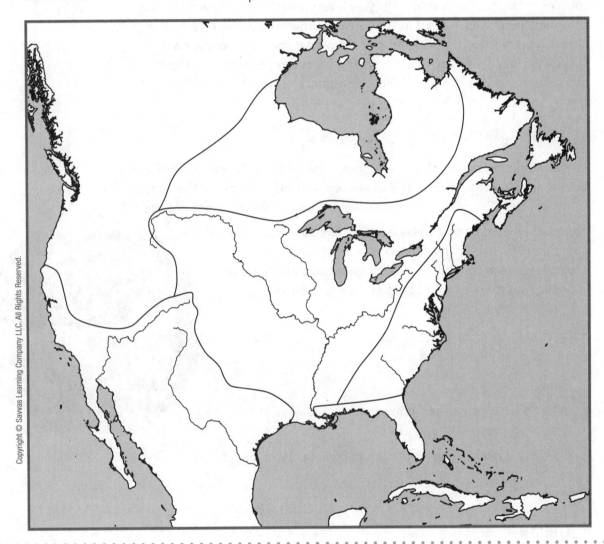

1650

1700

1750

25

European Colonization of North America

Quest

Project-Based Learning Inquiry

Examining the Colonial Environment

On this Quest, you are part of a group in England that must decide where to become colonists in the Americas. You will examine sources from this period to help you learn more about how previous colonists lived and thrived in their environments. At the end of the Quest, you will create a digital portfolio that includes maps, charts, and other visuals so the group can see how the physical environment has influenced the economy and population across the colonies.

① Ask Questions (See Student Text, page 54)

As you begin your Quest, keep in mind the Guiding Question: **How did the environment influence the economy and population of the British colonies?** Also, consider the Essential Question: **Why do people move?**

What other questions do you need to ask to answer these questions? Consider the following aspects of the physical environments in the colonies. Two questions are filled in for you. Add at least two questions in each category.

Theme Water and Natural Resources

Sample questions:

What role did water and other natural resources play in the locations of colonial settlements?

How did water influence the ease and frequency of trade?

Theme Farming, Agriculture, and Industry

Theme Society, Arts, Ideas, and Education

Theme Government and Warfare

Theme My Additional Questions

INTERACTIVE

For extra help with Step 1, review the
21st Century Tutorial: **Ask Questions**.

Quest CONNECTIONS

2 Investigate

As you read about the British colonies, collect five connections from your text to help you answer the Guiding Question and understand how the colonists made a living. Three connections are already chosen for you.

Connect to the Environment

Lesson 3 How Did People Live in the Towns of New England?
(See Student Text, page 88)

Here's a connection! Read the section titled The Environment Influences Economic Activity. In what ways was the environment helpful to people looking to make a living?

In what ways was the environment a challenge?

Connect to the Middle Colonies

Lesson 4 Daily Life in the Middle Colonies (See Student Text, page 96)

Here's another connection! The Middle Colonies were extremely successful. How was the environment there more favorable than in New England?

What impact did the environment have on the economy and population?

Connect to Tidewater and Backcountry

Lesson 5 How Did Two Regions Develop Differently?
(See Student Text, page 106)

What does this connection tell you about how a worker would benefit from living in the Tidewater?

How would a worker benefit from living in the backcountry?

It's Your Turn! **Find two more connections. Fill in the title of your connections, then answer the questions. Connections may be images, primary sources, maps, or text.**

Your Choice | Connect to

Location in text

What is the main idea of this connection?

What does this tell you about how the environment influenced the economy and population of the colonies?

Your Choice | Connect to

Location in text

What is the main idea of this connection?

What does this tell you about how the environment influenced the economy and population of the colonies?

③ Conduct Research (See Student Text, page 126)

You will need to conduct research on maps, graphs, charts, and/or models that describe the physical environment, economic activities, and population distribution of the colonies. Use the chart below to organize your sources and understand your data. Be sure to include source citations so that you can find them again.

Source Citation	Description

INTERACTIVE

For extra help with Step 3, review the 21st Century Tutorials: **Read Charts, Graphs, and Tables**; **Read Physical Maps**; and **Read Special-Purpose Maps**.

Quest FINDINGS

4 Create a Digital Portfolio (See Student Text, page 126)

Now it's time to put together all of the information you have gathered and use it to create a digital portfolio so your group can make informed decisions.

1. **Prepare to Write** You have collected connections and explored primary and secondary sources that contain maps, graphs, charts, and/or models that describe the British colonies' geographical features, natural resources, and industry. Use the chart to synthesize your information by region. Then, create your digital portfolio based on your teacher's instructions.

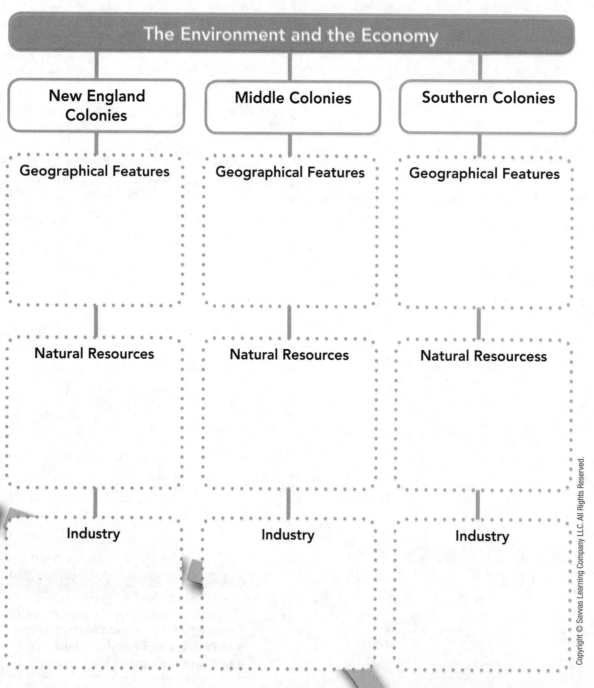

2. **Write a Recommendation** In your introduction paragraph, address the relationship between the geography, economy, and population distribution for each region. For focus, use the Guiding Question, the Essential Question, and your digital portfolio. In the body, outline the portfolio contents and the main points each piece conveys. Conclude with recommendations for settlement location and the role each person in the settlement will assume.

3. **Make Group Decisions** Each team member will make a five-minute portfolio presentation. As a group, compare cover letters to identify similarities and differences. Develop consensus on as many issues as possible. Determine the order of your presentation, ensuring that each person is presenting some element of the digital portfolio. As a group, end your presentation with your team's recommendations, including differing viewpoints team members may have on issues that didn't have consensus.

4. **Reflect on the Quest** Think about your experience completing this topic's Quest. What did you learn about the environment and its effects on the British colonies? What questions do you still have? How will you answer them?

Reflections

INTERACTIVE

For extra help with Step 4, review the 21st Century Tutorials: **Identify Trends**, **Analyze Data and Models**, and **Support Ideas with Evidence**.

Take Notes

Literacy Skills: Summarize Use what you have read to complete the table. Write two or three sentences that summarize each major idea. Then, combine them to form a summary of the chapter. The first one has been completed for you.

Conquistadors and Exploration	Colonization and Settlement of New Spain	Transatlantic Slave Trade
The Spanish wanted gold and glory, and explorers were required to send one-fifth of their treasure back to Spain. Some of the reasons they conquered the Aztecs and Incas included superior weapons, disease, and fighting between the two empires.		

Summary

INTERACTIVE

For extra help, review the 21st Century Tutorial: **Summarize**.

Practice Vocabulary

Sentence Builder Finish the sentences below with a key term from this section. You may have to change the form of the words to complete the sentences.

Word Bank

conquistador   pueblo   presidio   mission

peninsular   Creole   mestizo

1. Settlements made up of people whose goal is to convert others to Christianity are called

   ....

2. People of mixed Spanish and Indian background are known as

   ....

3. People who were born in Spain and were at the top of the social ladder in the Indies were known as

   ....

4. A Spanish word for *conqueror* is

   ....

5. Those born in America to parents of Spanish origin are known as

   ....

6. The towns in Spanish settlements were called

   ....

7. Soldiers lived in forts with thick, high walls called

   ....

Take Notes

Literacy Skills: Sequence Use what you have read to complete the chart. Sequence three to five events that led up to the formal establishment of colonies for the French, Dutch, and English settlers. The first event has been entered for you.

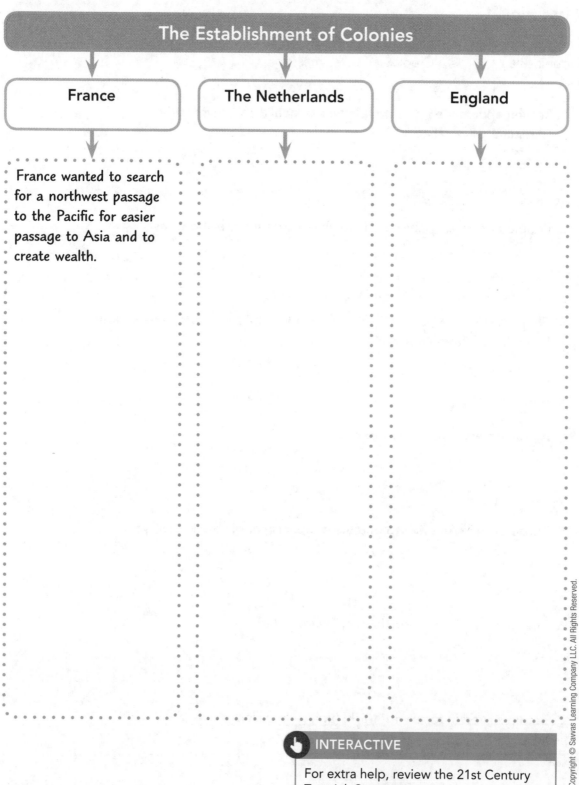

The Establishment of Colonies

France

France wanted to search for a northwest passage to the Pacific for easier passage to Asia and to create wealth.

The Netherlands

England

👆 **INTERACTIVE**

For extra help, review the 21st Century Tutorial: **Sequence**.

Practice Vocabulary

For each question below, write an answer that shows your understanding of the boldfaced key term.

1. Which country established a **representative government** in Virginia, and what does it mean to have one?

2. What are **alliances**, and why were they important for the colonists?

3. What was the **northwest passage**?

4. What are **charters**, and how did they influence the establishment of colonies?

5. Who were the **coureurs de bois**?

6. What happened during **Bacon's Rebellion**, and what were the consequences?

7. What is a **burgess**, and what is its significance?

Take Notes

Literacy Skills: Compare and Contrast Use what you have read to complete the chart. Compare and contrast the formation of government in the New England colonies. Include in your notes how religion influenced the development and changes in each colony. The first one has been completed for you.

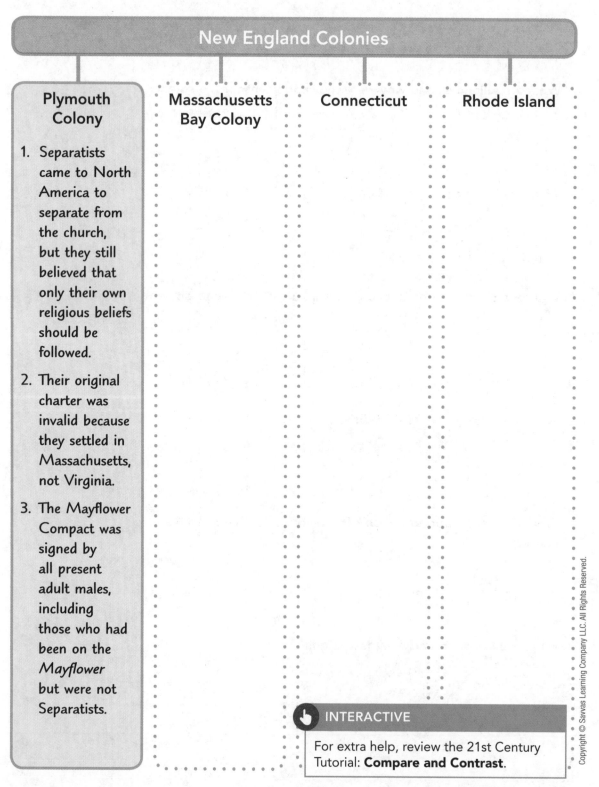

New England Colonies

Plymouth Colony

1. Separatists came to North America to separate from the church, but they still believed that only their own religious beliefs should be followed.

2. Their original charter was invalid because they settled in Massachusetts, not Virginia.

3. The Mayflower Compact was signed by all present adult males, including those who had been on the *Mayflower* but were not Separatists.

Massachusetts Bay Colony

Connecticut

Rhode Island

INTERACTIVE

For extra help, review the 21st Century Tutorial: **Compare and Contrast**.

Practice Vocabulary

True or False? Decide whether each statement below is true or false. Circle T or F, and then explain your answer. Be sure to include the underlined vocabulary word in your explanation. The first one is done for you.

1. **T / F** The <u>Pilgrims</u> were Separatists who founded the colony at Plymouth.
   True; The <u>Pilgrims</u> wanted to separate from the Church of England and won a charter to set up a colony in northern Virginia.

2. **T / F** <u>Religious tolerance</u> is a willingness to let others practice their own beliefs.

3. **T / F** The <u>Mayflower Compact</u> was a type of bag brought onto the *Mayflower* to keep track of personal belongings.

4. **T / F** At <u>town meetings</u> colonists discussed and voted on issues that were important to their communities.

5. **T / F** The <u>General Court</u> was a court designed to solve problems in Rhode Island.

6. **T / F** <u>Puritans</u> did not want to separate entirely from the Church of England. They wanted to simplify worship by eliminating practices inherited from the Roman Catholic Church.

7. **T / F** <u>Persecution</u> is when people are honored because of their religious beliefs.

Quick Activity Write a Letter

Imagine that you are a Pilgrim preparing to get on the *Mayflower*. Write a letter persuading other Separatists to join you on the journey across the Atlantic Ocean.

Team Challenge! In small groups, share your letters. Who do you think was more persuasive? What do you think made the arguments stronger?

Take Notes

Literacy Skills: Analyze Text Structure Use what you have read to complete the table. For each main idea, provide two or three supporting details. The first one has been completed for you.

The Development of the Middle Colonies	
Main Idea	**Supporting Details**
New Netherland became New York.	England wanted New Amsterdam for themselves. Dutch governor Peter Stuyvesant was unpopular, and the colonists refused to help him, so the English won without a fight. King Charles II of England gave New Netherland to his brother, the Duke of York, and it was renamed New York.
New Jersey formed out of New York and became a royal colony.	
Pennsylvania was established as a model of fairness.	
The middle colonies thrived.	

INTERACTIVE

For extra help, review the 21st Century Tutorial: **Support Ideas with Evidence.**

Practice Vocabulary

Matching Logic Using your knowledge of the underlined vocabulary words, draw a line from each sentence in Column 1 to match it with the sentence in Column 2 to which it logically belongs.

Column 1	Column 2
1. <u>Quakers</u> were Protestant reformers who fled persecution in England.	Direct rule from the English monarch tended to be harsh.
2. The Duke of York established New Jersey as a <u>proprietary colony</u>.	They exported so much grain that they became known as the Breadbasket Colonies.
3. The middle colonies thrived largely on <u>cash crops</u>.	They believed that all people were equal and rejected all war.
4. The <u>Pennsylvania Dutch</u> got their name because people could not pronounce the word *Deutsch*.	The king gave some loyal men the land in exchange for yearly payment.
5. New Jersey became a <u>royal colony</u>.	They included the Amish and Mennonites, who liked the idea of people of different religions living peacefully together.

Take Notes

Literacy Skills: Classify and Categorize Use what you have read to complete the charts. Categorize two to three details from each important element of life in the regions of the Tidewater and the backcountry. Examine how the two regions developed differently. The first detail has been completed for you.

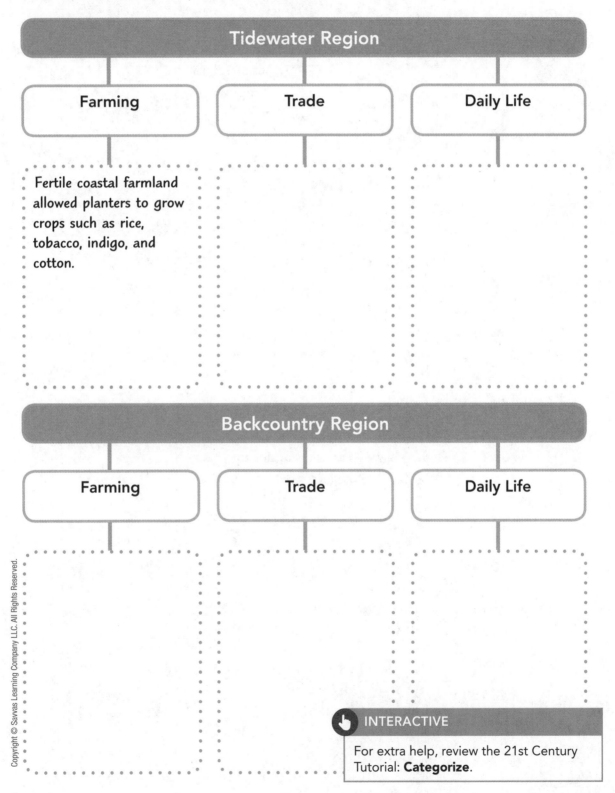

Tidewater Region

Farming	Trade	Daily Life
Fertile coastal farmland allowed planters to grow crops such as rice, tobacco, indigo, and cotton.		

Backcountry Region

Farming	Trade	Daily Life

INTERACTIVE

For extra help, review the 21st Century Tutorial: **Categorize**.

Practice Vocabulary

Vocabulary Quiz Show Some quiz shows ask a question and expect the contestant to give the answer. In other shows, the contestant is given an answer and must supply the question. If the blank is in the Question column, write the question that would result in the answer in the Answer column. If the question is supplied, write the answer.

Question	Answer
1.	1. Act of Toleration
2.	2. slave codes
3. What is the name of the plant used to make blue dye?	3.
4. What is the belief that one race is superior to another?	4.
5.	5. debtor

Take Notes

Literacy Skills: Summarize Use what you have read to complete the table. Provide details about each aspect of colonial life. Then, use these details to summarize this lesson. The first one has been started for you.

Structure	Arts and Education	Religion and Ideas
Distinct social classes included gentry, middle class, lower class, and enslaved.		

Summary

INTERACTIVE

For extra help, review the 21st Century Tutorial: **Summarize**.

Practice Vocabulary

Sentence Revision Revise each sentence so that the underlined vocabulary word is used logically. Be sure not to change the vocabulary word. The first one is done for you.

1. During the <u>Great Awakening</u>, many colonists totally gave up religion.
   During the <u>Great Awakening</u>, many colonists questioned their religion and changed their beliefs.

2. The <u>Enlightenment</u> was a movement to reject all forms of religion.

3. The <u>Gullah</u> language emerged as a combination of English and Dutch.

4. <u>Libel</u> is when you say something that is true that can damage a person's reputation.

5. <u>Dame schools</u> were institutions where girls could go to live and study.

6. The <u>gentry</u> class included tradespeople and represented the majority of the population.

7. The <u>middle class</u> consisted of people who agreed to work without wages in exchange for passage across the ocean.

8. Sometimes a boy would become an <u>apprentice</u> so he could remain in school his whole life.

Quick Activity Newspaper Headlines

With a partner or small group, imagine that you are preparing the front page of a newspaper in one of the colonies. Write three headlines that you think would represent the biggest stories of the day.

Team Challenge! With your partner(s), select one of your headlines and create an illustration that would go with it. Then, post your illustration and headline to the class board.

Featured Illustration

Take Notes

Literacy Skills: Draw Conclusions Use what you have read to complete the chart. Examine aspects of colonial trade and colonial foundations of government, and record each topic's details. Draw conclusions about how both led to a push for colonial independence. The first detail has been completed for you.

Trade and the English Colonies	Foundations of Government
England wanted tight control over trade with the colonies so that England would profit the most.	

Conclusions

INTERACTIVE

For extra help, review the 21st Century Tutorial: **Draw Conclusions**.

Practice Vocabulary

Use a Word Bank Choose one word from the word bank to fill in each blank. When you have finished, you will have a short summary of important ideas from the section.

Word Bank

Yankees	Glorious Revolution	legislature	English Bill of Rights
mercantilism	Navigation Acts	export	triangular trade
import	bill of rights		

The British believed strongly in the idea of ....

They also believed that countries should ....

more goods than they .... to make

a profit. England wanted all the profits of its colonies, so the

.... was passed so that the colonies could

only trade with England. Merchants from New England, nicknamed

.... , dominated colonial trade. One trade

route known as the .... had three points

of contact: New England, West Africa, and the West Indies. As the

colonies started to govern themselves more, elements of government

from England became more important. Many colonies established a

.... , or a representative assembly. In the 1680s,

the .... in England resulted in the dethroning

of King James II. Soon after, the .... was

signed. A .... is a list of freedoms that

the government promises to protect. All of these developments greatly

influenced how the colonies ultimately established a new government.

Writing Workshop Narrative Essay

As you read, build a response to this prompt: **Write an essay from the perspective of a newly arrived settler in the thirteen colonies.** The prompts below will help walk you through the process.

Lessons 1 and 2: Introduce Characters (See Student Text, pages 64 and 77)

Imagine you are a colonist living in North America. Fill in the first row of the chart with your name, your role in society, and two or three sentences describing who you are and what your life is like. Use details from the text. Fill in the second and third rows of the chart for two people your character interacts with. Explain what these people do for a living and how they know your character. You will use this information for a narrative essay you will write at the end of this topic.

Characters	
Name and Role	**Description**

Lesson 3: Establish Setting (See Student Text, page 89)

Describe the setting where your character lives in the colonies. Incorporate details from the topic.

Lessons 4 and 5: Organize Sequence of Events
(See Student Text, pages 99 and 109)

Make an ordered list to show what will happen to your character in your essay.

Lessons 6 and 7: Use Narrative Techniques, Descriptive Details, and Sensory Language (See Student Text, pages 120 and 125)

Brainstorm and fill in the table with other writing elements you may use in your essay.

Narrative Techniques	Descriptive Details	Sensory Language

Writing Task (See Student Text, page 127)

Imagine that you are a newly arrived colonist. Use the notes you made to write a narrative essay, from the perspective of a newly arrived settler in the thirteen colonies, in which you describe daily life. Give a detailed account about who you are, who you might interact with, and what challenges you face.

The Revolutionary Era Preview

Essential Question When is war justified?

Before you begin this topic, think about the Essential Question by answering the following questions.

1. What are good reasons for going to war? Put a check mark next to the reasons that you think would prompt a justifiable war.

___ Too many taxes

___ No voice in government

___ Government cuts off trade with the world

___ Government punishes illegal acts of civil disobedience

___ Government keeps soldiers among the people in times of peace

___ Government forces people to house soldiers

___ Government officers inspect the cargoes of ships for no reason

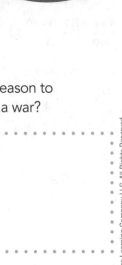

2. Look at the items you checked. Is any one, by itself, a good enough reason to go to war? Or would it take more than one of these reasons to justify a war?

Timeline Skills

As you read, write and/or draw at least three events from the topic. Draw a line from each event to its correct position on the timeline.

1750	1760	1770

Map Skills

Using maps throughout the topic, label the outline map with the places listed. Then color in the territory claimed by Britain and Spain.

New Hampshire	Massachusetts	New York	Connecticut
Rhode Island	New Jersey	Pennsylvania	Delaware
Maryland	Virginia	North Carolina	South Carolina
Georgia			

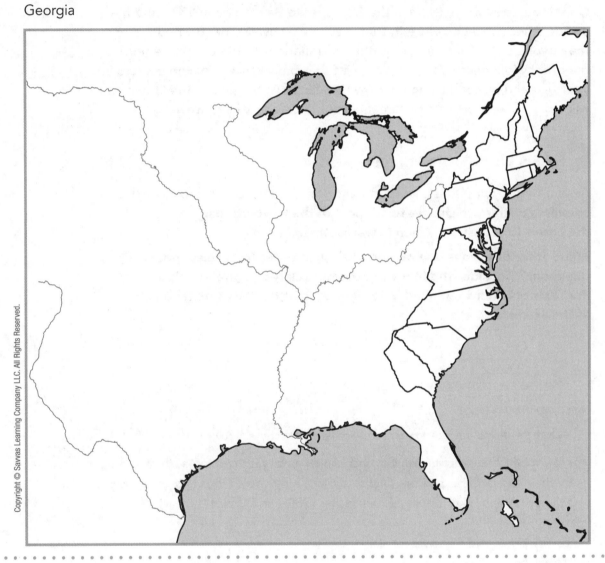

1780

1790

Quest
Project-Based Learning Inquiry

Choosing Sides

On this Quest, you are living in the Chesapeake Bay region in 1776 and must decide whether to become a Patriot, become a Loyalist, or stay neutral in the Revolutionary War. You will gather information about how the region's geography influenced people's views on the conflict by examining sources in your text and by conducting your own research. At the end of the Quest you will write a blog post that documents your decision-making process.

1 Ask Questions (See Student Text, page 132)

As you begin your Quest, keep in mind the Guiding Question: **How did colonists decide which side to support in the Revolutionary War?** and the Essential Question: **When is war justified?**

What other questions do you need to ask in order to answer these questions? Consider the following themes related to the Revolutionary Era. Two questions are filled in for you. Add at least two questions for each category.

Theme Historical Factors

Sample questions:

What problems did the French and Indian War cause between Britain and its colonies?

How might the colonists' belief in their rights as English citizens, such as those protected by the Magna Carta and the English Bill of Rights, have influenced their views on the Stamp Act and other British actions in the 1760s and 1770s?

Theme Society and Demographics

Theme Geography and Economy

Theme Land and the Proclamation of 1763

Theme Government and Laws

Theme My Additional Questions

INTERACTIVE

For extra help with Step 1, review the
21st Century Tutorial: **Ask Questions**.

Quest CONNECTIONS

2 Investigate

As you read about the Revolutionary Era, collect five connections from your text to help you answer the Guiding Question. Three connections are already chosen for you.

Connect to Chesapeake Region Trade

Lesson 2 Why Did the Stamp Act Anger Colonists? (See Student Text, page 146)

Here's a connection! Look at the Chesapeake region trade map in your text. Which colonies were in the Chesapeake region? In what way was Britain involved in the economy of the region? What does this map tell you about the importance of trade to the Chesapeake region?

What does this map tell you about why British policies that restricted trade might have angered the people of Chesapeake Bay?

Connect to Thomas Paine's Ideas

Lesson 4 What Did Thomas Paine Say in *Common Sense*?
(See Student Text, page 167)

Here's another connection! Thomas Paine was a British-born writer who lived in Philadelphia and tried to encourage colonists to resist the British government and King George III. What does the excerpt from his writing say about the importance of kings compared to ordinary, honest men?

How do you think colonists might have reacted to this argument?

Connect to *Common Sense*

Primary Source Thomas Paine, *Common Sense*
(See Student Text, page 177)

What arguments does this connection offer to those who were deciding whether to support the Patriots or Britain? Thomas Paine's pamphlet was distributed throughout the colonies. Was he a Patriot or a Loyalist? What does Paine have to say to those who felt an obligation to the king?

According to the essay, why did Britain offer help and protection to the colonies?

It's Your Turn! **Find two more connections. Fill in the title of your connections, then answer the questions. Connections may be images, primary sources, maps, or text.**

Your Choice | Connect to

Location in text

What is the main idea of this connection?

What does it tell you about how the colonists decided which side to support during the Revolutionary War?

Your Choice | Connect to

Location in text

What is the main idea of this connection?

What does it tell you about how the colonists decided which side to support during the Revolutionary War?

③ Conduct Research (See Student Text, page 190)

Form teams based on your teacher's instructions. Meet to decide who will create each segment of your blog. In the chart below, record which team member will perform which task.

You will research further only the segment that you are responsible for. Use the ideas in the connections to further explore the subject you have been assigned. Pick who or what you will write about, and find more sources about that subject.

Be sure to find valid sources, and take good notes so you can properly cite your sources. Record key information about your area of research here.

Team Member	Segment	Specific Topic of Segment
Historical Factors		
Society and Demographics		
Geography and Economy		

👆 INTERACTIVE

For extra help with Step 3, review the 21st Century Tutorials: **Work in Teams, Search for Information on the Internet,** and **Avoid Plagiarism**.

**FINDINGS**

4 Create Your Blog (See Student Text, page 190)

Now it's time to put together all the information you have gathered and use it to write your segment of the blog.

1. **Prepare to Write** You have collected connections and explored primary and secondary sources that tell you about the Chesapeake Bay region during colonial times. Look through your notes and decide which facts would help you decide whether to be a Patriot, Loyalist, or neutral colonist. Record them here.

2. **Write a Draft** Decide as a team which side of the war you will support. Then write a draft of your segment of the blog, explaining how your assigned theme affected your team's decision. Include any maps or images that might help illustrate your position. Be sure to include evidence that you have gathered and citations for the evidence used.

3. **Share with a Partner** Once you have finished your draft, ask one of your team members to read your draft and provide comments on the clarity and flow of the information. Revise the segment based on his or her comments, and comment on his or her segment, if possible.

4. **Put Together Your Blog** Once all team members have written and revised their segments, it's time to put them together. As a team, discuss how you will organize your information. Be sure to write smooth transitions from one segment to the next and finish with a strong conclusion.

5. **Present Your Blog** Present your completed blog to your classmates as a group. Listen to the other teams' blogs, and take notes on the information they shared using a separate sheet of paper.

6. **Reflect on the Quest** After all the presentations, discuss your thoughts on your blog and the other blogs. Reflect on the project and list what you might do differently next time so the teamwork goes more smoothly.

Reflections

 INTERACTIVE

For extra help with Step 4, review the 21st Century Tutorial: **Give an Effective Presentation**.

Take Notes

Literacy Skills: Sequence Use what you have read to complete the flow charts. Each box contains a specific event, and the boxes are placed in the order in which events happened. The first one has been completed for you.

George Washington and the French and Indian War

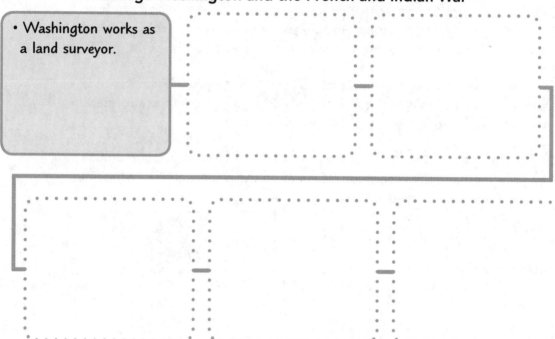

- Washington works as a land surveyor.

The French and Indian War from 1757 to 1763

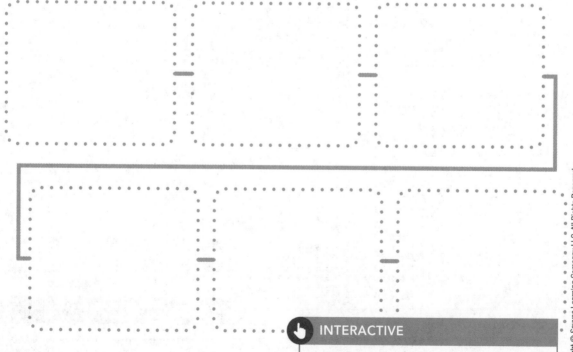

👆 **INTERACTIVE**

For extra help, review the 21st Century Tutorial: **Sequence**.

Practice Vocabulary

Word Map Study the word map for the term *French and Indian War*. Characteristics are words or phrases that relate to the word or words in the center of the word map. Non-characteristics are words and phrases not associated with the word or words. Use the blank word map to explore the meaning of the term *Treaty of Paris*. Then make word maps of your own for these terms: *ally* and *Albany Plan of Union*.

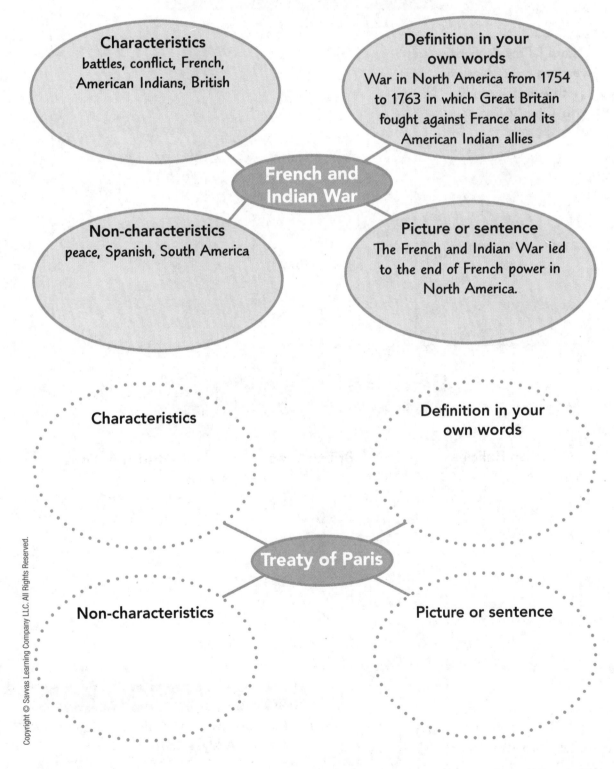

Characteristics
battles, conflict, French, American Indians, British

Definition in your own words
War in North America from 1754 to 1763 in which Great Britain fought against France and its American Indian allies

French and Indian War

Non-characteristics
peace, Spanish, South America

Picture or sentence
The French and Indian War led to the end of French power in North America.

Characteristics

Definition in your own words

Treaty of Paris

Non-characteristics

Picture or sentence

Take Notes

Literacy Skills: Identify Cause and Effect Use what you have read to complete the charts. The top box contains the effect and the boxes below contain the causes. The first one has been completed for you.

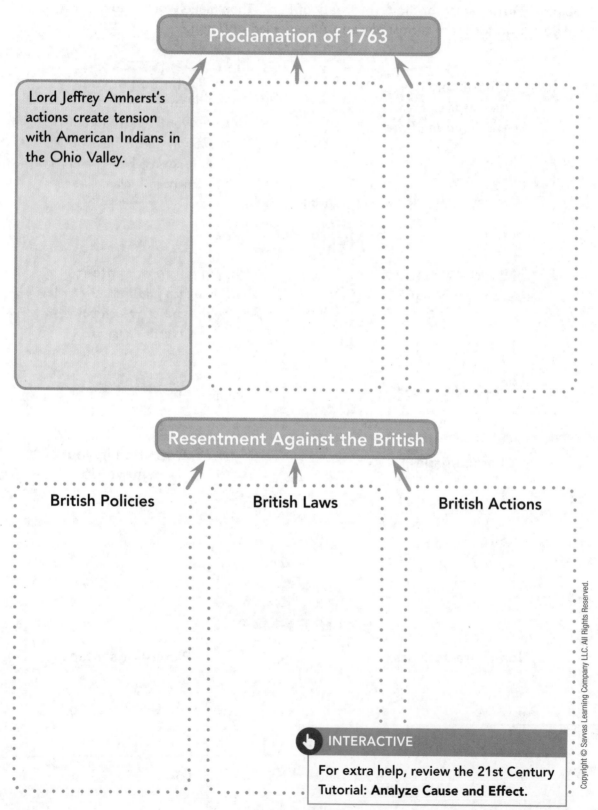

Proclamation of 1763

Lord Jeffrey Amherst's actions create tension with American Indians in the Ohio Valley.

Resentment Against the British

British Policies

British Laws

British Actions

INTERACTIVE

For extra help, review the 21st Century Tutorial: **Analyze Cause and Effect.**

Practice Vocabulary

Sentence Builder Finish the sentences below with a vocabulary term from this section. You may have to change the form of the words to complete the sentences.

Word Bank

petition   boycott   repeal

writ of assistance   committee of correspondence

1. A formal written request signed by a group of people is called a

2. Parliament cancelled the Stamp Act, which means that the act was

3. Legal documents that allowed British customs officers to inspect a ship's cargo without giving a reason were called

4. When the colonists refused to buy British tea, they were

                                  the tea.

5. Colonists who joined letter-writing campaigns to protest British policies were members of a

Quick Activity Make a Timeline

With a partner or small group, examine this painting of George Washington during the Battle of Monongahela during the French and Indian War.

What does this portrayal of George Washington tell you about how he was viewed? How did the French and Indian War lead to conflicts and actions that contributed to the start of the American Revolution?

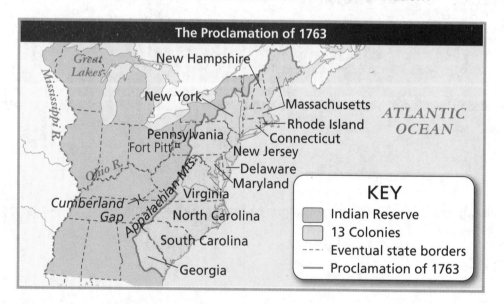

Team Challenge! How does this map relate to the causes of the American Revolution? Create a timeline of major events and ideas that led to the American Revolution, such as the ones depicted in these images. Add events and ideas as you read and explain the significance of each. Add some images to help illustrate your timeline.

Take Notes

Literacy Skills: Summarize Summarize the content of the main headings in this lesson using the tables on this page. As you work, pay special attention to the subheadings in the reading. The first main idea has been completed for you.

The Boston Tea Party	How Did King George III Strike Back at Boston?	The Battles of Lexington and Concord
Main Idea: Colonists protest the Tea Act.	**Main Idea:**	**Main Idea:**
Details: Parliament kept the tax on tea when it repealed all other taxes with the Townsend Act. The Tea Act of 1773 cut out American merchants from the tea trade. Americans boycotted tea and drank coffee.	**Details:**	**Details:**

The Fighting Continues	Opposing Sides at War
Main Idea:	Main Idea:
Details:	Details:

INTERACTIVE

For extra help, review the 21st Century Tutorial: **Summarize**.

Practice Vocabulary

Vocabulary Quiz Show Some quiz shows ask a question and expect the contestant to give the answer. In other shows, the contestant is given an answer and must supply the question. If the blank is in the Question column, write the question that would result in the answer in the Answer column. If the question is supplied, write the answer.

Question

1. What is the name for colonial volunteers who were ready to fight at any time?

2.

3.

4.

5. What is the term for an army of citizens who serve as soldiers during an emergency?

Answer

1.

2. Loyalists

3. civil disobedience

4. Patriots

5.

Take Notes

Literacy Skills: Use Evidence Use what you have read to complete the concept webs. Enter evidence in the outer circles that supports the main idea in the center circle. The first circle has been filled in for you.

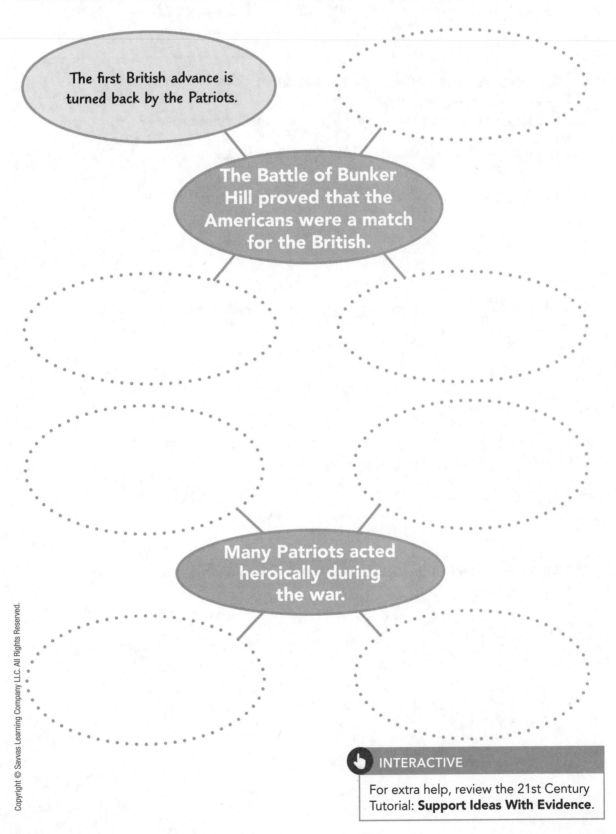

The first British advance is turned back by the Patriots.

The Battle of Bunker Hill proved that the Americans were a match for the British.

Many Patriots acted heroically during the war.

● INTERACTIVE

For extra help, review the 21st Century Tutorial: **Support Ideas With Evidence**.

Practice Vocabulary

True or False? Decide whether each statement below is true or false. Circle T or F, and then explain your answer. Be sure to include the underlined vocabulary word or words in your explanation. The first one is done for you.

1. **T / F** <u>Unalienable rights</u> are rights that cannot be claimed by citizens and can only be granted by governments.
   False; <u>Unalienable rights</u> are rights that governments cannot take away from citizens.

2. **T / F** A <u>traitor</u> is a person who fights for his or her country.

3. **T / F** King George III used <u>mercenaries</u> from Germany to help fight the colonists.

4. **T / F** The British used a <u>blockade</u> of colonial ports to help trade move smoothly between the colonies and Britain.

5. **T / F** The <u>preamble</u> of the Declaration of Independence declares that "all men are created equal."

6. **T / F** <u>Natural rights</u> are those that belong to all kings and queens from birth.

Quick Activity Edit the Declaration

Thomas Jefferson wrote the first draft of the Declaration of Independence in June 1776. Afterward, he made some revisions to the document himself, and Benjamin Franklin and John Adams also made some changes. When the Declaration was presented to the Second Continental Congress, still other changes were made.

Here is the original version of Thomas Jefferson's Preamble to the Declaration.

Did you know?

After the 1941 bombing of Pearl Harbor, the Declaration was placed in a padlocked bronze container, guarded by Secret Service agents, and temporarily moved from the National Archives to Fort Knox.

> We hold these truths to be sacred & undeniable; that all men are created equal & independent, that from that equal creation they derive rights inherent & inalienable, among which are the preservation of life, & liberty, & the pursuit of happiness. . . .

Working in pairs, one partner should write the original version of the Preamble on a piece of paper. The other should write any phrases from the final version of the Preamble (below) that differ from this original version on sticky notes. For example, you will have one sticky note that reads *self-evident*. Also use blank sticky notes to "cross out" words. Work together to use your sticky notes to change the original Preamble until it reads as the final version does.

> We hold these Truths to be self-evident, that all Men are created equal, that they are endowed by their Creator with certain unalienable Rights, that among these are Life, Liberty, and the Pursuit of Happiness.

Team Challenge! Work with your partner to answer this question: Why were these changes made to the Preamble? Give a possible reason for each change that was made.

Take Notes

Literacy Skills: Sequence Use what you have read to complete the timeline. Look for key events that fall within the dates on the timeline as you read. Add those events to the timeline by entering the event in one of the spaces provided and then connecting the event to the appropriate place on the timeline. The first one has been completed for you.

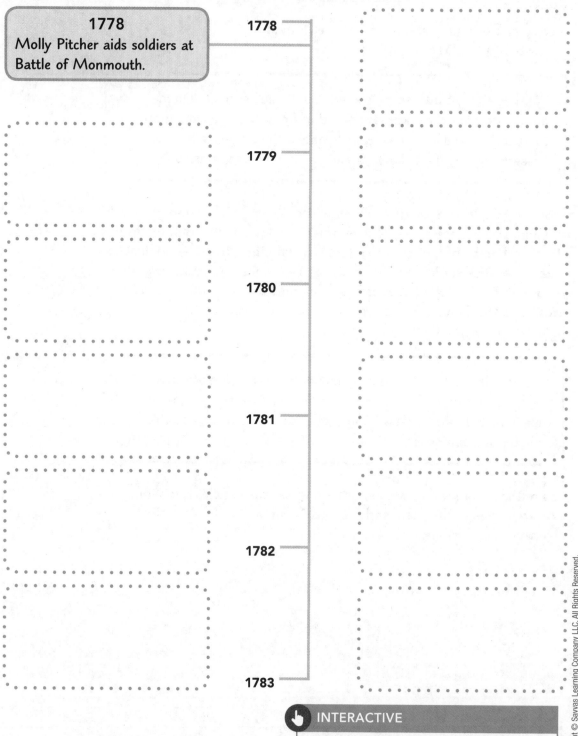

1778
Molly Pitcher aids soldiers at Battle of Monmouth.

1778

1779

1780

1781

1782

1783

INTERACTIVE

For extra help, review the 21st Century Tutorial: **Sequence**.

Practice Vocabulary

Matching Logic Using your knowledge of the underlined vocabulary words, draw a line from each sentence in Column 1 to match it with the sentence in Column 2 to which it logically belongs.

Column 1	Column 2
1. More than 16,000 American and French troops laid <u>siege</u> to the general's army of fewer than 8,000.	The troops appeared suddenly out of the swamps, attacked quickly, and retreated swiftly back into the swamps.
2. Congress <u>ratified</u> the Treaty of Paris after eight years of war.	Casimir Pulaski trained troops to fight from horseback.
3. American forces included a <u>cavalry</u>.	Less than three weeks later, the British surrendered.
4. Militia led by the Swamp Fox used <u>guerrilla</u> tactics against the British.	The British recognized the United States as an independent nation.

Writing Workshop Explanatory Essay

As you read, build a response to this question: **Why was there an American Revolution?** The prompts below will help walk you through the process.

Lesson 1 Writing Task: Consider Your Purpose and Audience
(See Student Text, page 140)

Write a sentence that states the purpose of your essay and identifies your audience.

Lesson 2 Writing Task: Develop a Clear Thesis (See Student Text, page 152)

In one sentence, express the most important reason for why the American Revolution happened. This will be your thesis statement for the explanatory essay you will write at the end of the topic.

Lesson 3 Writing Task: Support Thesis with Details (See Student Text, page 163)

Now add details from lessons 1, 2, and 3 to support your thesis statement.

Lesson 1

Lesson 2

Lesson 3

Lesson 4 Writing Task: Pick an Organizing Strategy
(See Student Text, page 176)

Make an outline of your essay. You can organize your essay any way you like. For example, you might focus first on British actions and then on changes in the colonial perspective. Or you might choose to organize by major themes, such as taxes. Use the chart below to decide on a strategy and outline how you will carry it out in each paragraph of your essay.

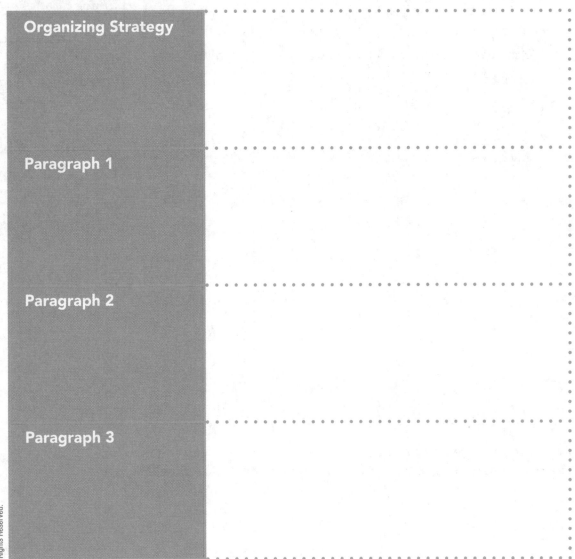

Organizing Strategy	
Paragraph 1	
Paragraph 2	
Paragraph 3	

Lesson 5 Writing Task: Write an Introduction (See Student Text, page 188)

On a separate sheet of paper, write a short paragraph that introduces the thesis of your essay about the American Revolution.

Writing Task (See Student Text, page 191)

Using the outline you created, answer the following question in a three-paragraph explanatory essay: Why was there an American Revolution?

4 A Constitution for the United States Preview

Essential Question How much power should the government have?

Before you begin this topic, think about the Essential Question by answering the following questions.

1. Read over the following list of powers. Put a check mark in front of each power that you think the government should have.

___declare war   ___protect the environment   ___build roads

___appoint a king   ___tax the people   ___fund schools

___censor newspapers   ___spy on citizens   ___make laws

2. For each item you did not check off, explain why you think the government should not have this power.

> **TWO TREATISES OF Government:**
> In the former,
> *The false Principles and Foundation* OF
> Sir *ROBERT FILMER,*
> And his FOLLOWERS,
> ARE
> Detected and Overthrown.
> The latter is an
> ## ESSAY
> CONCERNING
> The True Original, Extent, and End OF
> Civil - Government.
>
> The Second Edition Corrected.
>
> *LONDON,* Printed for *Awnsham* and *John Churchill* at the *Black Swan* in *Pater-noster-Row,* 1694.

Timeline Skills

As you read, write and/or draw at least three events from the topic. Draw a line from each event to its correct position on the timeline.

1770	1780	1790

Map Skills

Using maps throughout the topic, label the outline map with the places listed. Then shade the disputed western lands one color, Spanish territory a second color, and British territory a third color.

Georgia	Delaware	Connecticut	Virginia
South Carolina	New Jersey	Rhode Island	New York
North Carolina	Pennsylvania	Massachusetts	New Hampshire
Maryland			

1800   1810

Senate Representation

On this Quest, you will explore sources and gather information about representation in the Senate from the perspective of a U.S. Senator. Then, you will participate in a civic discussion with other legislators about the Guiding Question.

1 Ask Questions (See Student Text, page 196)

As you begin your Quest, keep in mind the Guiding Question: **Should representation in the Senate be based on population?** and the Essential Question: **How much power should the government have?**

What other questions do you need to ask in order to answer these questions? Consider themes such as the government established by the Articles of Confederation, the concerns of the delegates who attended the Constitutional Convention, the ideas that influenced the Framers of the Constitution, and the debates within the states over ratification. Two questions are filled in for you. Add at least two questions for each of the other categories.

Theme The Articles of Confederation

Sample questions:

What was a major concern of the states when they agreed to the Articles of Confederation?

How was representation in Congress determined under the Articles?

Theme The Constitutional Convention

Theme Ideas and Traditions That Influenced the Framers

Theme Debates Over Ratification

Theme My Additional Questions

INTERACTIVE

For extra help with Step 1, review the
21st Century Tutorial: **Ask Questions**.

2 Investigate

As you read about the events leading up to and following the drafting of the Constitution, collect five connections from your text to help you answer the Guiding Question. Three connections are already chosen for you.

Connect to Alexander Hamilton

Primary Source Federalist and Antifederalist Writings
(See Student Text, page 223)

Here's a connection! Read the excerpt from Framer Alexander Hamilton. To what criticism of the proposed Constitution is he responding?

According to Hamilton, what is accomplished by equal representation in the Senate?

Connect to The Virginia and New Jersey Plans

Lesson 2 Disagreements Over a New Government (See Student Text, page 206)

Here's another connection! Read the discussion of the Virginia and New Jersey plans in your text. What was the main difference between the two plans?

How did the states respond to these two plans?

Connect to Representation in Congress

Lesson 5 The Legislative Branch—Congress (See Student Text, page 229)

What does this connection tell you about how the number of representatives is decided in each body that makes up the legislative branch? How many representatives does each state get in the House? How many representatives does each state get in the Senate?

Which states have the largest and smallest numbers of representatives?

It's Your Turn! **Find two more connections. Fill in the title of your connections, then answer the questions. Connections may be images, primary sources, maps, or text.**

Your Choice | Connect to

Location in text

What is the main idea of this connection?

What does it tell you about how representation in the Senate should be determined?

Your Choice | Connect to

Location in text

What is the main idea of this connection?

What does it tell you about how representation in the Senate should be determined?

A Constitution for the United States

③ Examine Primary Sources (See Student Text, page 254)

Examine the primary and secondary sources provided online or from your teacher. Fill in the chart to show how these sources provide further information about whether representation in the Senate should be based on population. The first one is completed for you.

Should Representation in the Senate be Based on Population?	
Source	**Yes or No? Why?**
"Democracy-Proof"	YES, because equal representation unfairly allows a small minority to pass or block laws.
"Democracy's False Prophet"	
"America the Undemocratic?"	

> **INTERACTIVE**
>
> For extra help with Step 3, review the 21st Century Tutorials: **Compare viewpoints** and **Read Charts, Graphs, and Tables**.

Quest FINDINGS

4 Discuss! (See Student Text, page 254)

Now that you have collected clues and explored documents about representation in Congress, you are ready to discuss with your fellow representatives the Guiding Question: **Should representation in the Senate be based on population?** Follow the steps below, using the spaces provided to prepare for your discussion.

You will work with a partner in a small group of Senators. Try to reach consensus, a situation in which everyone is in agreement, on the question. The people of your state are depending on you!

1. **Prepare Your Arguments** You will be assigned a position on the question, either YES or NO.

My position:

Work with your partner to review your Quest notes from the Quest Connections and Quest Sources.

- If you were assigned YES, agree with your partner on what you think were the strongest arguments from Scialabba.

- If you were assigned NO, agree on what you think were the strongest arguments from Gordon and Zakaria.

2. **Present Your Position** Those assigned YES will present their arguments and evidence first. As you listen, ask clarifying questions to gain information and understanding.

What is a Clarifying Question?	
These types of questions do not judge the person talking. They are only for the listener to be clear on what he or she is hearing.	
Example: Can you tell me more about that?	Example: You said [x]. Am I getting that right?

 INTERACTIVE

For extra help with Step 4, review the 21st Century Tutorial: **Participate in a Discussion or Debate**.

While the opposite side speaks, take notes on what you hear in the space below.

3. **Switch!** Now NO and YES will switch sides. If you argued YES before, now you will argue NO. Work with your same partner and use your notes. Add any arguments and evidence from the clues and sources. Those *now* arguing YES go first.

When both sides have finished, answer the following:

Before I started this discussion with my fellow legislators, my opinion was that the Senate	*After* I started this discussion with my fellow legislators, my opinion was that the Senate
_____should be based on population.	_____should be based on population.
_____should not be based on population.	_____should not be based on population.

4. **Point of View** Do you all agree on the answer to the Guiding Question?

- ——Yes

- ——No

If not, on what points do you all agree?

Take Notes

Literacy Skills: Summarize Use what you have read to complete the flowchart. For each main heading in the reading, write the important points under that heading. Then use the information you have collected to summarize that section of the lesson in the top box. The first one has been completed for you.

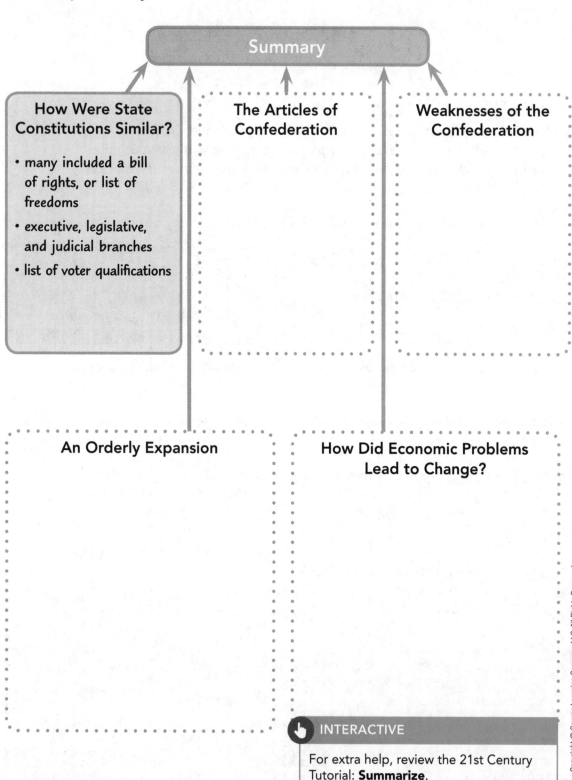

Summary

How Were State Constitutions Similar?

- many included a bill of rights, or list of freedoms
- executive, legislative, and judicial branches
- list of voter qualifications

The Articles of Confederation

Weaknesses of the Confederation

An Orderly Expansion

How Did Economic Problems Lead to Change?

INTERACTIVE

For extra help, review the 21st Century Tutorial: **Summarize**.

Practice Vocabulary

True or False? Decide whether each statement below is true or false. Circle T or F, and then explain your answer. Be sure to include the underlined vocabulary word in your explanation. The first one is done for you.

1. **T / F** States list the structure and powers of government in a <u>bill of rights</u>.
   False. States list the basic freedoms that government promises to protect in a <u>bill of rights</u>.

2. **T / F** A document that sets out the basic laws, principles, organization, and processes of a government is called a <u>constitution</u>.

3. **T / F** The <u>Articles of Confederation</u> was the first American constitution; it created a loose alliance of 13 independent states.

4. **T / F** To <u>cede</u> land means to claim it for your state.

5. **T / F** The Continental Congress authorized the printing of paper money, or <u>currency</u>.

6. **T / F** <u>Shays's Rebellion</u> occurred because leaders from several states decided that the Articles of Confederation did not work.

7. **T / F** The <u>Northwest Ordinance</u> outlawed slavery in the thirteen colonies.

Take Notes

Literacy Skills: Compare and Contrast Use what you have read to complete the Venn diagram. In the main circles, write characteristics of the Great Compromise and the Three-Fifths Compromise. In the overlapping area, write two ways in which these compromises are alike. The first item has been completed for you.

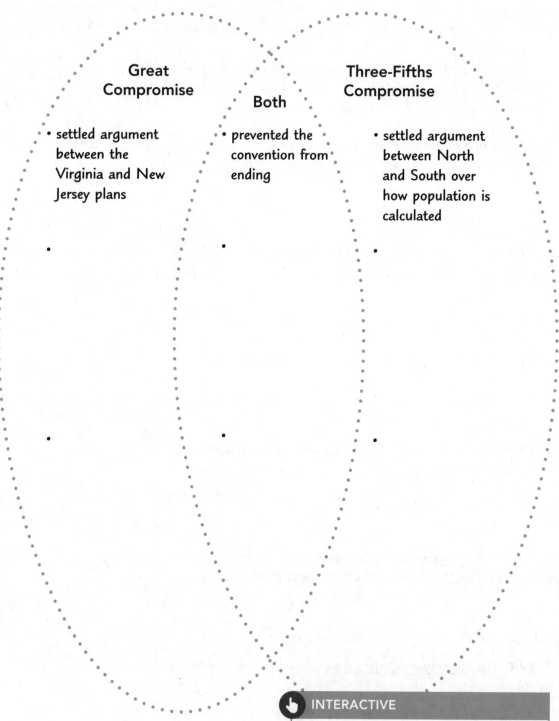

Great Compromise

- settled argument between the Virginia and New Jersey plans

•

•

Both

- prevented the convention from ending

•

Three-Fifths Compromise

- settled argument between North and South over how population is calculated

•

•

👆 **INTERACTIVE**

For extra help, review the 21st Century Tutorial: **Compare and Contrast**.

Practice Vocabulary

Vocabulary Quiz Show Some quiz shows ask a question and expect the contestant to give the answer. In other shows, the contestant is given an answer and must supply the question. If the blank is in the Question column, write the question that would result in the answer in the Answer column. If the question is supplied, write the answer.

Question	Answer
1.	1. Constitutional Convention
2. Under which plan was the number of representatives based on population?	2.
3.	3. New Jersey Plan
4.	4. compromise
5. What is the name of the compromise that solved the issue of representation in Congress?	5.
6.	6. Three-Fifths Compromise

Quick Activity Focus on a Framer

With a partner or small group, examine this short biography of framer James Madison.

James Madison Jr. was the eldest of ten children. He grew up at Montpelier, a 5,000-acre plantation in Virginia. Frequently ill and painfully shy, at 12 he began studying Greek, Latin, French, geography, mathematics, and literature. Later he attended the College of New Jersey at Princeton. In 1776, Madison was elected to the Virginia Constitutional Convention, where he impressed members with his grasp of political philosophy. He next served in the Continental Congress, and then the state legislature. During this time, Madison spent long hours poring over books of history, government, and law. In 1787, he traveled to Philadelphia as one of Virginia's delegates to the Constitutional Convention. Many years later, he served as the fourth President of the United States.

James Madison's father was a leading landowner in Virginia. What are two other key features of James Madison's background?

The excerpt below is taken from the notes James Madison took during the Constitutional Convention. In it, he is arguing against the New Jersey Plan.

[James Madison] enumerated [listed] the objections against an equality of votes in the second branch. . . . 1. The minority could [negate] the will of the majority of the people. 2. They could extort [get by force] measures, by making them a condition of their assent [agreement] to other necessary measures. 3. They could obtrude [force] measures on the majority, by virtue of the peculiar powers which would be vested in the Senate. 4. The evil, instead of being cured by time, would increase with every new State that should be admitted, as they must all be admitted on the principle of equality.

— *James Madison, Debates in the Federal Convention of 1787, July 14, 1787*

Team Challenge! What point is James Madison making in this excerpt? Work together to draw conclusions about the relationship between Madison's background and the point of view he expresses in the excerpt. Write a short paragraph explaining your conclusions.

Take Notes

Literacy Skills: Classify and Categorize Use what you have read to complete the table. Write the most important ideas from each group that influenced the founders as they wrote the Constitution. The first one has been completed for you.

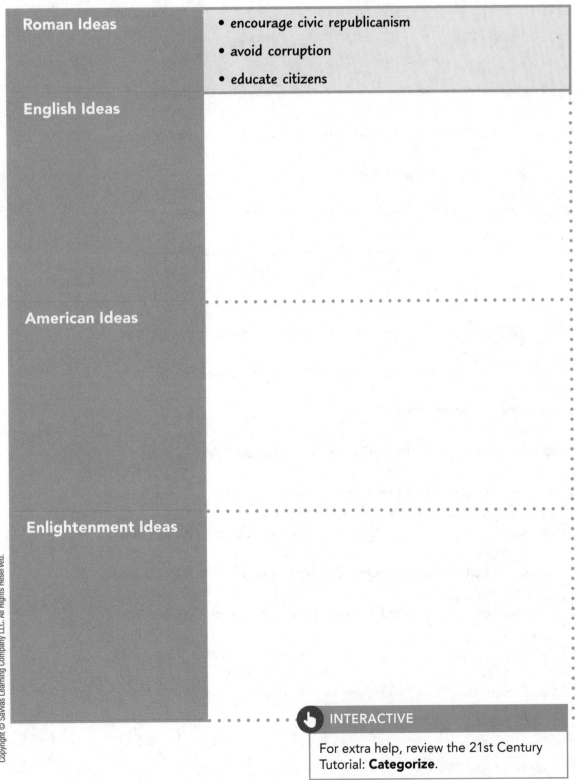

Roman Ideas	• encourage civic republicanism • avoid corruption • educate citizens
English Ideas	
American Ideas	
Enlightenment Ideas	

INTERACTIVE

For extra help, review the 21st Century Tutorial: **Categorize**.

Practice Vocabulary

Use a Word Bank **Choose one word from the word bank to fill in each blank. When you have finished, you will have a short summary of important ideas from the section.**

Word Bank

republic   dictatorship   Magna Carta

English Bill of Rights   separation of powers

The Framers of the Constitution drew on many ideas as they worked

to create a new government for the United States. They looked to

ancient Rome, for example, which was a ....,

a government in which citizens rule themselves through elected

representatives. They also considered the ideas put forward in great

English documents. The .... stated that

kings had to obey the law and that the nobles had certain rights. Other

important ideas, such as the right to trial by jury, were found in a

document created in 1689, the ....

In addition to protecting the rights of the people, the Framers also

knew it was important to make sure the new government would not

become a ...., a government in which one

person or a small group of people holds all the power. To prevent this

from happening, they included important principles in the Constitution,

such as the ...., which says that the powers

of government should be divided up among several branches.

Lesson 4 Federalists, Antifederalists, and the Bill of Rights

Take Notes

Literacy Skills: Sequence Use what you have read to complete the timeline. Determine the date for each of the events listed. Then, draw a line from each event to its correct position on the timeline.

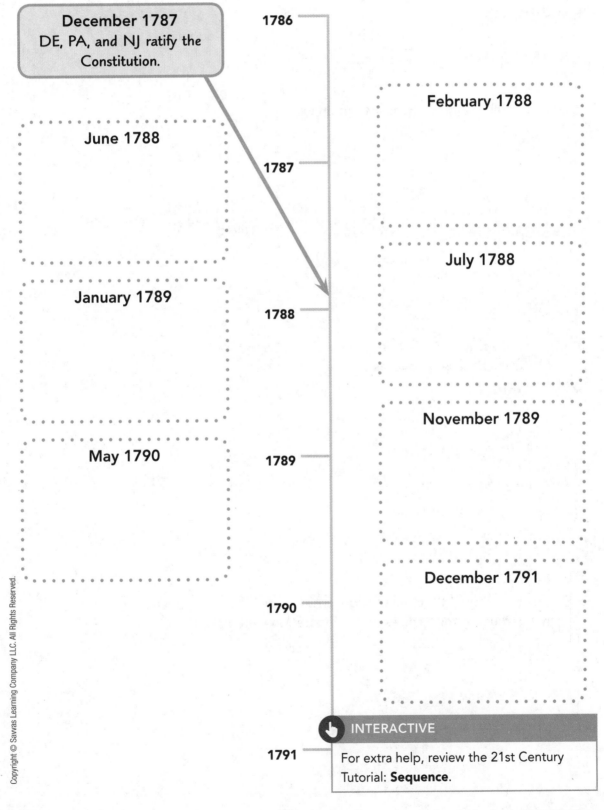

December 1787
DE, PA, and NJ ratify the Constitution.

June 1788

January 1789

May 1790

1786

1787

1788

1789

1790

1791

February 1788

July 1788

November 1789

December 1791

👆 INTERACTIVE

For extra help, review the 21st Century Tutorial: **Sequence**.

Practice Vocabulary

Sentence Builder Finish the sentences below with a key term from the Word Bank. You may have to change the form of the words to complete the sentences.

Word Bank

ratify   Federalist   Antifederalist

Federalist Papers   amend

1. To add a Bill of Rights, the Constitution was

2. People who opposed the new Constitution were called

3. A series of essays written to explain and defend the new Constitution became known as the

4. After they were written, the new amendments had to be

5. People who thought the national government needed more power than it had under the Articles of Confederation were called

Take Notes

Literacy Skills: Classify and Categorize Use what you have read to complete the table. Place each key term under its proper category. The first one has been completed for you.

Key Terms

Preamble

27 amendments

Preamble

Popular sovereignty

Executive

Vice President and executive
 departments

Checks and balances

Judicial

Federalism

Seven articles

President

District courts

Limited government

Legislative

Separation of powers

House of Representatives

Individual rights

Republicanism

Supreme Court

Senate

Basic Principles	Constitution	Government Structure
	Preamble	

> **INTERACTIVE**
>
> For extra help, review the 21st Century Tutorial: **Categorize**.

Practice Vocabulary

Word Map Study the word map for the word *veto*. Characteristics are words or phrases that relate to the word in the center of the word map. Non-characteristics are words and phrases not associated with the word. Use the blank word map to explore the meaning of the word *bill*. Then make word maps of your own for these words: *popular sovereignty*, *override*, and *impeach*.

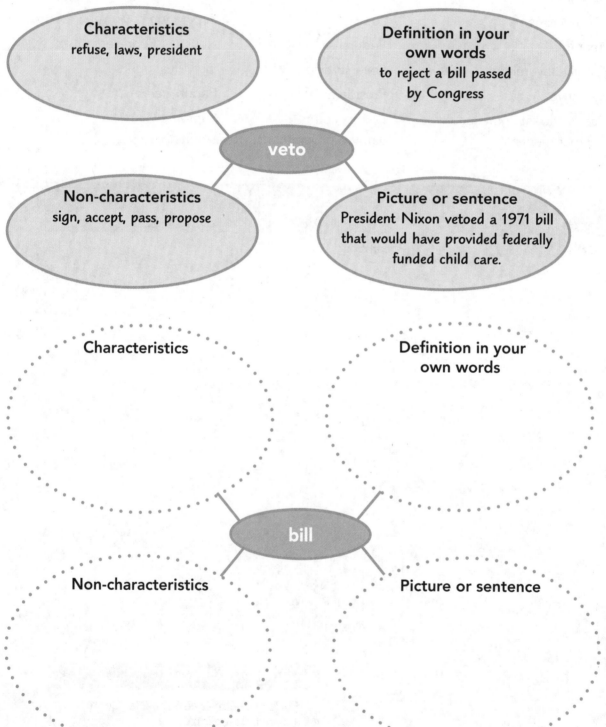

Characteristics
refuse, laws, president

Definition in your own words
to reject a bill passed by Congress

veto

Non-characteristics
sign, accept, pass, propose

Picture or sentence
President Nixon vetoed a 1971 bill that would have provided federally funded child care.

Characteristics

Definition in your own words

bill

Non-characteristics

Picture or sentence

Take Notes

Literacy Skills: Summarize Use what you have read to complete the chart. List the most important points from each section of the text in the lower boxes. Then summarize the entire lesson in the top box. The first section has been completed for you.

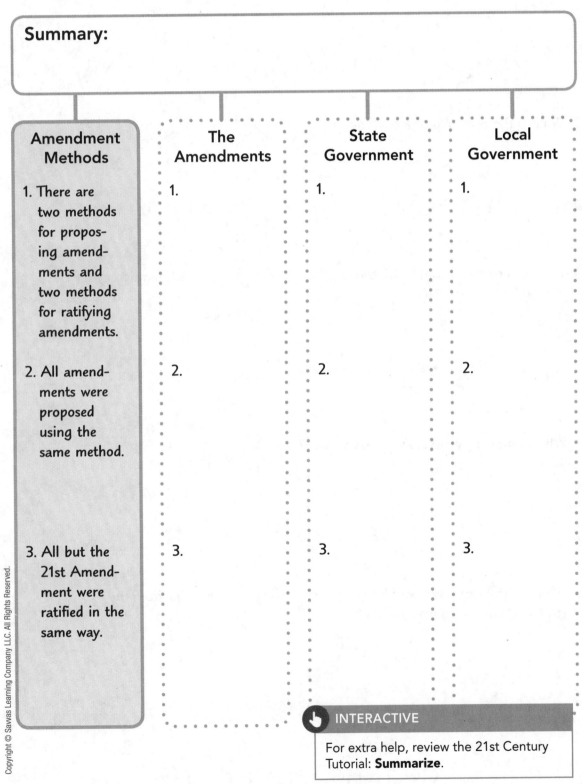

Summary:

Amendment Methods

1. There are two methods for proposing amendments and two methods for ratifying amendments.

2. All amendments were proposed using the same method.

3. All but the 21st Amendment were ratified in the same way.

The Amendments

1.

2.

3.

State Government

1.

2.

3.

Local Government

1.

2.

3.

👆 INTERACTIVE

For extra help, review the 21st Century Tutorial: **Summarize**.

Practice Vocabulary

Words in Context For each question below, write an answer that shows your understanding of the boldfaced key term.

1. What is the **Bill of Rights**, and why is it important to all Americans?

2. What is the opposite of a **civil** trial?

3. What is a **constitutional initiative** and how is it an example of democracy at work?

4. What is meant by a state's **infrastructure**?

5. What is **local government** and in what major way does it differ from the state and national governments?

Quick Activity Explore Free Speech

With a partner or small group, examine this cartoon related to the Bill of Rights. It was created when George W. Bush was president.

To which amendment from the Bill of Rights does this cartoon relate? What point is the artist making with the signs in people's yards? Why does the man walking down the street say "America the Beautiful"?

Team Challenge! Are there ever times when speech should not be protected? Consider the situations below and discuss with your group whether or not each should be allowed. Put a check mark beside the examples of speech you think should be protected.

___blog that criticizes a member of Congress

___book that gives information that endangers national security

___ad that falsely claims a product will make you smarter

___speech that urges protestors to attack the police

___editorial that accuses a governor of stealing money

___burning a cross in someone's front yard

___protestors chanting in front of the White House

___network news story exposing wrongdoing by the president

Take Notes

Literacy Skills: Use Evidence to Support Ideas Use what you have read to complete the chart. Use the evidence in the lower boxes to arrive at a conclusion. Write your conclusion in the top box.

Conclusion:

At least one parent is a U.S. citizen.	You were naturalized.	You were 18 or younger when your parents were naturalized.

Conclusion:

Citizens have a duty to obey the laws.	Citizens have a duty to help defend the nation.	Citizens have a duty to serve on juries.

INTERACTIVE

For extra help, review the 21st Century Tutorial: **Support Ideas with Evidence.**

Practice Vocabulary

1. A <u>citizen</u> is a person who owes loyalty to no particular nation and is entitled to no rights or protections.
   A <u>citizen</u> is a person who owes loyalty to a particular nation and is entitled to all its rights and protections.

2. If you have not yet completed the official legal process for becoming a citizen, you are a <u>naturalized</u> citizen.

3. An <u>immigrant</u> is a person who leaves a country in order to return to his or her country of birth.

4. An immigrant must receive permission to remain in the United States as a <u>resident alien</u>, or citizen living out of the country.

5. <u>Civic virtue</u> is the willingness of the government to grant all American citizens equal rights under the law.

6. <u>Patriotism</u> is a feeling of love and devotion toward other countries.

7. Every citizen has the responsibility to report for <u>jury duty</u>, meaning to decide whether a jury reached the correct decision.

Writing Workshop Arguments

As you read, build a response to this question: **How much power should the federal government have, and what should its responsibilities be?** The prompts below will help walk you through the process.

Lesson 1 Writing Task: Introduce Claims (See Student Text, page 203)

Write a brief paragraph introducing the two sides of the argument about how much power the government should have.

Lessons 2 and 3 Writing Tasks: Support Claims and Distinguish Claims from Opposing Claims (See Student Text, pages 209 and 215)

Based on the information in Lessons 1, 2, and 3, write a few sentences that support each claim about how much power the government should have. Then, for each claim, write a counterclaim. Be sure to use logical reasoning and support your position with evidence.

	Supporting Details	Counterclaim
Claim 1		
Claim 2		

Lesson 4 Writing Task: Use Credible Sources (See Student Text, page 222)

On additional paper, make a list of sources you might use to support or oppose claims about how much power the federal government should have.

Lessons 5 and 6 Writing Tasks: Use Transition Words and Shape Tone
(See Student Text, pages 236 and 245)

Transition words and phrases can help compare ideas (*similarly*), contrast them (*but, on the contrary*), or clarify them (*to put it another way*). Think of more transition words and phrases and write them here. Then, think about the tone you want to take in your argument. To help shape your tone, write a few sentences that reflect your viewpoint about the subject matter, while maintaining the formal style and informative approach required in presenting an argument.

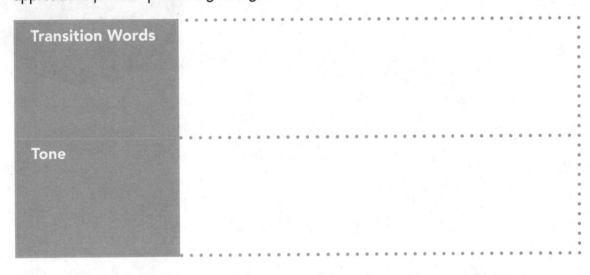

Transition Words

Tone

Lesson 7 Writing Task: Write a Conclusion (See Student Text, page 252)

Now that you have formed your own viewpoint about how much power the government should have, write a conclusion for your argument.

Writing Task (See Student Text, page 252)

Using the claims, evidence, and sources you have listed here, answer the following question in a three-paragraph argument: How much power should the federal government have, and what should its responsibilities be?

Essential Question How much power should the federal government have, and what should it do?

Before you begin this topic, think about the Essential Question by completing the following activity.

1. Write a short blog post that explains how much power the federal government should have, and why.

Timeline Skills

As you read, write and/or draw at least three events from the topic. Draw a line from each event to its correct position on the timeline.

1780	1790	1800

Map Skills

Using maps throughout the topic, label the outline map with the places listed. Then color in the bodies of water.

Louisiana Purchase

land from Great Britain 1783

thirteen states in 1783

land from Spain 1819

Great Lakes

land from Great Britain 1818

Mississippi River

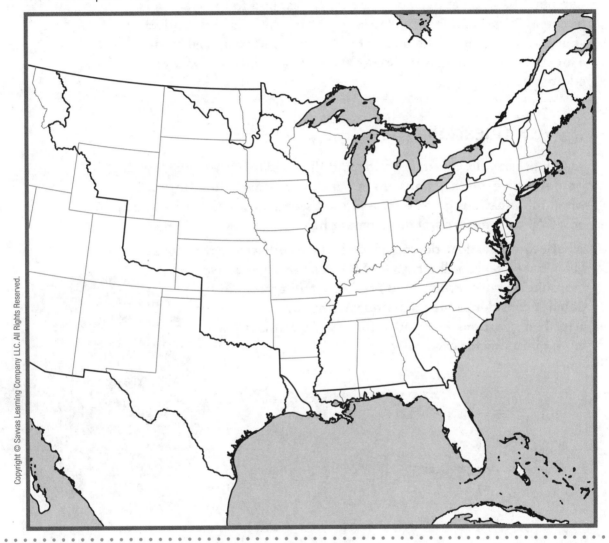

| 1810 | 1820 | 1830 | 1840 |

Quest
Project-Based Learning Inquiry

Stay Out? Or Get Involved?

On this Quest, you are working as a member of President Jefferson's Cabinet. The Cabinet must decide how to respond to the war between Britain and France. You will examine sources and conduct your own research. At the end of the Quest, your group will hold a mock Cabinet meeting to discuss the issue and the best way to address it.

① Ask Questions (See Student Text, page 260)

As you begin your Quest, keep in mind the Guiding Question: **How do we determine which actions are in the best interest of the United States when other nations go to war?** and the Essential Question: **How much power should the federal government have, and what should it do?**

What other questions do you need to ask in order to answer these questions? Consider the nature of the relationships between the United States, Britain, and France. What factors did the Cabinet consider as they debated whether or not to go to war? Two questions are filled in for you. Add at least two more questions for each category.

Theme Political

Sample questions:

What were the political objectives of the new nation?

Did the United States still have obligations to its ally France?

Theme Economic

Theme Relations with Other Countries

Theme My Additional Questions

INTERACTIVE

For extra help with Step 1, review the
21st Century Tutorial: **Ask Questions**.

Quest CONNECTIONS

2 Investigate

As you read about the Early Republic, collect five connections to help you answer the Guiding Question. Three connections are already chosen for you.

Connect to President Washington's Foreign Policy

Lesson 1 How Did Americans React to the French Revolution?
(See Student Text, page 270)

Here's a connection! Read this section in your text. What does it tell you about how the United States reacted to the war in Europe? Why did the President choose this course of action? What did it establish?

How did President Washington enforce his policy?

Connect to the XYZ Affair

Lesson 3 Conflict With France (See Student Text, page 282)

Here's another connection! Read this section in your text. Think about the XYZ Affair and the way that President Adams responded to French attacks on American ships. What do these events suggest about dealing with conflicts?

How did Americans respond to these events?

Connect to American Embargo

Lesson 4 A Ban on Trade (See Student Text, page 301)

What does this connection tell you about the pros and cons of President Jefferson's ban on trade?

Could Jefferson's actions have started a war?

It's Your Turn! **Find two more connections. Fill in the title of your connections, then answer the questions. Connections may be images, primary sources, maps, or text.**

Your Choice | Connect to

Location in text

What is the main idea of this connection?

What does it tell you about how the United States reacted to war in other nations? What does it tell you about how the United States established its foreign policy?

Your Choice | Connect to

Location in text

What is the main idea of this connection?

What does it tell you about how the United States reacted to the war in other nations? What does it tell you about how the United States established its foreign policy?

③ Conduct Research (See Student Text, page 330)

Explore primary and secondary sources about events leading up to 1793, when war broke out between Britain and France. Fill in the chart to show how these sources provide further information about how we determine which actions are in the best interest of the United States when other nations go to war. The first entry is completed for you.

Source	How do we determine which actions are in the best interest of the United States when other nations go to war?
Washington's Farewell Address	Maintaining a policy of neutrality is the best policy for the nation at this time.

👆 INTERACTIVE

For extra help with Step 3, review the 21st Century Tutorial: **Analyze Primary and Secondary Sources**.

Quest FINDINGS

4 Write a Position Paper (See Student Text, page 330)

Now it is time to put together all of the information you have gathered and use it to hold a mock Cabinet meeting with your team to review notes, decide on the best course of action, and document this problem-solving process. In a small group, write a position paper summarizing the chosen solution.

1. **Prepare to Write** You have collected connections and explored primary and secondary sources about how the United States regarded the affairs of other nations. Look through your notes and decide which events and statements you want to highlight in your position paper. Record them here.

Events and Statements

2. **Write a Draft** Using evidence from the text and the documents you explored, write a draft of the position paper based on the outcome of the mock Cabinet meeting.

3. **Share with a Partner** Exchange your draft with a partner. Tell your partner what you like about his or her draft and suggest any improvements you think are necessary.

4. **Finalize Your Paper** Revise your position paper as needed. Correct any grammatical or spelling errors.

5. **Reflect on the Quest** Think about your experience completing this topic's Quest. What did you learn about the United States and its position on foreign affairs in the early days of the Republic? Do you still have questions about the position of the United States on foreign events at that time? How will you answer them?

Reflections

 INTERACTIVE

For extra help, review the 21st Century Tutorials: **Work in Teams** and **Make Decisions**.

Take Notes

Literacy Skills: Summarize Use what you have read to complete the chart. Add details related to the challenges facing the new government in each box. The first entry has been completed for you.

Challenges Facing the New Government

The Government

- In 1789, Congress creates the departments of State, Treasury, and War and the offices of Attorney General and Postmaster General.

- Washington sets a precedent by choosing well-known leaders to serve in his Cabinet—Thomas Jefferson and Alexander Hamilton.

- Congress passes the Judiciary Act of 1789 establishing the Supreme Court.

The Economy

Foreign Affairs

INTERACTIVE

For extra help, review the 21st Century Tutorial: **Summarize**.

Practice Vocabulary

Matching Logic Using your knowledge of the underlined vocabulary words, draw a line from each sentence in Column 1 to match it with a sentence in Column 2 to which it logically belongs.

Column 1	Column 2
In his first major task as President, Washington chose talented people to fill his <u>Cabinet</u>.	James Madison did not approve of investors making a profit in this way.
Washington's presidency, being the first, established <u>precedents</u> that are still used today.	In 1789, Congress passed this tax on imported goods to protect their products.
On April 30, at Federal Hall, the <u>inauguration</u> of George Washington took place.	The number of executive departments has more than tripled. There are now fourteen executive departments.
Faced with the conflict between France and Britain, President Washington chose to remain <u>neutral</u>.	Hamilton's plan proposed using these to promise payment to citizens.
To help pay off war debts, the government issued <u>bonds</u> with a promise to repay the loans with interest.	In 1796, he decided not to run for a third term. Not until 1940 did any President seek a third term.
Hamilton believed a <u>tariff</u> would help with the new government's debt.	Britain made matters difficult for the United States when it seized cargo from American ships.
<u>Speculators</u> bought war bonds in the hopes of making a profit.	This ceremony starts a new presidency.

Take Notes

Literacy Skills: Compare and Contrast Use what you have read to complete the table. Compare and contrast the political views of the first political parties. The first entry is completed for you.

The First Political Parties	
Federalists	**Democratic-Republicans**
strong national government	limited national government

INTERACTIVE

For extra help, review the 21st Century Tutorial: **Compare and Contrast**.

Practice Vocabulary

True or False? Decide whether each statement below is true or false.
Circle T or F, and then explain your answer. Be sure to include the
underlined word in your explanation. The first one is done for you.

1. **T / F** The legislative branch has the final word on whether or not a law
   is <u>unconstitutional</u>.
   False; The Supreme Court has the final word on whether or not a law
   is <u>unconstitutional</u>.

2. **T / F** The <u>Federalists</u> gained wide support from farmers, southern
   planters, and workers.

3. **T / F** Differing views on what the nation should become led to <u>factions</u>
   and the rise of political parties.

4. **T / F** <u>Democratic Republicans</u> favored a loose interpretation
   of the Constitution.

Quick Activity Take Sides

Look at the political cartoon. Clearly, despite President Washington's warning against political parties, Americans were deeply divided over how the nation should be run.

With a partner or small group, discuss the issues over which Democratic Republicans and Federalists disagreed. Decide whether you would support Hamilton's or Jefferson's views on the role of government.

Team Challenge! Still working with a partner or small group, list what you consider to be the strengths and weaknesses of having political parties in a nation. Use this list to write a three or four sentence paragraph explaining why you favor or oppose having political parties.

Strengths	Weaknesses

Take Notes

Literacy Skills: Identify Main Ideas Use what you have read to complete the concept webs. In the first concept web, list the main idea and details of the foreign policy issues John Adams faced during his presidency. The first entry is completed for you. In the second concept web, list the changes Jefferson made to the government during his presidency.

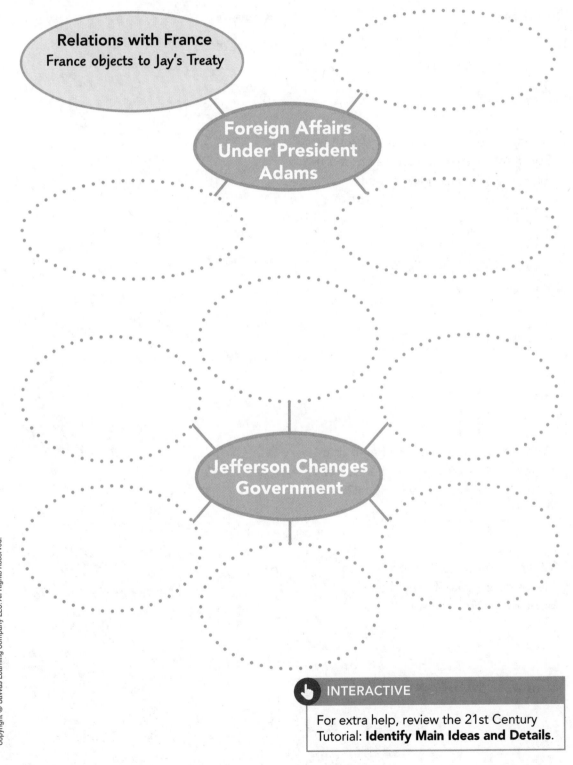

Relations with France
France objects to Jay's Treaty

Foreign Affairs Under President Adams

Jefferson Changes Government

🖑 INTERACTIVE

For extra help, review the 21st Century Tutorial: **Identify Main Ideas and Details**.

Practice Vocabulary

Vocabulary Quiz Show Some quiz shows ask a question and expect the contestant to give the answer. In other shows, the contestant is given an answer and must supply the question. If the blank is in the Question column, write the question that would result in the answer in the Answer column. If the question is supplied, write the answer.

Question	Answer
1.	1. tribute
2. What new power given to the Supreme Court established a balance among the three branches of government?	2.
3.	3. sedition
4.	4. laissez faire
5. What theory supports the belief that states can determine whether or not a federal law is unconstitutional?	5.
6. What action did Jefferson believe states could take if they did not approve a federal law?	6.

Take Notes

Literacy Skills: Analyze Text Structure Use what you have read to complete the outline. Add details to explain the significance of the Louisiana Purchase and foreign trade during Jefferson's presidency. The first entries are completed for you.

I. Jefferson's Presidency
   A. Louisiana Purchase
      1. Buying the land
         a. Western farmers rely on Mississippi River to ship goods.
         b. Livingston and Monroe negotiate to buy Louisiana for $15 million.
         c. Jefferson determines presidents can buy land as part of a treaty.
      2. Exploring the land

         a.

         b.

         c.

   B. Foreign Affairs

      1.

         a.

      2. A Ban on Trade

         a.

         b.

INTERACTIVE

For extra help, review the 21st Century Tutorial: **Summarize**.

Practice Vocabulary

Words in Context For each question below, write an answer that shows your understanding of the boldfaced key term.

1. What is the **continental divide**?

2. Why were Americans upset about the British navy's use of **impressment**?

3. What was the significance of the Lewis and Clark **expedition**?

4. What led to an increase in **smuggling**?

5. Why did the **embargo** become a major issue in the election of 1808?

Quick Activity Explore

President Jefferson instructed Lewis and Clark to explore a possible overland route to the Pacific and determine if the Missouri River offered "the most direct and practicable water communication across [the] continent." Jefferson was also interested in the port city of New Orleans, which was a part of the Louisiana Purchase.

With a partner or a small group, discuss why the President insisted on these goals as part of the expedition. Why were rivers so important?

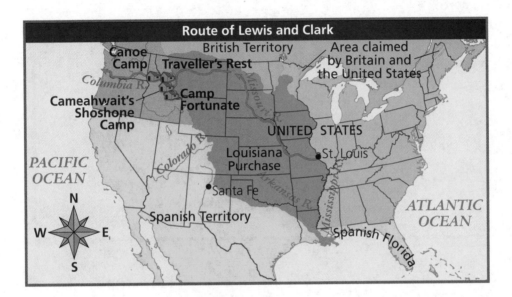

Team Challenge! With your partner or group, write an entry that a member of the Lewis and Clark expedition might have written in their journal years after their expedition to describe how rivers changed life in the United States. Share your journal entry with the class.

Take Notes

Literacy Skills: Sequence Use what you have read to complete the flowchart. Provide the sequence of events that led to the War of 1812. The first entry is completed for you.

Relations with Great Britain were strained. Britain provided weapons and support to American Indians who attacked American settlers in the West.

INTERACTIVE

For extra help, review the 21st Century Tutorial: **Sequence**.

Practice Vocabulary

Word Map Study the word map for the word *nationalism.*
Characteristics are words or phrases that relate to the word in the
center of the word map. Non-characteristics are words and phrases
not associated with the word. Use the blank word map to explore the
meaning of the term *War Hawks.* Then make word maps of your own
for the word *confederation.*

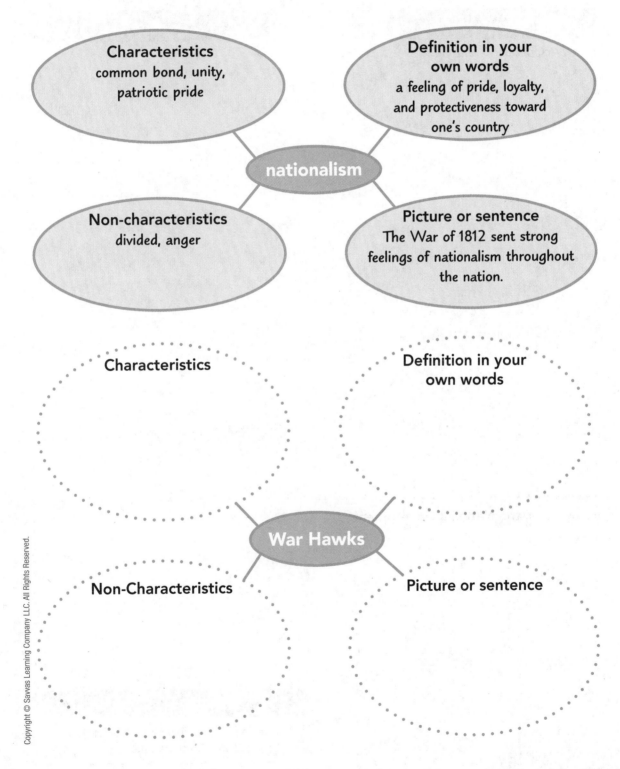

Characteristics
common bond, unity, patriotic pride

Definition in your own words
a feeling of pride, loyalty, and protectiveness toward one's country

nationalism

Non-characteristics
divided, anger

Picture or sentence
The War of 1812 sent strong feelings of nationalism throughout the nation.

Characteristics

Definition in your own words

War Hawks

Non-Characteristics

Picture or sentence

Take Notes

Literacy Skills: Draw Conclusions Use what you have read to draw conclusions about the effect of several Supreme Court decisions on the way the government was run. Complete the flowchart outlining the cases and the decisions. In the bottom box, write one or two sentences about how these Supreme Court decisions affected the U.S. government. The first one has been started for you.

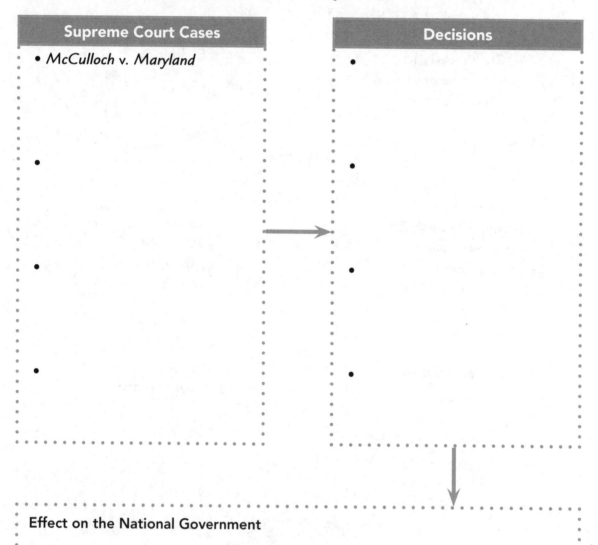

Supreme Court Cases	Decisions
• *McCulloch v. Maryland*	

Effect on the National Government

INTERACTIVE

For extra help, review the 21st Century Tutorial: **Draw Conclusions**.

Practice Vocabulary

Use a Word Bank **Choose one word from the word bank to fill in each blank. When you have finished, you will have a short summary of important ideas from the section.**

Word Bank

sectionalism

interstate commerce

intervention

American System

Monroe Doctrine

Nationalism sparked President Monroe's presentation of a plan to improve the economy of the nation. The three-part plan, designed by Henry Clay, was called the .... The plan would unify the economy of the states into a national economy. During the Monroe administration, several landmark Supreme Court decisions promoted national unity by strengthening the federal government. One decision, *Gibbons* v. *Ogden*, stated that .... could be regulated only by the federal government. At the same time nationalism was uniting the country, loyalty to one's region or .... was threatening to drive the country apart. The economy, slavery, and states' rights were major issues.

Events elsewhere in the Americas loomed large. Presenting the United States as a world power and protector of Latin America, the .... firmly stated that European .... would not be tolerated.

Writing Workshop Research Paper

As you read, build a response to this prompt: **Research the country's physical landscapes, political divisions, and territorial expansion during the early republic.** The prompts below will help you walk through the process.

Lesson 1 Writing Task: Generate Questions to Focus Research
(See Student Text, page 272)

At the end of this topic, you will write a research paper describing the country's physical geography, political divisions, and expansion during the terms of its first four Presidents. Make a list of questions that would need to be answered in order to write a research paper on this subject, such as: What were the political parties of this period?

Lesson 2 Writing Task: Find and Use Credible Sources
(See Student Text, page 279)

You will need more information to write your paper. List three credible sources of information you can use to research about the early republic's physical landscapes, political divisions, or territorial expansion.

Lesson 3 Writing Tasks: Choose an Organizing Strategy
(See Student Text, page 290)

How will you organize your research paper? Will you have one section for each topic? Chronologically? Choose an organizing strategy for your paper and describe it here.

Lesson 4 Writing Task: Support Thesis with Details (See Student Text, page 302)

Gather specific details from each lesson that you can use in your research paper. Write those details in the table below.

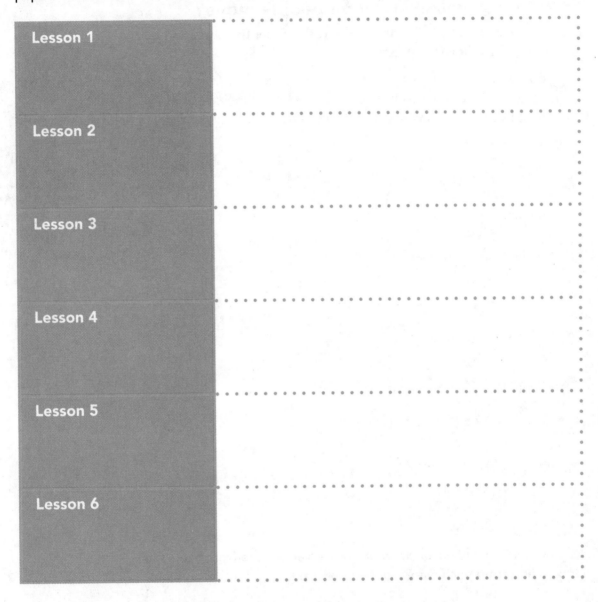

Lesson 1	
Lesson 2	
Lesson 3	
Lesson 4	
Lesson 5	
Lesson 6	

Lesson 5 Writing Task: Clarify Relationships with Transition Words (See Student Text, page 315)

What are some transition words that you can use to show the relationship between facts in your paper? Write those words on a separate sheet of paper.

Lesson 6 Writing Task: Visuals (See Student Text, page 328)

What graphics and formatting will you use to help convey information in an engaging way? Make a list on a separate sheet of paper.

Writing Task (See Student Text, page 331)

Using your notes, write a research paper describing the country's physical geography, political divisions, and expansion during the terms of the first four Presidents.

6 The Age of Jackson and Westward Expansion Preview

Essential Question Why do people move?

Before you begin this topic, think about the Essential Question by answering the following questions.

1. If you had the option to move to any city or country in the world, where would you choose to go and why? Include at least three reasons why you chose that location.

Timeline Skills

As you read, write and/or draw at least three events from the topic. Draw a line from each event to its correct position on the timeline.

1820 | **1830**

Map Skills

Using maps throughout the topic, label the outline map with the places listed. Then, color in the bodies of water.

Gadsen Purchase

Pacific Ocean

Texas Annexation

Land ceded by Britain in 1818

Louisiana Purchase

Oregon Country

Mexico

Gulf of Mexico

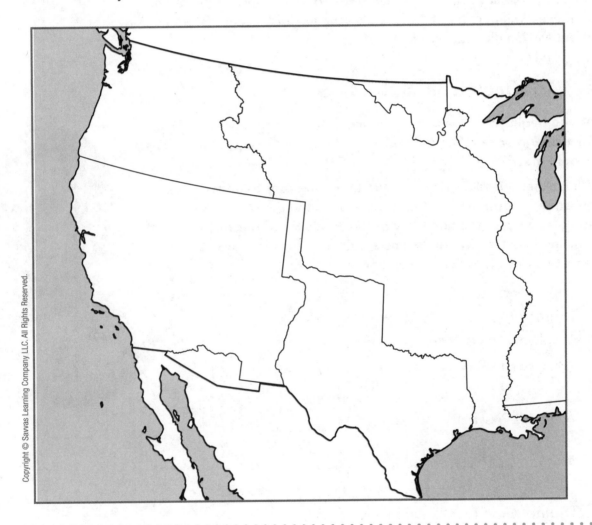

1840	1850	1860

Civic Discussion Inquiry

The Mexican-American War

On this Quest, you will explore sources and gather information about the Mexican-American War in the role of a modern historian. Then, you will participate in a civic discussion with other historians about the Guiding Question.

① Ask Questions (See Student Text, page 336)

As you begin your Quest, keep in mind the Guiding Question: **Was the Mexican-American War justified?** and the Essential Question: **Why do people move?**

What other questions do you need to ask in order to answer these questions? Consider that the dispute between the United States and Mexico over the boundary of the southern border of Texas remained hostile. Two questions are filled in for you. Add at least two questions for each category.

Theme Troubles with Mexico

Sample questions:

What were the hostilities about?

What was President Polk's view?

Theme Manifest Destiny and Westward Expansion

Theme Public Response to the War

Theme Effects of the War

Theme My Additional Questions

 INTERACTIVE

For additional help with Step 1, review the 21st Century Tutorial: **Ask Questions**.

Quest CONNECTIONS

② Investigate

As you read about the Mexican-American War, collect five connections to help you answer the Guiding Question. Three connections are already chosen for you.

Connect to Colonies in Texas

Lesson 6 Americans Colonize Mexican Texas (See Student Text, page 386)

Here's a connection! Read this section in your text. What does this event tell you about the significance of Texas and Mexico to the United States?

How did the United States' relationship with Mexico develop after Mexican independence from Spain?

Connect to Causes of the Mexican-American War

Lesson 7 The Mexican-American War (See Student Text, page 394)

Here's another connection! Read this section in your text.
What events led to the start of the war with Mexico?

How did most Americans feel about the war?

Connect to Effects of the Mexican-American War

Lesson 7 Mormons Settle the Mexican Cession (See Student Text, page 397)

What does this connection tell you about the immediate effect of the war's end?

What were the long-term effects of the war for the United States?

It's Your Turn! **Find two more connections. Fill in the title of your connections. Then, answer the questions. Connections may be images, primary sources, maps, or text.**

Your Choice | Connect to

Location in text

What is the main idea of this connection?

What does it tell you about the relationship between the United States and Mexico?

Your Choice | Connect to

Location in text

What is the main idea of this connection?

What does it tell you about the relationship between the United States and Mexico?

3 **Examine Primary Sources** (See Student Text, page 402)

Examine the primary and secondary sources provided online or from your teacher. Fill in the chart to show how these sources provide further information about whether the Mexican-American War was justified. The first one is completed for you.

Was the Mexican-American War Justified?	
Source	**Yes or No? Why?**
"The Borderlands on the Eve of War"	YES. Events in Mexico had weakened the government, revolts were breaking out, there was political chaos and a poor economy. In addition, Mexicans no longer felt a sense of loyalty to the government.
Message on War with Mexico	
The War with Mexico	
The History of Mexico	

 INTERACTIVE

For extra help with Step 3, review the 21st Century Tutorials: **Compare Viewpoints** and **Read Charts, Graphs, and Tables**.

Quest FINDINGS

4 Discuss! (See Student Text, page 402)

Now that you have collected evidence and explored primary and secondary sources about the Mexican-American War, you are ready to discuss with your fellow historians the Guiding Question: **Was the Mexican-American War justified?**

You will work with a partner in a small group of historians. Try to reach a consensus, or a situation in which everyone is in agreement, on the question. Can you do it?

1. **Prepare Your Arguments** You will be assigned a position on the question, either YES or NO.

   My position: ....

   Work with your partner to review your Quest notes from the Quest Connections and Quest Sources.

   - If you were assigned YES, agree with your partner on what you think were the strongest arguments from Weber and Polk.

   - If you were assigned NO, agree on what you think were the strongest arguments from Lincoln and Corkwood.

2. **Present Your Position** Those assigned YES will present their arguments and evidence first. As you listen to the opposing side, ask clarifying questions to gain information and understanding.

What is a Clarifying Question?	
These types of questions do not judge the person talking. They are only for the listener to be clear on what he or she is hearing.	
Examples: Can you tell me more about that?	Examples: You said [x]. Am I getting that right?

🔊 INTERACTIVE

For extra help with Step 4, review the 21st Century Tutorial: **Participate in a Discussion or Debate**.

While the opposite side speaks, take notes on what you hear in the space below.

3. **Switch!** Now NO and YES will switch sides. If you argued YES before, now you will argue NO. Work with your same partner and use your notes. Add any arguments and evidence from the clues and sources. Those *now* arguing YES go first.

When both sides have finished, answer the following:

Before I started this discussion, my opinion was that the Mexican-American War:	*After* this discussion, my opinion is that the Mexican-American War:
____was justified. ____was not justified.	____was justified. ____was not justified.

4. **Point of View** Do you all agree on the answer to the Guiding Question?
   - ____ Yes
   - ____ No
   If not, on what points do you all agree?

Take Notes

Literacy Skills: Identify Cause and Effect Use what you have read to complete the chart below. List the causes and effects of Jacksonian Democracy on the nation. The first entry is done for you.

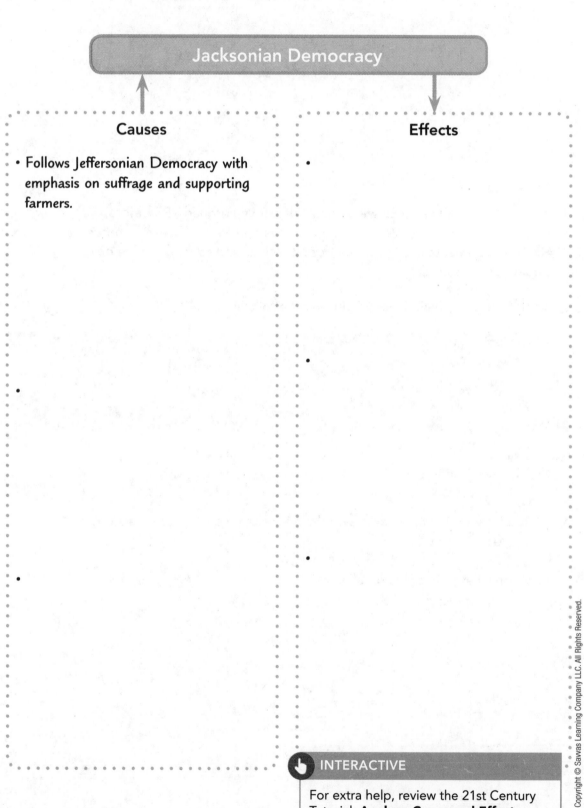

Jacksonian Democracy

Causes

- Follows Jeffersonian Democracy with emphasis on suffrage and supporting farmers.

Effects

-

INTERACTIVE

For extra help, review the 21st Century Tutorial: **Analyze Cause and Effect**.

Practice Vocabulary

Sentence Revision Revise each sentence so that the underlined vocabulary word is used logically. Be sure not to change the vocabulary word. The first one is done for you.

1. Andrew Jackson's opponents supported the <u>spoils system</u>.
   Andrew Jackson's opponents did not support the <u>spoils system</u>.

2. The spread of political power to the people during Jackson's presidency granted <u>suffrage</u> to women and all males.

3. In the election of 1824, John Quincy Adams won the <u>majority</u> of the popular vote.

4. Members of the <u>Whig Party</u> believed less government involvement improved business pursuits.

5. The <u>Democratic Party</u> platform in the 1830s saw a strong federal government involved in the economy and more privileges for the wealthy as the cornerstone of a strong republic.

Quick Activity

American Equality When Tocqueville arrived in the United States, he wrote, "What struck me during my stay [was] the equality of conditions." Consider the following:

- Tocqueville came from a country where wealthy citizens, or the aristocracy, greatly influenced society.

- Equality at that time in America was different from equality today.

Team Challenge! Work with a partner to create a short "quote" of something Tocqueville might say about equality in America today. Write your quote below and on a sticky note to post for the class.

Take Notes

Literacy Skills: Compare and Contrast Use what you have read to compare and contrast the rising sectional differences among the North, West, and South. Fill in the chart below with information about the economy, federal vs. state government, tariffs, and free and slave states. The first entry has been completed for you.

Rising Sectional Differences

North	South	West
Economy	**Economy**	**Economy**
manufacturing economy	agricultural economy; cash crops	farming
Federal vs. State Government	**Federal vs. State Government**	**Federal vs. State Government**
Tariffs	**Tariffs**	**Tariffs**
Free/Slave States	**Free/Slave States**	**Free/Slave States**

INTERACTIVE

For extra help, review the 21st Century Tutorial: **Compare and Contrast**.

Practice Vocabulary

Vocabulary Quiz Show Some quiz shows ask a question and expect the
contestant to give the answer. In other shows, the contestant is given
an answer and must supply the question. If the blank is in the Question
column, write the question that would result in the answer in the
Answer column. If the question is supplied, write the answer.

Question	Answer
1. What is a period of severe economic slump and a loss of jobs?	1.
2.	2. states' rights
3. At which event did political parties meet to choose candidates for an upcoming election?	3.
4.	4. Nullification Act
5.	5. caucus

Take Notes

Literacy Skills: Cite Evidence Use what you have read in Lesson 3 to respond to the following statement: **The lives of American Indians were radically changed when settlers arrived.** Fill in the concept web below with evidence from the text that supports the statement. The first entry has been completed for you.

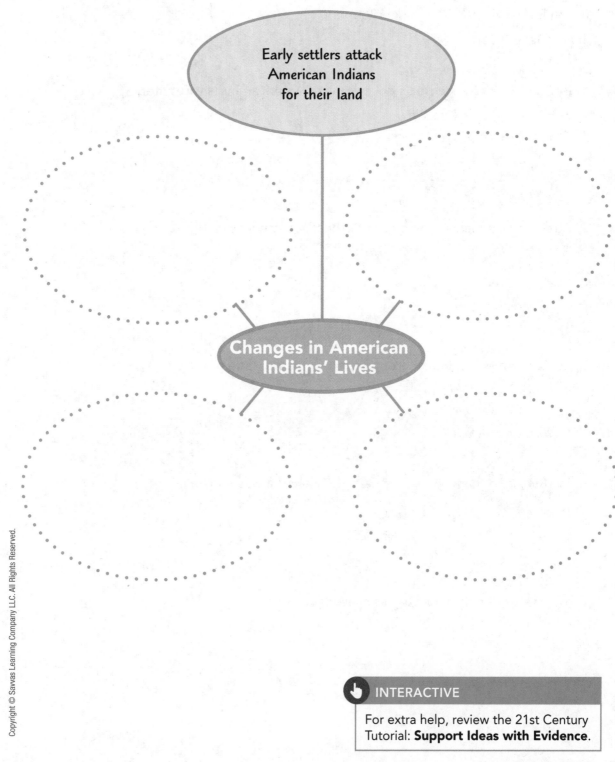

Early settlers attack American Indians for their land

Changes in American Indians' Lives

INTERACTIVE

For extra help, review the 21st Century Tutorial: **Support Ideas with Evidence**.

Practice Vocabulary

Sentence Builder Finish the sentences below with a key term from this section. You may have to change the form of the words to complete the sentences.

Word Bank

frontier   *Worcester* v. *Georgia*

Indian Removal Act   Indian Territory

Trail of Tears

1. By 1838, Andrew Jackson's policy toward American Indians resulted in the

2. A region that marks the point of furthest settlement in a territory is called the

3. In 1830, American Indian groups resisted the passage of the

4. In 1854, land that is presently part of Oklahoma was known as

5. The status of states' rights was challenged by

Take Notes

Literacy Skills: Classify and Categorize Use what you have read to complete the table below about the westward movement. The first entry has been completed for you.

Moving Westward		
New territories	Why people moved there	Life in the West
Oregon country	Northwest Ordinance opens up opportunities to buy and settle land	farming
Missouri territory		
Texas		
Land from Mexican cession		

INTERACTIVE

For extra help, review the 21st Century Tutorial: **Categorize**.

Practice Vocabulary

True or False? Decide whether each statement below is true or false. Circle T or F, and then explain your answer. Be sure to include the underlined vocabulary word in your explanation. The first one is done for you.

---

1. T / F As the first steam-powered boats, <u>flatboats</u> helped to revolutionize travel and trade.

False: <u>Flatboats</u> were not steam powered and were used to transport wagons and people along rivers.

---

2. T / F The <u>National Road</u> was the first step in a federal government-funded transportation system.

3. T / F The Constitution states that all <u>revenue</u> or income collected by the government should originate in the House of Representatives.

4. T / F As canals became important in American travel, <u>*Clermont*</u> became the first canal for transporting goods.

5. T / F In spite of high expectations, the <u>Erie Canal</u> failed to improve water transportation and trade between New York City and Buffalo, New York.

Take Notes

Literacy Skills: Summarize Use what you have read to complete the outline below. For each main idea, provide the details needed to write a summary of the topic. The main idea and details for the first entry have been completed for you.

Settling Oregon

I. Exploring the territory
    a. geography
    b. weather
    c. how the land was explored
II. Who came to the area?

    a.

    b.

    c.

III. The fur trade

    a.

    b.

IV. Negotiations with Britain

    a.

INTERACTIVE

For extra help, review the 21st Century Tutorial: **Summarize**.

Practice Vocabulary

Use a Word Bank Choose one term from the word bank to fill in each blank. When you have finished, you will have a short summary of important ideas from the section.

Word Bank

Oregon Country   mountain men

Oregon Trail   rugged individualists

Between 1800 and 1840, thousands of settlers poured into

.... While the rich, virgin soil drew many,

there was also a prosperous fur trade. Fur companies often hired fur

trappers who became known as .... Many

people admired them as .... When the fur

trade declined, many .... hired themselves

out as guides along the ....

Take Notes

Literacy Skills: Sequence Use what you have read to complete the flowchart below. In each space, write the events that led to the independence of Texas. The first event is filled in for you.

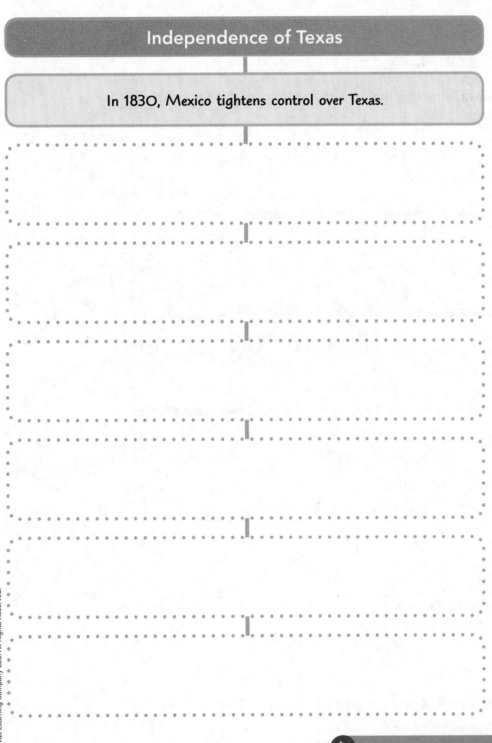

Independence of Texas

In 1830, Mexico tightens control over Texas.

INTERACTIVE

For extra help, review the 21st Century Tutorial: **Sequence**.

Practice Vocabulary

Words in Context For each question below, write an answer that shows your understanding of the **boldfaced** key term.

1. Why was the **Alamo** significant?

2. How did Santa Anna's actions as a **dictator** spark the Texas fight for independence?

3. Why did **missions** continue to spread throughout California?

4. Why were **vaqueros** a part of California tradition?

5. How did the **Santa Fe trail** affect trade routes in the United States?

6. Why is the thirteen-day **seige** of the Alamo significant?

7. Who were the **Puebloans**?

8. How did missions in California become **self-sufficient**?

Take Notes

Literacy Skills: Identify Cause and Effect Use what you have read to complete the chart below. In each box, write the effects of the expansion of the West between 1840 and 1870. The first entry is done for you.

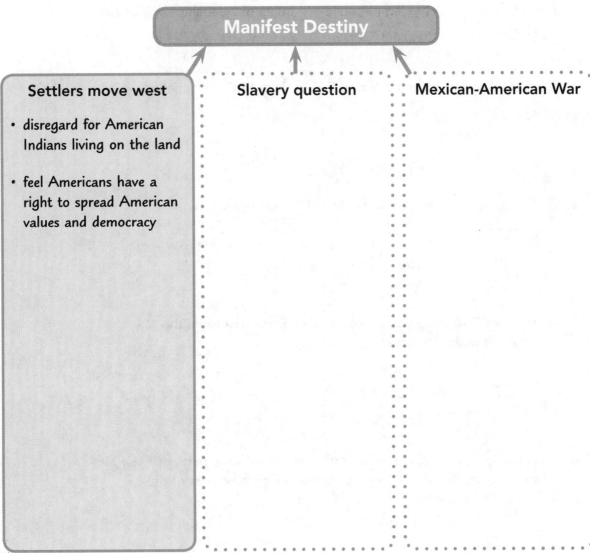

Manifest Destiny

Settlers move west

- disregard for American Indians living on the land

- feel Americans have a right to spread American values and democracy

Slavery question

Mexican-American War

INTERACTIVE

For extra help, review the 21st Century Tutorial: **Analyze Cause and Effect**.

Practice Vocabulary

Sentence Builder Finish the sentences below with a key term from this section. You may have to change the form of the words to complete the sentences.

Word Bank

Manifest Destiny   Bear Flag Republic   Treaty of Guadalupe-Hidalgo

Mexican Cession   forty-niner

1. These gold seekers, who rushed to California in 1849, became known as

2. The recognition of Texas as part of the United States was part of

3. After James Polk's election, the goal of expansion became the government policy known as

4. Present-day California, Nevada, Utah, most of Arizona, parts of New Mexico, Colorado, Wyoming, and Texas became part of the United States in the

5. Rebels, led by John C. Fremont, declared California independent of Mexico and called their new land the

Quick Activity The Importance of Water

With a partner, study the photo of the miners seeking gold during the California Gold Rush. What does it tell you about water shortages in the West?

Team Challenge! With your partner, draw a picture showing other effects of water shortages on the West. Post your drawing to share with the class. Explain the message behind your drawing.

Writing Workshop Narrative Essay

As you read, build a response to this prompt: **It is 1844 and your family has decided to move to Oregon. Write a journal entry describing the trip.** The prompts below will help walk you through the process.

Lesson 1 Writing Task: Introduce Characters (See Student Text, page 347)

List the characters who will play important roles in your journal entry and explain why your family has decided to move west.

Lesson 2 Writing Task: Establish a Setting (See Student Text, page 358)

Describe the trail from your point of view. How does the setting affect your experiences?

Lesson 3 Writing Task: Organize Sequence of Events (See Student Text, page 367)

Anecdotes are short, amusing or interesting stories about an incident or person. Create an outline for your journal entry. Start with the planning of your trip. Then identify three anecdotes you could tell about your family's trip.

Planning for Trip	
Anecdotes	

Lessons 4 and 5 Writing Tasks: Narrative Techniques
(See Student Text, pages 374 and 381)

A good journal entry will use narrative techniques—such as dialogue, description, and similes—to make it more lively and interesting to read. Identify a narrative technique, and write a sentence based on the lesson's content that uses that technique.

Lesson 6 Writing Task: Descriptive Details and Sensory Language
(See Student Text, page 391)

Choose one of your anecdotes. Is it interesting enough? Rewrite it, adding descriptive details or sensory language.

Lesson 7 Writing Task: Strong Conclusion (See Student Text, page 401)

How will your journal entry end? Draft an ending for your entry that will be memorable for your readers.

Writing Task (See Student Text, page 403)

Using the characters, setting, and anecdotes you've identified, write a journal entry about your family's trip to Oregon. Be sure to use narrative techniques, descriptive details, and sensory language in your writing. Capture the readers' attention in your opening, and end with a strong conclusion to your entry.

7 Society and Culture Before the Civil War Preview

Essential Question Why is culture important?

Before you begin this topic, think about the Essential Question by completing the following activity.

1. Think of one way that music, art, or books have inspired you. Then think of one song, piece of art, or book that an artist created because of something happening in the world. For example, *Uncle Tom's Cabin* is a novel by Harriet Beecher Stowe that was inspired by the evils of slavery.

The [song, art, book] inspired me to

The [song, art, book] was inspired by

Timeline Skills

As you read, write and/or draw at least three events from the topic. Draw a line from each event to its correct position on the timeline.

1810	1820	1830

Map Skills

Using maps throughout the topic, label the outline map showing the various travel times from New York City. Then, create a key for each of the various travel times and use the key to color the map.

1 day, 1857	1 week, 1857	4 weeks, 1857
1 day, 1800	1 week, 1800	4 weeks, 1800

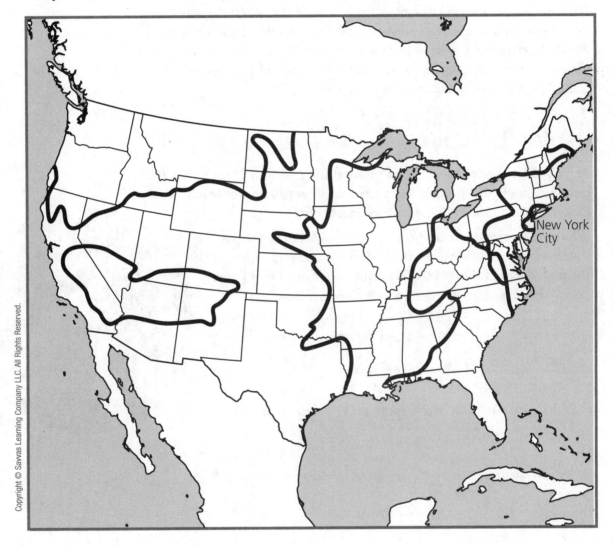

| 1840 | 1850 | 1860 | 1880 |

Quest
Document-Based Writing Inquiry
Slavery and Abolition

On this Quest, you will examine the views of those who opposed and those who supported slavery. You will examine sources from the 1800s to gain insight into these viewpoints. At the end of the Quest, you will write an essay about the tensions, related to slavery and abolition, that arose before the Civil War.

1 Ask Questions (See Student Text, page 408)

As you begin your Quest, keep in mind the Guiding Question: **What points of view did people have toward slavery and abolition?** and the Essential Question: **Why is culture important?**

What other questions do you need to ask in order to answer these questions? Consider the following aspects of life in the United States in the 1800s. Two questions are filled in for you. Add at least two questions for each category.

Theme Economy

Sample questions:

What was the basis of the southern economy in the 1800s?

What was the basis of the northern economy in the 1800s?

Theme Culture

Theme History

Theme New Inventions and Technology

Theme My Additional Questions

 INTERACTIVE

For extra help with Step 1, review the
21st Century Tutorial: **Ask Questions**.

Quest CONNECTIONS

2 Investigate

As you read about society and culture before the Civil War, collect five connections from your text to help you answer the Guiding Question. Three connections are already chosen for you.

Connect to the Abolition Movement

Lesson 2 African Americans Face Discrimination (See Student Text, page 429)

Here's a connection! Look at this section in your text. Who were William Whipper and John Russwurm? What do the accomplishments of these men reveal about the lives of free African Americans in the North in the mid-1800s?

What position do you think men such as Whipper and Russwurm took toward slavery?

Connect to the South's Economic Dependence

Lesson 3 Reliance on Plantation Agriculture (See Student Text, page 435)

Here's another connection! What does this section of the text tell you about the interaction between the southern and northern economies? On what was the southern economy based?

How might this situation have influenced the South's views on slavery?

Connect to Opponents of Slavery

Lesson 4 How Did Abolitionism Gain Momentum? (See Student Text, page 445)

What does this connection tell you about the two groups of people who opposed slavery?

What clue can you find in this section about how the abolitionists were received by those who supported slavery?

It's Your Turn! **Find two more connections. Fill in the title of your connections, then answer the questions. Connections may be images, primary sources, maps, or text.**

Your Choice | Connect to

Location in text

What is the main idea of this connection?

What does it tell you about the differing viewpoints in the United States toward slavery and abolition?

Your Choice | Connect to

Location in text

What is the main idea of this connection?

What does it tell you about the differing viewpoints in the United States toward slavery and abolition?

3 Examine Primary Sources (See Student Text, page 472)

Examine the primary and secondary sources provided online or from your teacher. Fill in the chart to show how these sources demonstrate points of view on both sides of the slavery issue. The first one is completed for you.

Source	Point of View
British Anti-Slavery Society Medallion, 1795	Abolition/Anti-slavery
"No Compromise With the Evil of Slavery"	
"Inhumanity of Slavery"	
The Southern Address of 1849	
1837 Broadside	
Cannibals All! Or, Slaves Without Masters	

INTERACTIVE

For extra help with Step 3, review the 21st Century Tutorials: **Analyze Primary and Secondary Sources** and **Compare and Contrast**.

Quest FINDINGS

4 Write Your Essay (See Student Text, page 472)

Now it's time to put together all of the information you have gathered and use it to write your essay.

1. **Prepare to Write** You have collected connections and explored primary and secondary sources that show the conflicting points of view about slavery held by Americans in the 1800s. Look through your notes and summarize these viewpoints. Record them here.

Viewpoints on Slavery and Abolition

2. **Write a Draft** Using evidence from the clues you found and the documents you explored, write a draft of your essay. Introduce the various viewpoints you have identified, then describe the cultural differences and personal attitudes behind them. Be sure to use vivid details that spring from evidence in the documents you've studied in this Quest.

3. **Share with a Partner** Exchange your draft with a partner. Tell your partner what you like about his or her draft and suggest any improvements.

4. **Finalize Your Essay** Revise your essay. Correct any grammatical or spelling errors. Be sure you have clearly described what you learned from the documents and how you used evidence from them to support your main points.

5. **Reflect on the Quest** Think about your experience completing this topic's Quest. What did you learn about the differing viewpoints on slavery and abolition? What questions do you still have about these views? How will you answer them?

Reflections

 INTERACTIVE

For extra help with Step 4, review the 21st Century Tutorial: **Write an Essay**.

Take Notes

Literacy Skills: Cite Evidence Use what you have read to complete the table. In the first column, write one conclusion from the text. In the second column, write any evidence you can find in the text that supports this conclusion. The first one has been completed for you.

Conclusions	Evidence
New machines transformed the textile industry in England.	• In 1764, James Hargreaves developed the spinning jenny, allowing workers to spin several threads at once. • In the 1780s, Edmund Cartwright built a loom powered by water that allowed a worker to produce a great deal more cloth in a day than was possible before.

INTERACTIVE

For extra help, review the 21st Century Tutorial: **Support Ideas with Evidence**.

Practice Vocabulary

True or False? Decide whether each statement below is true or false. Circle T or F, and then explain your answer. Be sure to include the underlined vocabulary word in your explanation. The first one is done for you.

1. **T / F** The <u>Industrial Revolution</u> was a fight between factory workers and wealthy factory owners.
False; The <u>Industrial Revolution</u> was a long, slow process that completely changed the way goods were produced and where people lived and worked.

2. **T / F** Setting up a new business requires <u>capital</u>, or money for investment.

3. **T / F** A <u>capitalist</u> is a person who is trained to use new technologies, such as the spinning jenny and water-powered loom.

4. **T / F** When factories cannot get enough raw materials, the supply of goods drops. <u>Supply</u> is the amount of goods available to sell.

5. **T / F** A large amount of goods, known as <u>scarcity</u>, causes prices to rise.

6. **T / F** Eli Whitney's idea of <u>interchangeable parts</u> meant that the parts of an object could be sold for a low price.

7. **T / F** The young women from nearby farms who came to work in the Lowell mills came to be called the <u>Lowell girls</u>.

8. **T / F** As industry grew, many people left farms for work in city factories, causing less <u>urbanization</u>.

Take Notes

Literacy Skills: Identify Main Ideas Use what you have read to complete the table. Use the details to identify the main idea. The first one has been completed for you.

What Changes Did the Age of Steam Power Bring?	How Did Workers Respond to Challenges?	How Did Ethnic Minorities Fare in the North?
Main Idea: The harnessing of steam power transformed many aspects of life in the United States. **Details:** Rail lines spread across the country. Factories also began to use steam, resulting in the expansion of industry and more affordable goods. Industrialization improved the standard of living.	**Main Idea:** **Details:**	**Main Idea:** **Details:**

A Reaction Against Immigrants	African Americans Face Discrimination
Main Idea: **Details:**	**Main Idea:** **Details:**

INTERACTIVE

For extra help, review the 21st Century Tutorial: **Identify Main Ideas and Details**.

Practice Vocabulary

Vocabulary Quiz Show Some quiz shows ask a question and expect the contestant to give the answer. In other shows, the contestant is given an answer and must supply the question. If the blank is in the Question column, write the question that would result in the answer in the Answer column. If the question is supplied, write the answer.

Question	Answer
1. What is another term for a skilled worker?	**1.**
2.	**2.** famine
3.	**3.** discrimination
4. What action, in which workers refused to do their jobs until their demands were met, was illegal in many parts of the country in the early 1800s?	**4.**
5.	**5.** Know-Nothing Party
6.	**6.** nativists
7. What groups were formed when artisans united to protest poor working conditions and low wages?	**7.**

Take Notes

Literacy Skills: Compare and Contrast Use what you have read to complete the charts comparing and contrasting aspects of life in the South. The first one has been completed for you.

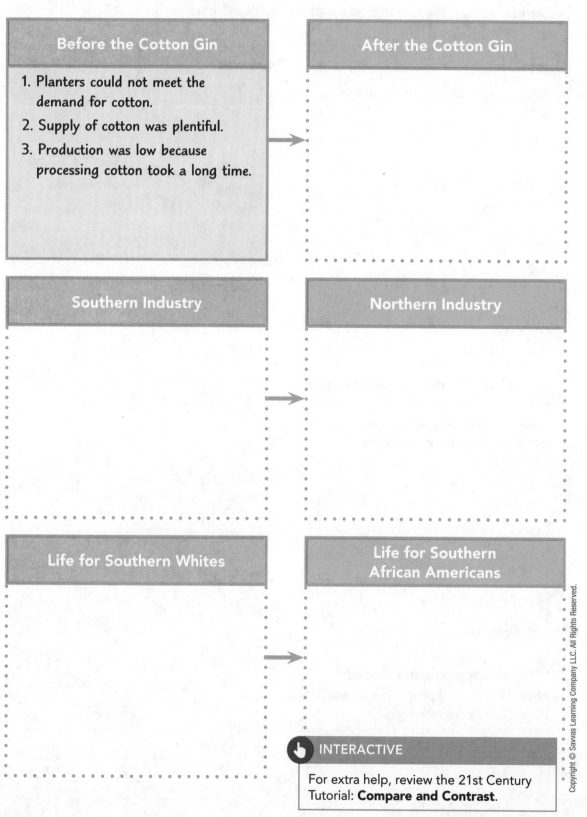

Before the Cotton Gin	After the Cotton Gin
1. Planters could not meet the demand for cotton. 2. Supply of cotton was plentiful. 3. Production was low because processing cotton took a long time.	

Southern Industry	Northern Industry

Life for Southern Whites	Life for Southern African Americans

👆 **INTERACTIVE**

For extra help, review the 21st Century Tutorial: **Compare and Contrast**.

Practice Vocabulary

Matching Logic Using your knowledge of the underlined vocabulary words, draw a line from each sentence in Column 1 to match it with the sentence in Column 2 to which it logically belongs.

Column 1	Column 2
1. The views and way of life of the "cottonocracy" dominated the South.	Before planting, farmers must prepare the land.
2. This idea of the extended family had its roots in Africa.	Swift growth in cotton production meant that by 1850, planters were producing more than 2 million bales of cotton a year.
3. Under the slave codes, enslaved African Americans could not leave their owner's land without a written pass.	These wealthy planter families lived mainly in the cotton belt of the lowland South and in coastal areas of South Carolina, Georgia, and Louisiana.
4. The invention of the cotton gin meant that planters needed more land to cultivate.	They were designed to keep enslaved African Americans from running away or rebelling.
5. Slavery spread as a result of the cotton boom.	Grandparents, parents, children, aunts, uncles, and cousins formed a close-knit group.

Take Notes

Literacy Skills: Summarize Use what you have read to complete the
table. In each space, write an important point related to that topic.
Then summarize the lesson. The first one has been completed for you.

What Form Did Early Opposition to Slavery Take?	How Did Abolitionism Gain Momentum?	Who Opposed the Abolitionists?
Slavery in the 1800s Slavery was gradually ended in the North; religious beliefs led some to oppose slavery; slavery was banned in the Northwest Territory.	Abolitionists	Northerners Against Abolition
The Colonization Movement The American Colonization Society proposed to end slavery by setting up an independent colony in Africa for Africans and African Americans.	Civil Disobedience and the Underground Railroad *Uncle Tom's Cabin*	Southerners Defend Slavery Against the North

Summary:

 INTERACTIVE

For extra help, review the 21st Century
Tutorial: **Summarize**.

Practice Vocabulary

Sentence Builder Finish the sentences below with a vocabulary term from this section. You may have to change the form of the words to complete the sentences.

Word Bank

American Colonization Society   abolitionist

The Liberator   Underground Railroad

civil disobedience

1. A person who wanted to end slavery in the United States was known as a(n)

....
.
.
....

2. "Conductors" guided runaways to "stations" where they could spend the night on the

....
.
.
....

3. Disobeying laws that one feels are unjust is known as

....
.
.
....

4. The group that President Monroe helped to set up a colony in western Africa was called the

....
.
.
....

5. William Lloyd Garrison called his antislavery newspaper

....
.
.
....

Quick Activity Abolitionists Speak Out

With a partner or small group, examine this 1859 flyer announcing the sale of enslaved people.

NEGROES FOR SALE.

I will sell by Public Auction, on Tuesday of next Court, being the 29th of November, *Eight Valuable Family Servants*, consisting of one Negro Man, a first-rate field hand, one No. 1 Boy, 17 years o' age, a trusty house servant, one excellent Cook, one House-Maid, and one Seamstress. The balance are under 12 years of age. They are sold for no fault, but in consequence of my going to reside North. Also a quantity of Household and Kitchen Furniture, Stable Lot, &c. Terms accommodating, and made known on day of sale.

Jacob August.
P. J. TURNBULL, *Auctioneer.*
Warrenton, October 28, 1859.

Printed at the *News* office, Warrenton, North Carolina.

How might an abolitionist use the information in this flyer to point out some of the evils of slavery? Refer to specific parts of the flyer in your answer.

We do not preach rebellion—no, but submission and peace. Our enemies may accuse us of striving to stir up the slaves to revenge but their accusations are false, and made only to excite the prejudices of the whites, and to destroy our influence. We say, that the possibility of a bloody insurrection at the south fills us with dismay; and we avow, too, as plainly, that if any people were ever justified in throwing off the yoke of their tyrants, the slaves are that people. It is not we, but our guilty countrymen, who put arguments into the mouths, and swords into the hands of the slaves. Every sentence that they write—every word that they speak—every resistance that they make, against foreign oppression, is a call upon their slaves to destroy them. Every Fourth of July celebration must embitter and inflame the minds of the slaves.

— William Lloyd Garrison, Editorial, *The Liberator* (January 8, 1831)

Team Challenge! The excerpt above is from an 1831 editorial. An editorial is a newspaper article that gives an opinion on a particular issue. Work with your group to write an editorial about the work of abolitionists that might have appeared in your local newspaper in the 1850s. Find an image from your text or online that you might use to illustrate the editorial, then design the article and illustration to look like a real page from a newspaper.

 Society and Culture Before the Civil War

Lesson 5 Reform and Women's Rights

Take Notes

Literacy Skills: Draw Conclusions Use what you have read to complete the table. In the right column, write conclusions that can be drawn from the information in the box to the left. The first one has been completed for you.

Main Idea	Conclusion
Reformers fought to end slavery, increase access to education, improve conditions in prisons, expand women's rights, and more.	Conflict likely erupted between reformers and those who wanted things to stay as they were.
Women often played a leading role in reform movements.	
By the 1850s, most northern states had set up free tax-supported elementary schools.	
Women had few legal or political rights at this time.	
The *Declaration of Sentiments* was modeled on the Declaration of Independence.	
Women won new opportunities in education and employment.	

INTERACTIVE

For extra help, review the 21st Century Tutorial: **Draw Conclusions**.

Practice Vocabulary

Use a Word Bank Choose one word from the word bank to fill in each blank. When you have finished, you will have a short summary of important ideas from the section.

Word Bank

social reform	women's rights movement
debtors	temperance movement
Seneca Falls Convention	Second Great Awakening

Some Americans saw many things that needed to be fixed during the Era of Reform. Dorothea Dix convinced state prison systems to stop cruel punishment and the treatment of .... as criminals. Those who took part in the .... urged people to drink less alcohol or stop drinking altogether. Much of the impulse toward .... at this time had its roots in the .... that swept the nation. This movement taught that people could save their souls by their actions.

Inspired by religion and their work on other causes, women met at the .... in 1848 to discuss equal rights for women. This meeting was the beginning of the long- and still-continuing ....

Quick Activity An Echo Across Time

In 1776, the founders of the United States declared their independence from Britain with these ringing words:

> . . . The history of the present King of Great Britain is a history of repeated injuries and usurpations, all having in direct object the establishment of an absolute Tyranny over these States. To prove this, let Facts be submitted to a candid world.
>
> He has refused his Assent to Laws, the most wholesome and necessary for the public good.
>
> He has forbidden his Governors to pass Laws of immediate and pressing importance.
>
> —The Declaration of Independence (1776)

More than seventy years later, the women who attended the Seneca Falls Convention declared their own independence. Underline words and phrases that are the same in the two declarations.

> The history of mankind is a history of repeated injuries and usurpations on the part of man toward woman, having in direct object the establishment of an absolute tyranny over her. To prove this, let facts be submitted to a candid world.
>
> He has never permitted her to exercise her inalienable right to the elective franchise.
>
> He has compelled her to submit to laws, in the formation of which she had no voice.
>
> —The Declaration of Sentiments and Resolutions, 1848

Team Challenge! With a partner or small group, explore the similarities between the Declaration of Independence and the Declaration of Sentiments. Then answer this question: Why do you think the writers of the Declaration of Sentiments chose to model their work on the earlier document?

Take Notes

Literacy Skills: Identify Cause and Effect Use what you have read to complete the diagrams. Two causes have been completed for you.

Effect: By the mid-1800s, Americans developed a new pride in their country and its culture.

Cause

The Hudson River School and other artists painted scenes of American life and American landscapes.

Cause

Cause

Effect: Henry David Thoreau writes about civil disobedience.

Cause

Transcendentalism develops.

Cause

Cause

👆 **INTERACTIVE**

For extra help, review the 21st Century Tutorial: **Analyze Cause and Effect**.

Practice Vocabulary

Word Map Study the word map for the term *Hudson River School.* Characteristics are words or phrases that relate to the term in the center of the word map. Non-characteristics are words and phrases not associated with that term. Use the blank word map to explore the meaning of the word *transcendentalist.* Then make a word map of your own for the word *individualism.*

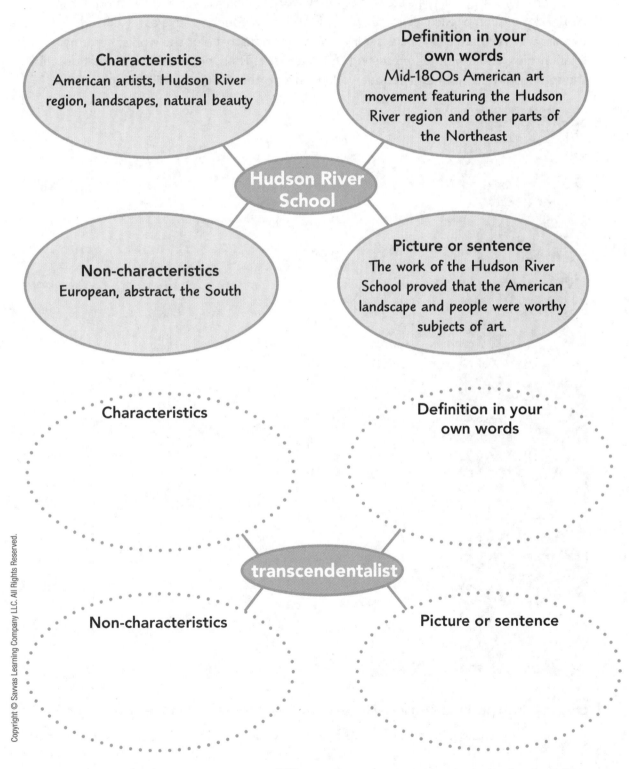

Characteristics
American artists, Hudson River region, landscapes, natural beauty

Definition in your own words
Mid-1800s American art movement featuring the Hudson River region and other parts of the Northeast

Hudson River School

Non-characteristics
European, abstract, the South

Picture or sentence
The work of the Hudson River School proved that the American landscape and people were worthy subjects of art.

Characteristics

Definition in your own words

transcendentalist

Non-characteristics

Picture or sentence

Writing Workshop Narrative Essay

As you read, build a response to this topic: **Write a three-paragraph narrative essay from the point of view of a young person working in northern industry during this time period.** The prompts below will help walk you through the process.

Lessons 1 and 2 Writing Tasks: Introduce Characters and Establish Setting
(See Student Text, pages 420 and 430)

Your narrative essay will tell a story, and every story has characters and a setting. Write a brief description of each character who will appear in your narrative essay. Include details such as where each character lives, in which industry he or she works, his or her relationships, and any other interesting characteristics. Then, write a sentence that describes the setting in which your story about working in a northern industry will take place.

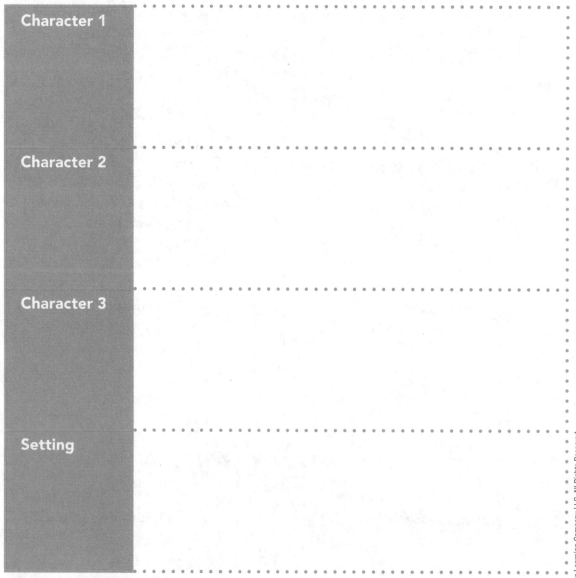

Character 1	
Character 2	
Character 3	
Setting	

Lesson 3 Writing Task: Organize Sequence of Events (See Student Text, page 442)

On a separate sheet of paper, plan the events of your story in the order they will happen.

Lessons 4 and 5 Writing Tasks: Use Narrative Techniques, Descriptive Details, and Sensory Language (See Student Text, pages 449 and 463)

Will you tell your story using the first person point of view—"I lived . . ." or "I saw . . ."? Or the third person—"He lived . . ." or "He saw . . ."? Will you use present or past tense? Will you include dialogue? After deciding these points, think about how to bring your story to life. Write some descriptive words and sensory language about where you are sitting right now. Then, write descriptive words and sensory language related to your story.

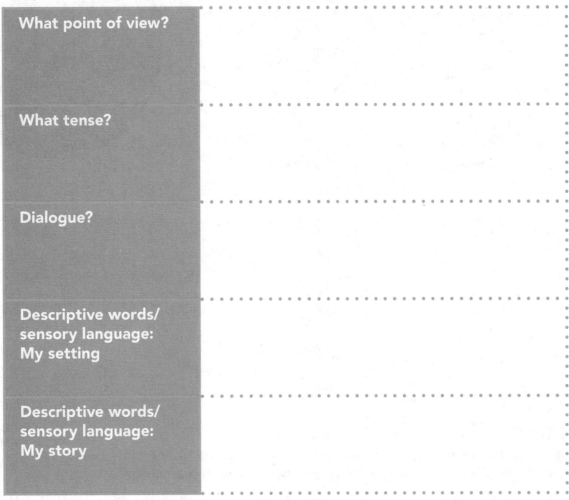

What point of view?	
What tense?	
Dialogue?	
Descriptive words/ sensory language: My setting	
Descriptive words/ sensory language: My story	

Lesson 6 Writing Task: Prepare a Final Draft (See Student Text, page 471)

Using the details you have fleshed out here, write a first draft of your story. After you have finished, review your work. Check your structure, spelling, and grammar, and prepare a final draft.

Writing Task (See Student Text, page 473)

Read your final draft. Does the story follow the plan you set out here? Does it accurately describe life for a young person working in a northern industry during the Industrial Revolution? Once you are satisfied with your work, trade essays with a partner. Make any corrections or improvements your partner suggests.

Sectionalism and Civil War Preview

Essential Question When is war justified?

Before you begin this topic, think about the Essential Question by completing the following activity.

1. What factors justify going to war? Read the list below, then write a paragraph explaining which of these factors would justify going to war and which would not.

economic factors   religious factors

political factors   social factors

Timeline Skills

As you read, write and/or draw at least three events from the topic. Draw a line from each event to its correct position on the timeline.

1820	1830	1840

Map Skills

Using maps throughout the topic, add the state abbreviations for those states that are missing labels. Then use different colors to shade the Union states, the Border states, the Confederate states, and the territories.

California	Georgia	Kansas	Kentucky
Mississippi	New York	Ohio	South Carolina
Texas	Virginia	West Virginia	

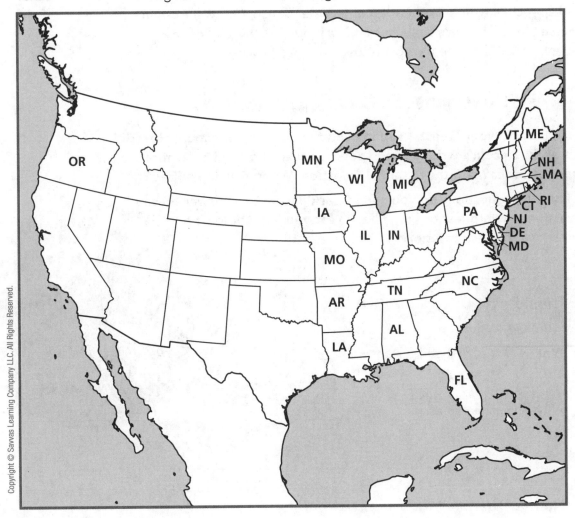

1850   1860   1870

Quest

Project-Based Learning Inquiry

A Lincoln Website

On this Quest, you need to compare Abraham Lincoln's writings and speeches to the Declaration of Independence. You will examine sources from Lincoln's speeches and writings. At the end of the Quest, you will create a website to share your findings.

1 Ask Questions (See Student Text, page 478)

As you begin your Quest, keep in mind the Guiding Question: **How did Abraham Lincoln's writings and speeches relate to the Declaration of Independence?** and the Essential Question: **When is war justified?**

What other questions do you need to ask in order to answer these questions? Two questions are filled in for you. Add at least two questions for each category.

Theme The Gettysburg Address

Sample questions:

What was the Gettysburg Address?

Why is it memorable?

Theme The Declaration of Independence

Theme Preserving the Union

Theme Election of 1864

Theme My Additional Questions

 INTERACTIVE

For extra help with Step 1, review the
21st Century Tutorial: **Ask Questions**.

2 Investigate

As you read about President Lincoln and the Civil War, collect five connections from your text to help you answer the Guiding Question. Three connections are already chosen for you.

Connect to the Lincoln/Douglas Debates

Lesson 2 How Did Abraham Lincoln Come to Lead the Republican Party? (See Student Text, page 497)

Here's a connection! Find the passage in the Declaration of Independence that explains the rights that all men should have. How do Lincoln's comments during his series of debates with Stephen Douglas support the ideas expressed in the Declaration of Independence?

What were Stephen Douglas's views on popular sovereignty? What were Lincoln's views?

Connect to the Right to Alter or to Abolish

Lesson 3 A Move Toward Civil War (See Student Text, page 503)

Here's another connection! What does the Declaration of Independence say about the people's displeasure with their current government?

What does Lincoln say about this in his speeches?

Secessionists leaving the Union.

Connect to the Emancipation Proclamation

Primary Source Abraham Lincoln, The Emancipation Proclamation
(See Student Text, page 531)

What does the Declaration of Independence say about the responsibility of government to protect the safety and happiness of the people?

How is this passage in the Declaration of Independence reflected in the Emancipation Proclamation?

It's Your Turn! **Find two more connections. Fill in the title of your connections, then answer the questions. Connections may be images, primary sources, maps, or text.**

Your Choice | Connect to

Location in text

What is the main idea of this connection?

What does it tell you about Lincoln's understanding of the Declaration of Independence?

Your Choice | Connect to

Location in text

What is the main idea of this connection?

What does it tell you about Lincoln's understanding of the Declaration of Independence?

3 Conduct Research (See Student Text, page 544)

Examine Abraham Lincoln's Emancipation Proclamation in your text. Then find additional writings and speeches from Lincoln in the text or online. List these additional sources in the chart and then note how they reveal the ways that Lincoln's speeches and writings relate to the Declaration of Independence. The first one is completed for you.

Abraham Lincoln's Writings/Speeches	Relation to the Declaration of Independence
Emancipation Proclamation (1863)	"All men are created equal," including enslaved people. Government is responsible for protecting the rights of all people, including the enslaved.

INTERACTIVE

For extra help with Step 3, review the 21st Century Tutorial: **Analyze Primary and Secondary Sources**.

Quest FINDINGS

④ Create a Website (See Student Text, page 544)

Now is the time to put together all of the information you have gathered and use it to create your two-page website. Work with a partner or team. Familiarize yourself with digital tools and software to help you create images and text for your website.

1. **Prepare to Write** You have collected connections and explored primary sources that show how Lincoln's speeches and writings reflected ideas in the Declaration of Independence. Look through your notes and decide which speeches and writings you want to highlight on your website. Record them here. Then, decide which team member will write and design each section of your website.

Lincoln's Writings and Speeches

2. Write a Draft Using evidence from the clues you found and the documents you explored, write a draft of your section of the website, including any visuals you plan to use.

3. Share with a Partner Exchange your draft with a partner. Tell your partner what you like about his or her draft and suggest any improvements.

4. Finalize Your Plans for Your Website. Make any revisions needed. Are your explanations clear? Do your images relate well to your content? Once you finalize your plans, create your website.

5. Reflect on the Quest Think about your experience completing this topic's Quest. What did you learn about Abraham Lincoln and his admiration for the ideas in the Declaration of Independence? What questions do you still have about his writings and how they reflect ideas in the Declaration of Independence? How will you answer them?

Reflections

👆 INTERACTIVE

For extra help with Step 4, review the 21st Century Tutorial: **Evaluate Web Sites**.

Take Notes

Literacy Skills: Compare and Contrast Use what you have learned to complete the Venn diagram. Compare and contrast the Missouri Compromise of 1820 and the Missouri Compromise of 1850. In what ways were the provisions different? In what ways were the provisions the same? The first entry has been completed for you.

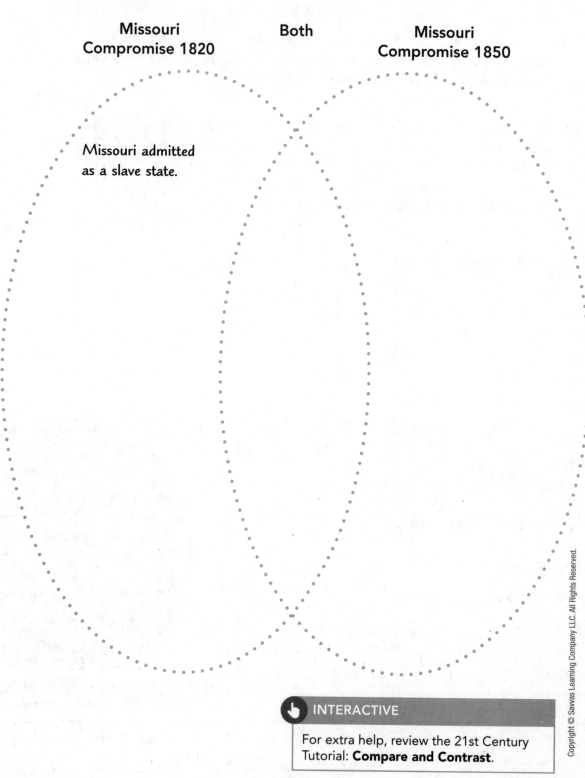

Missouri
Compromise 1820

Both

Missouri
Compromise 1850

Missouri admitted
as a slave state.

👆 INTERACTIVE

For extra help, review the 21st Century Tutorial: **Compare and Contrast**.

Practice Vocabulary

True or False? Decide whether each statement below is true or false. Circle T or F, and then explain your answer. Be sure to include the underlined vocabulary word in your explanation. The first one is done for you.

1. **T / F** The <u>Missouri Compromise</u> was a series of laws in 1820 that favored the admission of free states to the Union.
   False; The <u>Missouri Compromise</u> was a series of laws in 1820 and 1850 that maintained a balance between free and slave states admitted to the Union.

2. **T / F** The newly formed <u>Free-Soil Party</u>, whose members were mostly southerners, campaigned for popular sovereignty in the western territories.

3. **T / F** Southerners felt justified in the decision to <u>secede</u> because they said the North did not respect the compact between states as set forth in the Constitution.

4. **T / F** Bleeding Kansas was the result of the repeal of <u>popular sovereignty</u> in Kansas and Nebraska.

5. **T / F** The <u>Compromise of 1850</u> applied to the Louisiana Purchase and the Mexican Cession.

6. **T / F** The <u>Fugitive Slave Act</u> of 1850, with added provisions and heavier punishments, was more harsh than the Fugitive Slave Act passed in 1793.

7. **T / F** Daniel Webster felt the Compromise of 1850 would not prevent <u>civil war</u>.

8. **T / F** Personal liberty laws passed in the North allowed <u>fugitives</u> to argue their cases before a court.

Take Notes

Literacy Skills: Identify Cause and Effect Use what you have learned to complete the chart. Write the effects of each event on the North and on the South. The first one is completed for you.

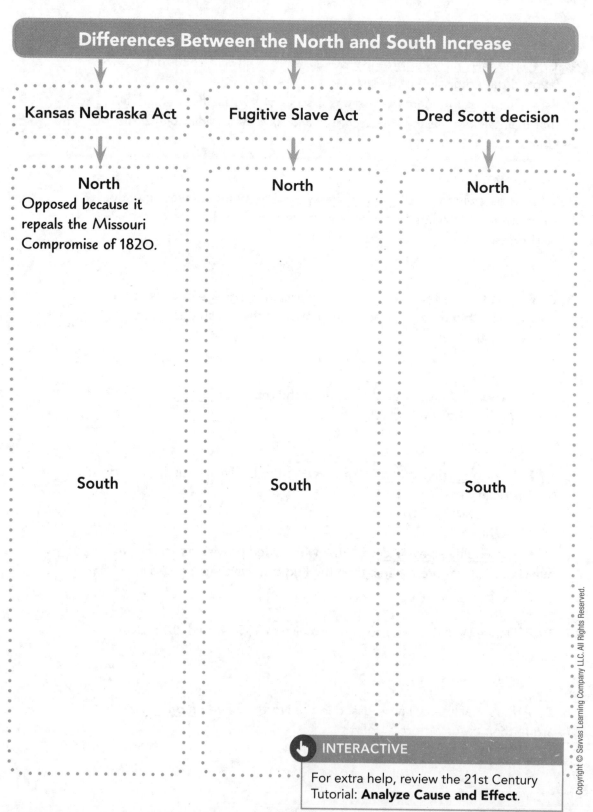

Differences Between the North and South Increase

Kansas Nebraska Act

Fugitive Slave Act

Dred Scott decision

North
Opposed because it repeals the Missouri Compromise of 1820.

North

North

South

South

South

👆 INTERACTIVE

For extra help, review the 21st Century Tutorial: **Analyze Cause and Effect**.

Practice Vocabulary

Vocabulary Quiz Show Some quiz shows ask a question and expect the contestant to give the answer. In other shows, the contestant is given an answer and must supply the question. If the blank is in the Question column, write the question that would result in the answer in the Answer column. If the question is supplied, write the answer.

Question

1.

2. What measure did Stephen Douglas propose to organize government in two territories?

3.

4. What said that Congress did not have the power to ban slavery in the territories?

5. Which proslavery group traveled to the Kansas-Nebraska territory to set up a government?

6.

7. What organization attracted people who were opposed to the spread of slavery in the western territories?

8. What is it called when informal military groups use hit-and-run tactics?

Answer

1. martyr

2.

3. arsenal

4.

5.

6. treason

7.

8.

Quick Activity Formerly a Slave

With a partner or small group, read the excerpt below. It is the narrative of an escaped slave, Nancy Howard. Her story is part of a collection of narratives of former slaves who escaped to Canada. The stories were gathered by Boston abolitionist Benjamin Drew.

> I was born in Arundel County, Maryland—was brought up in Baltimore. After my escape, I lived in Lynn, Mass., seven years. But I left there, through fear of being carried back, owing to the fugitive slave law. I have lived in St. Catherines [Ontario, Canada] less than a year.
>
> The way I got away was—my mistress was sick and went into the country for her health. I went to stay with her cousin. After a month, my mistress was sent back to the city to her cousin's and I waited on her. My daughter had been off [successfully escaped] three years. A friend said to me—"Now is your chance to get off." At last I concluded to go—the friend supplying me with money. I was asked no questions on the way north.
>
> —from Benjamin Drew, *The Refugee: Narratives of Fugitive Slaves in Canada Related by Themselves* (1856)

This is one story. Why did Nancy leave Massachusetts? Do you think her fears were justified? Explain your answer.

Team Challenge! The picture above shows African Americans arriving at a place where they can live in freedom. How do you think these people feel? If you were an enslaved person planning to escape, would your plans be influenced by the *Dred Scott* decision? Working with your partner or group, write a short narrative from the viewpoint of the enslaved person that tells whether or not you will keep your plans to escape in light of this decision. Share your stories with the class.

Take Notes

Literacy Skills: Compare and Contrast Use what you have read to complete the tables. List the differences between the North and South during the early years of the Civil War. The first entry is completed for you.

	North	South
Reason for fighting	• To preserve the Union	• To preserve their way of life
Advantages		
Disadvantages		

INTERACTIVE

For extra help, review the 21st Century Tutorial: **Compare and Contrast**.

Practice Vocabulary

Word Map Study the word map for the word *unamendable*. Characteristics are words or phrases that relate to the term in the center of the word map. Non-characteristics are words and phrases not associated with that term. Use the blank word map to explore the meaning of the word *acquiescence*. Then make a word map of your own for the term *border state*.

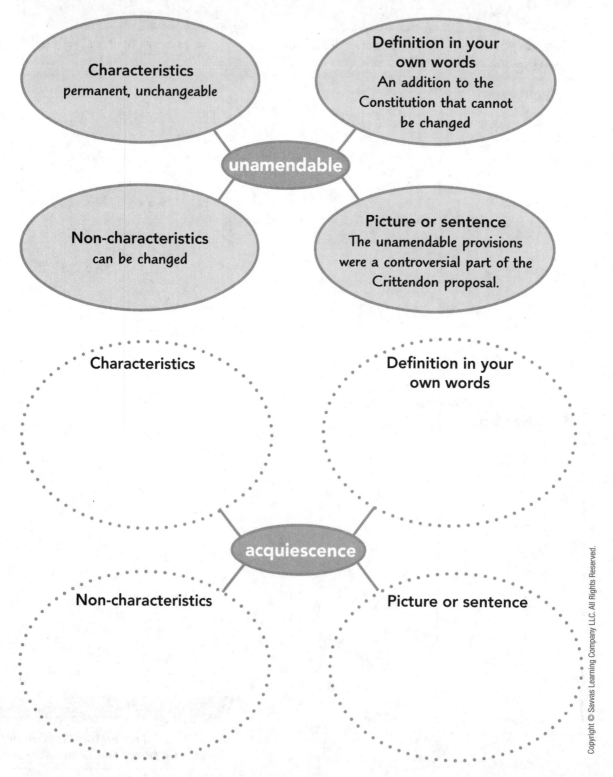

Characteristics
permanent, unchangeable

Definition in your own words
An addition to the Constitution that cannot be changed

unamendable

Non-characteristics
can be changed

Picture or sentence
The unamendable provisions were a controversial part of the Crittendon proposal.

Characteristics

Definition in your own words

acquiescence

Non-characteristics

Picture or sentence

Take Notes

Literacy Skills: Sequence Use what you have read to complete the timeline with the five important battles that occurred during 1862. Then, in the box at bottom, write the significance of each battle.

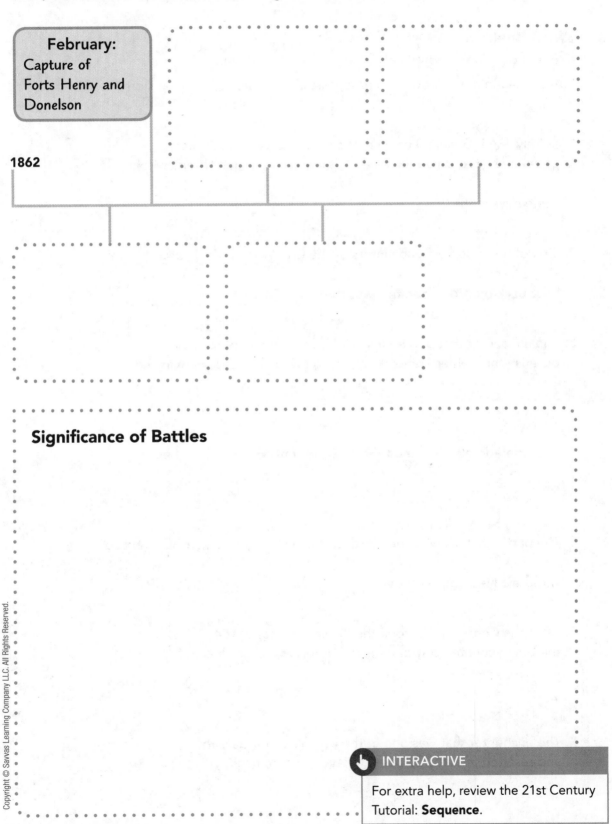

February:
Capture of
Forts Henry and
Donelson

1862

Significance of Battles

INTERACTIVE

For extra help, review the 21st Century Tutorial: **Sequence**.

Practice Vocabulary

Sentence Builder Finish the sentences below with a key term from this section. You may have to change the form of the words to complete the sentences.

Word Bank

Battle of Bull Run	Battle of Shiloh	*Monitor*
Battle of Antietam	Battle of Fredericksburg	Battle of Chancellorsville
Virginia		

1. In May 1863, General Lee, with the help of Stonewall Jackson, outmaneuvered Union forces and defeated the Union troops within

   three days in the ....

2. One of the bloodiest encounters of the Civil War, in which Grant's army

   beat back the Confederates, was the ....

3. The encounter that proved it would be a long and bloody war, because the Confederates stood up to the Union soldiers, was the

   ....

4. The Confederates renamed the USS *Merrimack* warship to the

   ....

5. The battle that allowed the North to claim victory because General Lee

   withdrew his troops was the ....

6. After the Confederates took the *Virginia* out for battle, the Union countered with their own ironclad, called the

   ....

7. The encounter that was one of the Union's worst defeats, and resulted in Burnside being relieved of command, was the

   ....

Take Notes

Literacy Skills: Summarize Use what you have read to complete the chart. After you have completed the chart, provide a summary describing how these factors changed or challenged the North and South during the Civil War. The first entry Is completed for you.

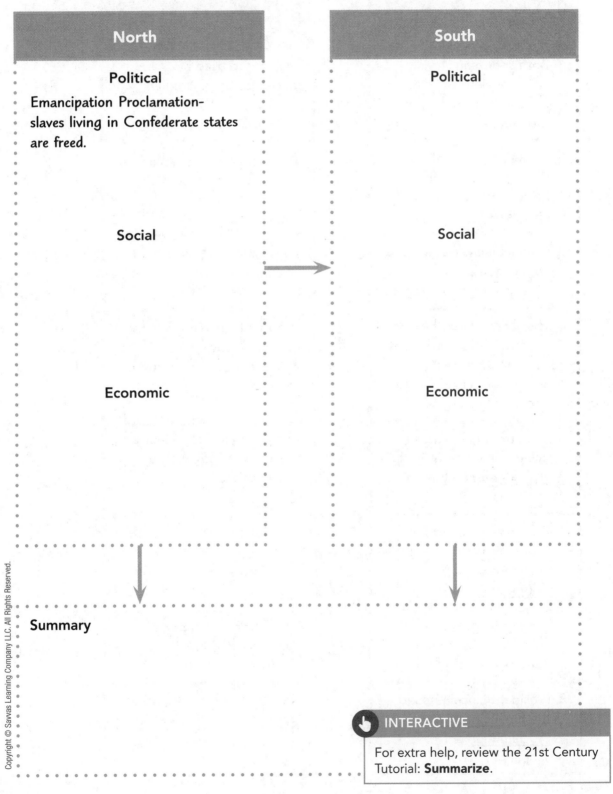

North	South
Political	**Political**
Emancipation Proclamation- slaves living in Confederate states are freed.	
Social	**Social**
Economic	**Economic**

Summary

INTERACTIVE

For extra help, review the 21st Century Tutorial: **Summarize**.

Practice Vocabulary

Matching Logic Using your knowledge of the underlined words, draw a line from each sentence in Column 1 to match it with the sentence in Column 2 to which it logically belongs.

Column 1	Column 2
1. Both Jefferson Davis and President Lincoln imposed a <u>draft</u> to raise their armies.	This group tried to persuade Union soldiers to desert.
2. He was accused of acting like a dictator when he suspended <u>habeas corpus</u>.	President Lincoln moved to end slavery in territory controlled by the Confederacy.
3. Colonel Shaw was a commander of the <u>54th Massachusetts Regiment</u>.	Opposition to this law led to riots and violence.
4. The sharp rise in the price of food in the South from $6 a month in 1861 to $68 a month in 1863 was a result of <u>inflation</u>.	President Lincoln stretched executive powers to suppress opposition during the war.
5. Even though the assault failed, the battle at <u>Fort Wagner</u> earned this unit distinction.	The Revenue Act included this measure to help pay war expenses.
6. One of two important economic laws passed to raise money was the <u>income tax</u>.	This volunteer unit was the first to accept African American soldiers.
7. <u>Copperheads</u>, or Peace Democrats, wanted peace with the South.	This occurs when prices rise and the value of money decreases.
8. President Lincoln issued the <u>Emancipation Proclamation</u> on January 1, 1863.	Nearly half of the regiment lost their lives in this attack.

Quick Activity Living through the War

As the war moved into its third year, the effect on civilians became more difficult. The account below is from Agnes, who lived in Richmond, Virginia.

> The crowd now rapidly increased and numbered, I am sure more than a thousand women and children. It grew and grew until it reached the dignity of a mob—a bread riot.
>
> —Agnes, quoted in *Reminiscences of Peace and War*

While the account is brief, it still creates a picture in the reader's mind. Working with a partner or a small group, give a one-minute news report of the situation. What do you know about the crowd? What was the mood? Who was affected? Then read the accounts of a soldier's life during the war.

> The first thing in the morning is drill. Then drill, then drill again. Then drill, drill, a little more drill. Then drill and lastly drill.

> Look at our company—21 have died of disease, 18 have become so unhealthy as to be discharged, and only four have been killed in battle.

Team Challenge! Working with a partner or a small group, explain how a Civil War correspondent on the front lines and a historian many years later might have used information from these and other primary sources to determine what the life of a soldier was like. What sort of sources would each use? What information might they have learned from these sources? Share your report with the class.

Take Notes

Literacy Skills: Sequence Use what you have read to complete the flowchart. Identify significant events during the last two years of the war (1863–1865). In the last box, describe the effect of the war on the nation. The first entry is completed for you.

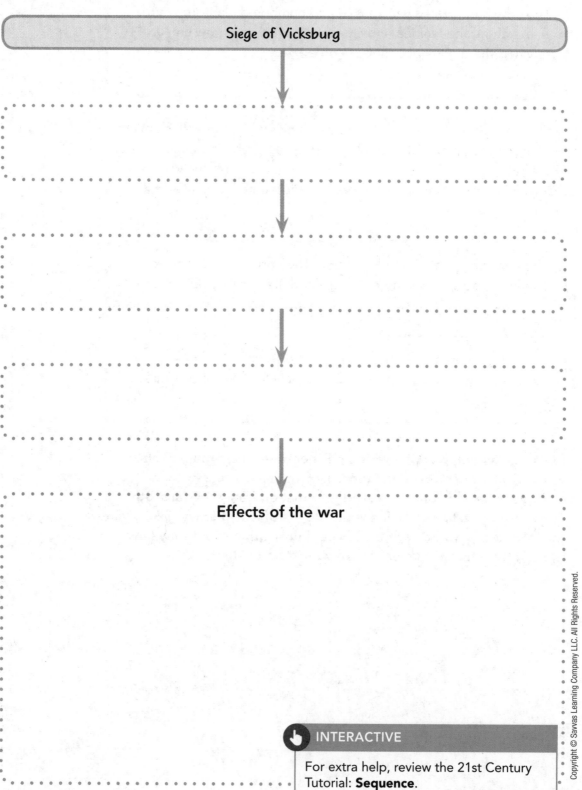

Siege of Vicksburg

Effects of the war

INTERACTIVE

For extra help, review the 21st Century Tutorial: **Sequence**.

Practice Vocabulary

Words in Context For each question below, write an answer that shows your understanding of the boldfaced key term.

1. Why was the meeting at **Appomattox Court House** significant?

2. How did **Pickett's Charge** change the course of the war?

3. Explain what happens during a military **siege**.

4. What happened at the **Battle of Gettysburg**?

5. What was Lincoln's goal in the **Gettysburg Address**?

Writing Workshop Informative Essay

As you read, build a response to this question: **What were the differences between the North and the South before, during, and after the Civil War?** The prompts below will help you walk through the process.

Lessons 1 and 2 Writing Tasks: Consider Your Purpose and Pick an Organizing Strategy (See Student Text, pages 487 and 499)

Describe what information you will provide to complete the task. Then, consider how you will present your information. Will you include visuals? Set out your plan below.

Lesson 3 Writing Task: Develop Your Thesis (See Student Text, pages 511)

Write one sentence that describes your ideas on the differences between the North and the South before, during, and after the Civil War. This will be your thesis statement.

Lesson 4 Writing Task: Support Thesis with Details (See Student Text, pages 519)

Review your thesis statement. Make any revisions you feel are necessary.
List details from Lessons 1, 2, 3, and 4 describing the differences
between the North and South. Use the table below to list these details.

North	South

Lesson 5 Writing Task: Write an Introduction (See Student Text, page 530)

Write the opening paragraph of your essay on another piece of paper. This
opening paragraph should introduce your thesis and be clear and concise.

Lesson 6 Writing Task: Draft Your Essay (See Student Text, page 543)

Use the details you have been gathering to write a first draft of your
essay about the differences between the North and South before, during,
and after the Civil War.

Writing Task (See Student Text, page 545)

Using the draft you created, answer the following question in a five-
paragraph informative essay: What were the differences between the
North and the South before, during, and after the Civil War?

The Reconstruction Era Preview

Essential Question How should we handle conflict?

Before you begin this topic, think about the Essential Question by answering the following questions.

1. Check the ideas that you think are helpful ways of resolving conflict.

   __compromising   __shouting   __speaking kindly

   __listening to everyone   __being open-minded   __name-calling

   __hitting   __seeing another perspective

2. Preview the topic by skimming lesson titles, headings, and graphics. List ideas that you think might have been sources of conflict after the Civil War.

Timeline Skills

As you read, write and/or draw at least three events from the topic. Draw a line from each event to its correct position on the timeline.

1865	1870

Map Skills

**Using maps throughout the topic, label the states listed below.
Then, color and number each military district.**

Alabama   Arkansas   Florida   Georgia

Louisiana   Mississippi   North Carolina   South Carolina

Texas   Virginia

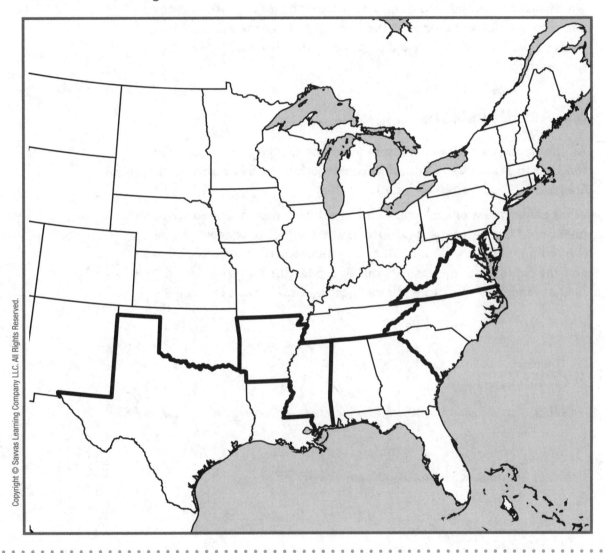

1875   1880

Civic Discussion Inquiry

The End of Reconstruction

On this Quest, in the role of an historian, you will explore sources and gather information about the ending of Reconstruction. Then, you will participate in a civic discussion with other historians about the Guiding Question.

1 Ask Questions (See Student Text, page 550)

As you begin your Quest, keep in mind the Guiding Question: **Should the United States have ended Reconstruction in 1877?** and the Essential Question: **How should we handle conflict?**

What other questions do you need to ask in order to answer these questions? Consider themes, such as the conflict that arose during rebuilding, Lincoln's plan, southern Democrats, northern Republicans, and the South and Reconstruction. Two questions are filled in for you. Add at least two questions for each of the other two categories.

Theme Rebuilding Brings Conflict

Sample questions:

What plan did white southern Democrats favor for rebuilding the South?

What plan did northern Republicans favor?

Theme Lincoln's Plan

Theme Southern Democrats

Theme Northern Republicans

Theme The South and Reconstruction

Theme My Additional Questions

 INTERACTIVE

For extra help with Step 1, review the
21st Century Tutorial: **Ask Questions**.

Quest CONNECTIONS

2 Investigate

As you read about the ending of Reconstruction, collect five connections to help you answer the Guiding Question. Three connections are already chosen for you.

Connect to Reconstruction Problems

Lesson 1 The Effects of the Civil War (See Student Text, page 552)

Here's a connection! Read this section in your text. What problems did the country face after the Civil War?

What problems would Reconstruction be expected to solve?

Connect to Frederick Douglass

Primary Source Frederick Douglass, "What the Black Man Wants"
(See Student Text, page 564)

Here's another connection! Frederick Douglass was an African American abolitionist, orator, and writer. What did Douglass want Reconstruction to achieve?

How did his goals for Reconstruction compare with those of others?

Connect to the End of Reconstruction

Lesson 4 New Restrictions on African American Rights
(See Student Text, page 577)

As troops withdrew from the South, what were some new ways that African Americans were prevented from exercising their rights?

Did Reconstruction successfully rebuild society?

It's Your Turn! **Find two more connections. Fill in the title of your connections, then answer the questions. Connections may be images, primary sources, maps, or text.**

Your Choice | Connect to

Location in text

What is the main idea of this connection?

What does this tell you about the events and legacy of Reconstruction?

Your Choice | Connect to

Location in text

What is the main idea of this connection?

What does this tell you about the events and legacy of Reconstruction?

3 **Examine Primary Sources** (See Student Text, page 580)

Examine the primary and secondary sources provided online or from your teacher. Fill in the chart to show how these sources provide further information about whether the United States should have ended Reconstruction in 1877. The first one is completed for you.

Should the United States have ended Reconstruction in 1877?	
Source	**Yes or No? Why?**
"Reconstruction Reassessed"	YES, because freed slaves were unequipped to succeed with control of the corrupt southern government, making the South vulnerable to "Northern adventures."
"The Supreme Court and the History of Reconstruction—and Vice-Versa"	
"The Use of Military Force to Protect the Gains of Reconstruction"	

INTERACTIVE

For extra help with Step 3, review the 21st Century Tutorial: **Compare Viewpoints**.

 **FINDINGS**

4 Discuss! (See Student Text, page 580)

Now that you have collected clues and explored documents about the end of Reconstruction, you are ready to discuss with your fellow historians the Guiding Question: **Should the United States have ended Reconstruction in 1877?** Follow the steps below, using the spaces provided to prepare for your discussion.

You will work with a partner in a small group of historians. Try to reach a consensus, a situation in which everyone is in agreement, on the question. Can you do it?

1. **Prepare Your Arguments** You will be assigned a position on the question, either YES or NO.

   My position: ⬚

   Work with your partner to review your Quest notes from the Quest Connections and Quest Sources.

   - If you were assigned YES, agree with your partner on what you think were the strongest arguments from Godkin and Foner.

   - If you were assigned NO, agree on what you think were the strongest arguments from Blair.

2. **Present Your Position** Those assigned YES will present their arguments and evidence first. As you listen, ask clarifying questions to gain information and understanding.

What is a Clarifying Question?
These types of questions do not judge the person talking. They are only for the listener to be clear on what he or she is hearing.

Example:	Example:
Can you tell me more about that?	You said [x]. Am I getting that right?

INTERACTIVE

For extra help with Step 4, review the 21st Century Tutorial: **Participate in a Discussion or Debate**.

While the opposite side speaks, take notes on what you hear in the space below.

3. **Switch!** Now NO and YES will switch sides. If you argued YES before, now you will argue NO. Work with your same partner and use your notes. Add any arguments and evidence from the clues and sources. Those *now* arguing YES go first.

When both sides have finished, answer the following:

Before I started this discussion with my fellow historians, my opinion was that the United States	*After* this discussion with my fellow historians, my opinion is that the United States
_____should have ended Reconstruction in 1877.	_____should have ended Reconstruction in 1877.
_____should not have ended Reconstruction in 1877.	_____should not have ended Reconstruction in 1877.

4. **Point of View** Do you all agree on the answer to the Guiding Question?

- _____Yes

- _____No

If not, on what points do you all agree?

Take Notes

Literacy Skills: Identify Cause and Effect Use what you have read to complete the chart. Draw a line connecting the cause to the effect. The first one has been completed for you.

Cause	Effect
Soldiers came home at the end of the war.	Environmental damage, including destruction of southern farms and forests, was widespread.
More battles took place in the South.	The Freedmen's Bureau was created to help with food, clothing, medical care, education, and jobs.
Freed African Americans needed help beginning new lives.	Many people were looking for jobs.
The Thirteenth Amendment banned slavery throughout the nation.	The South had to redefine its social and economic systems.

 INTERACTIVE

For extra help, review the 21st Century Tutorial: **Analyze Cause and Effect**.

Practice Vocabulary

Vocabulary Quiz Show Some quiz shows ask a question and expect the contestant to give the answer. In other shows, the contestant is given an answer and must supply the question. If the blank is in the Question column, write the question that would result in the answer in the Answer column. If the question is supplied, write the answer.

Question

1. What agency was established to help former slaves begin their new lives?

2. What is a government pardon called?

3.

4.

5. What name was given to describe the rebuilding of the nation?

Answer

1.

2.

3. freedmen

4. Thirteenth Amendment

5.

Quick Activity Debate with a Partner

In the roles of Congressional Republicans in 1864, debate with your partner the Ten Percent Plan versus the Wade-Davis Bill. Summarize your main ideas in this table.

Ten Percent Plan	Wade-Davis Bill

Team Challenge! Reconstruction of the South was a long process. When Andrew Johnson became president, his plan for Reconstruction called for a majority of voters in each Southern state to pledge loyalty to the United States and to ratify the Thirteenth Amendment, which banned slavery throughout the nation. Discuss how Johnson's plan compared to the Ten Percent Plan and the Wade-Davis Bill. Given how Reconstruction played out, how might the adoption of one of these alternative plans have changed the course of events?

Take Notes

Literacy Skills: Identify Supporting Details Use what you have read to complete the table. Respond to each main idea with two supporting details. The first one has been completed for you.

Main Idea	Supporting Details
Even after the Thirteenth Amendment passed, the rights of African Americans were still extremely restricted.	• Under the black codes, freedmen were not allowed to vote, own guns, or serve on juries. • In some states, freedmen were only permitted to work as servants or farm laborers.
Radical Republicans wanted to improve civil rights and equality.	
The Fourteenth Amendment was an important step toward civil rights.	
Congress and President Johnson disagreed on how to proceed with Reconstruction.	
After the passage of the Fifteenth Amendment, there was still a long way to go to achieve civil rights.	

 INTERACTIVE

For extra help, review the 21st Century Tutorial: **Support Ideas with Evidence**.

Practice Vocabulary

True or False? Decide whether each statement below is true or false. Circle T or F, and then explain your answer. Be sure to include the underlined vocabulary word in your explanation. The first one is done for you.

1. **T / F** The <u>black codes</u> were laws to help freedmen build new lives.
   False; The <u>black codes</u> were laws that severely restricted the rights of freed African Americans.

2. **T / F** <u>Radical Republicans</u> wanted to ensure freedmen received the right to vote.

3. **T / F** The <u>Reconstruction Act</u> of 1867 accepted all of the states back into the Union.

4. **T / F** The <u>Fourteenth Amendment</u> defined citizens as "all persons born or naturalized in the United States."

5. **T / F** The House of Representatives voted to <u>impeach</u> President Johnson because they agreed with him.

6. **T / F** The <u>Fifteenth Amendment</u> gave African American men over the age of 21 the right to vote.

Take Notes

Literacy Skills: Summarize Use what you have read to complete the table. In each box, list at least two details or ideas that describe the issue. Use your responses to summarize the lesson in three to five sentences. One has been completed for you.

New Political Groups	• white southern republicans •
Conservatives Resist Reform	
Political Problems Slow Progress	
Economic Problems in the South	

Summary

INTERACTIVE

For extra help, review the 21st Century Tutorial: **Summarize**.

Practice Vocabulary

Sentence Builder Finish the sentences below with a key term from this section. You may have to change the form of the words to complete the sentences.

Word Bank

Ku Klux Klan   carpetbagger

sharecropper   scalawag

1. A Southerner who helped Southern Republicans was referred to as a

2. Northerners who moved to the South were often called

3. Someone who farms a rented plot of land is called a

4. The most dangerous group who terrorized African Americans is called the

Take Notes

Literacy Skills: Draw Conclusions Use what you have read to complete the diagram. List ways that African Americans in the South were prevented from exercising their rights during this time. Then, make conclusions about the impact these restrictions had on these citizens. The first detail has been completed for you.

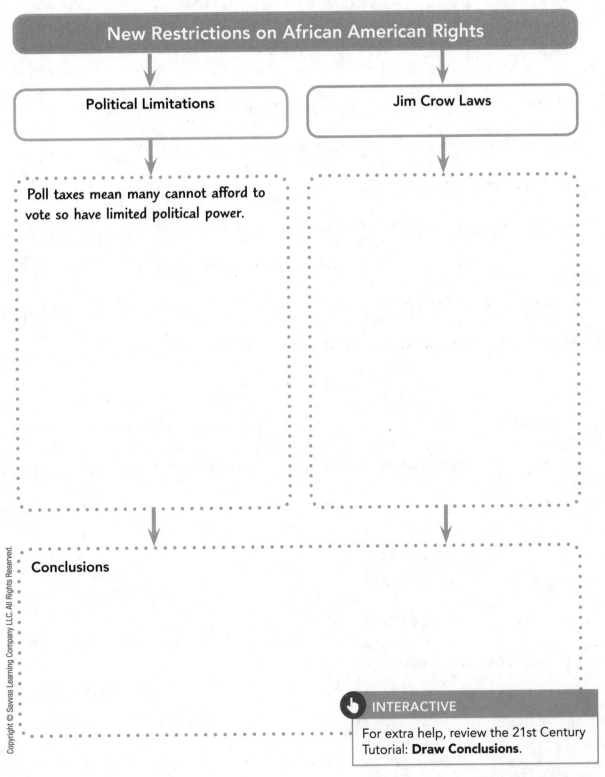

New Restrictions on African American Rights

Political Limitations	Jim Crow Laws

Poll taxes mean many cannot afford to vote so have limited political power.

Conclusions

👆 **INTERACTIVE**

For extra help, review the 21st Century Tutorial: **Draw Conclusions**.

Practice Vocabulary

Use a Word Bank Choose one word from the word bank to fill in each blank. When you have finished, you will have a short summary of important ideas from the section.

Word Bank

segregation	"New South"	poll tax
Compromise of 1877	Jim Crow laws	*Plessy* v. *Ferguson*
literacy test	grandfather clause	

With the .... and election of Rutherford B.

Hayes, Reconstruction ended. Laws to prevent African Americans from

exercising their rights included a ...., which

required voters to pay each time they voted. The laws also included

a ...., which required voters to read and

explain parts of the Constitution, and a ....

that stated if a voter's father or grandfather had been able to vote in

January 1867, then that voter did not have to take the literacy test.

After 1877, ..., or separation of the races,

became the law of the South. In 1896, the famous Supreme Court case

.... ruled that separate was legal as long

as facilities for blacks and whites were equal, even though they rarely

were. These laws were called the .... As the

economy in the South started to change and improve for some people,

it became referred to as the ....

Quick Activity Newspaper Editorial

Write a newspaper editorial supporting or opposing Samuel Tilden and the Democratic Party for choosing not to fight the commission's decision to award all of the disputed electors to Hayes. Use the chart below to help you organize your thinking.

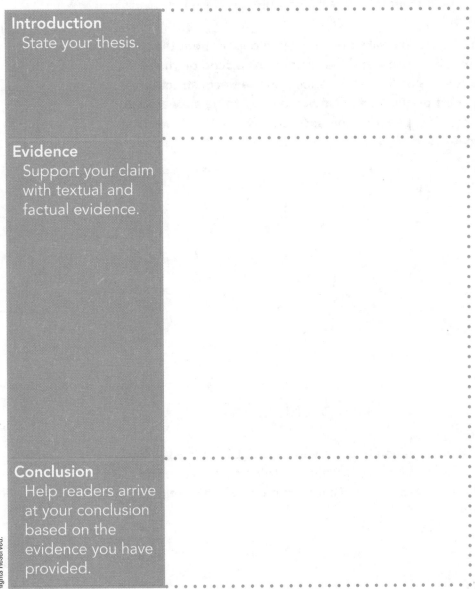

Introduction
State your thesis.

Evidence
Support your claim with textual and factual evidence.

Conclusion
Help readers arrive at your conclusion based on the evidence you have provided.

Team Challenge! Find a partner with a different opinion. Share your charts and talk about the differences. Practice listening to your partner's reasoning without arguing or making statements of your own. Instead, limit your responses to questions that help you better understand your partner's perspective and that help your partner develop and refine his or her opinion.

Writing Workshop Research Paper

As you read, build a response to the following research topic: **The Freedmen's Bureau, its effects, and the restrictions placed on the rights and opportunities of African Americans in the Reconstruction-era South.** The prompts below will help walk you through the process.

Lesson 1 Writing Task: Generate Questions to Focus Research
(See Student Text, page 557)

At the end of this topic, you will write a research paper about the Freedmen's Bureau, its effects, and the restrictions placed on the rights and opportunities of African Americans in the Reconstruction-era South. Make a list of questions that would need to be answered in order to write a research paper on this subject, such as: What was the Freedmen's Bureau?

Lesson 2 Writing Task: Find and Use Credible Sources
(See Student Text, page 563)

You will need more information to write your paper. List at least three credible sources of information you might use to research about the Freedmen's Bureau. Record the source information so you can find it again later.

Lesson 3 Writing Task: Support Ideas with Evidence
(See Student Text, page 572)

A thesis is a statement that a writer intends to support and prove. Write a thesis statement for your research paper. Then, outline your research paper by writing your main ideas. Under each main idea, write facts and other evidence that support that idea.

Thesis

Main Idea	Main Idea	Main Idea
Evidence	Evidence	Evidence

Lesson 4 Writing Task: Cite Sources (See Student Text, page 579)

Review the sources that you noted. Write citations for all of your sources, following the format provided by your teacher. Include the name of the article or text, the author, the publisher, the date of publication, and the web address (if applicable).

Writing Task (See Student Text, page 581)

Complete your research paper on the Freedmen's Bureau and its effects. Include a discussion of the limits placed on African Americans. Your paper should include a strong conclusion that summarizes your thesis and main ideas.

Essential Question How did America's economy, industries, and population grow after the Civil War?

Before you begin this topic, think about the Essential Question by answering the following question.

1. List five words or ideas that come to mind when you think about the word *growth*. Based on your list, do you feel that growth is usually **positive** or **negative**? Circle the bold word that matches your opinion.

Timeline Skills

As you read, write and/or draw at least three events from the topic. Draw a line from each event to its correct position on the timeline.

1860	1870	1880

Map Skills

Using maps throughout the topic, label the map with the places listed. Then use different colors to shade states admitted before 1867 and states admitted from 1867 to 1912. Be sure to create a key for your map.

Arizona (1912)   Colorado (1876)   Idaho (1890)

Montana (1889)   Nebraska (1867)   New Mexico (1912)

North Dakota (1889)   Oklahoma (1907)   South Dakota (1889)

Utah (1896)   Washington (1889)   Wyoming (1890)

Canada   Mexico   Pacific Ocean

Gulf of Mexico

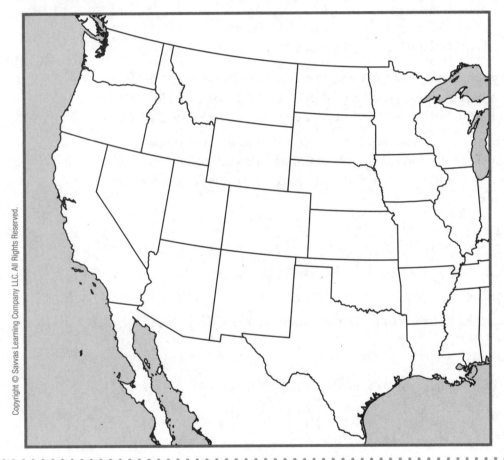

1890   1900   1910   1920

Quest

Civic Discussion Inquiry

High-Speed Rail

On this Quest, you will explore sources and gather information about the benefits and drawbacks of high-speed rail. Then, in the role of a member of the U.S. House of Representative's Subcommittee on Railroads, you will participate in a civic discussion with other representatives about the Guiding Question.

1 Ask Questions (See Student Text, page 586)

As you begin your Quest, keep in mind the Guiding Question: **Should America invest in high-speed rail?** and the Essential Question: **How did America's economy, industries, and population grow after the Civil War?**

What other questions do you need to ask in order to answer these questions? Consider the following aspects of life after the Civil War. Two questions are filled in for you. Add at least two questions for each of the other categories.

Theme Railroads

Sample questions:

What changes did railroads bring to the nation after the Civil War?

Were these changes good or bad for the country? Why?

Theme Industry

Theme Population

Theme Western Agriculture

Theme New Technologies

Theme My Additional Questions

 INTERACTIVE

For extra help with Step 1, review the
21st Century Tutorial: **Ask Questions.**

Quest CONNECTIONS

2 Investigate

As you read about the nation's economy and industries after the Civil War, collect five connections from your text to help you answer the Guiding Question. Three connections are already chosen for you.

Connect to a National Transportation System

Lesson 1 Creating a National Railroad Network

(See Student Text, page 593)

Here's a connection! What does this section tell you about the benefits of new transportation methods in the United States? What added benefits came from creating a network of rail lines that stretched across state lines?

How did networks change railroads?

Connect to Texas Ranchers and the Railroads

Lesson 2 How Did a Cattle Kingdom Start on the Plains?

(See Student Text, page 599)

Read about the Texas Cattle Kingdom and new opportunities for ranchers. In what way did the new railroads help bring about the cattle kingdom in Texas?

How does rail access change people's lives?

Connect to Thomas Edison

Primary Source Quotations from Thomas Edison

(See Student Text, page 645)

Here's another connection! Thomas Edison was a great inventor. How could new technology and inventions improve railroads?

What do you think Thomas Edison would have thought about the United States investing in high-speed rail? Explain your reasoning.

It's Your Turn! **Find two more connections. Fill in the title of your connections, then answer the questions. Connections may be images, primary sources, maps, or text.**

Your Choice | Connect to

Location in text

What is the main idea of this connection?

What does it tell you about whether the United States should invest in high-speed rail?

Your Choice | Connect to

Location in text

What is the main idea of this connection?

What does it tell you about whether the United States should invest in high-speed rail?

3 **Examine Primary Sources** (See Student Text, page 646)

Examine the primary and secondary sources provided online or from your teacher. Fill in the chart to show how these sources provide further information about whether America should invest in high-speed rail. The first one is completed for you.

Should America Invest in High-Speed Rail?	
Source	Yes or No? Why?
"Riled About Rail"	YES, because transportation in the United States is falling behind that of other industrialized nations.
"Myths/Facts"	
"A Case Against High-Speed Rail"	
"The Pragmatic Case Against High-Speed Rail"	

INTERACTIVE

For extra help with Step 3, review the 21st Century Tutorials: **Analyze Primary and Secondary Sources** and **Compare Viewpoints**.

4 Discuss! (See Student Text, page 646)

Now that you have collected clues and explored sources about high-speed rail, you are ready to discuss with your fellow representatives the Guiding Question: **Should America invest in high-speed rail?** Follow the steps below, using the spaces provided to prepare for your discussion.

You will work with a partner in a small group of representatives. Try to reach consensus, a situation in which everyone is in agreement, on the question. Can you do it?

1. **Prepare Your Arguments** You will be assigned a position on the question, either YES or NO.

   My position: ⸬⸬⸬⸬⸬⸬⸬⸬⸬⸬⸬⸬⸬⸬⸬⸬⸬⸬

   Work with your partner to review your Quest notes from the Quest Connections and Quest Sources.

   - If you were assigned YES, agree with your partner on what you think were the strongest arguments from Harrod and the Environmental Law & Policy Center.

   - If you were assigned NO, agree on what you think were the strongest arguments from Mobley and Staley.

2. **Present Your Position** Those assigned YES will present their arguments and evidence first. As you listen, ask clarifying questions to gain information and understanding.

What is a Clarifying Question?	
These types of questions do not judge the person talking. They are only for the listener to be clear on what he or she is hearing.	
Example: Can you tell me more about that?	Example: You said [x]. Am I getting that right?

👆 **INTERACTIVE**

For extra help with Step 4, review the 21st Century Tutorial: **Participate in a Debate or Discussion**.

While the opposite side speaks, take notes on what you hear in the space below.

[ ]

3. Switch! Now NO and YES will switch sides. If you argued YES before, now you will argue NO. Work with your same partner and use your notes. Add any arguments and evidence from the clues and sources. Those *now* arguing YES go first.

When both sides have finished, answer the following:

Before I started this discussion with my fellow representatives, my opinion was that America	*After* this discussion with my fellow representatives, my opinion is that America
_____should invest in high-speed rail.	_____should invest in high-speed rail.
_____should not invest in high-speed rail.	_____should not invest in high-speed rail.

4. Point of View Do you all agree on the answer to the Guiding Question?

• _____Yes

• _____No

If not, on what points do you all agree?

[ ]

Take Notes

Literacy Skills: Identify Cause and Effect Use what you have read to complete the flowcharts. In each space, write an effect of the event provided and support your answer with details from the text. The first one has been started for you.

Mining Booms in the West

Environmental Problems

- Forests are cut down.
- Mines and towns pollute water sources.

Completion of the Transcontinental Railroad

INTERACTIVE

For extra help, review the 21st Century Tutorial: **Analyze Cause and Effect**.

Practice Vocabulary

Vocabulary Quiz Show Some quiz shows ask a question and expect the contestant to give the answer. In other shows, the contestant is given an answer and must supply the question. If the blank is in the Question column, write the question that would result in the answer in the Answer column. If the question is supplied, write the answer.

Question	Answer
1. What word is used to describe the width of railroad track?	1.
2. What was a discount offered by railroads to big customers?	2.
3.	3. lode
4.	4. vigilante
5. What did the railroad owners form to end competition, which enabled them to fix high prices?	5.
6. What is a system of connected railroad lines?	6.
7.	7. transcontinental railroad
8.	8. subsidy
9.	9. consolidate

Take Notes

Literacy Skills: Classify and Categorize Use what you have read to complete the chart. In each space write details from the text that describe the type of challenge. The first one has been completed for you.

Challenges for Western Farmers

Land Rights Conflicts	Environmental Hardships	Economic Difficulties
• Ranchers let cattle roam free on the range; farmers had to build fences to protect their fields. • Land companies illegally got control of land from the Homestead Act; only 20% went to farmers for free.		

INTERACTIVE

For extra help, review the 21st Century Tutorial: **Categorize**.

Practice Vocabulary

Word Map Study the word map for the word *cow town*. Characteristics are words or phrases that relate to the term in the center of the word map. Non-characteristics are words and phrases not associated with that term. Use the blank word map to explore the meaning of the word *sodbuster*. Then make word maps of your own for these words: *vaquero, cattle drive, cooperative, Morrill Acts, wholesale,* and *inflation*.

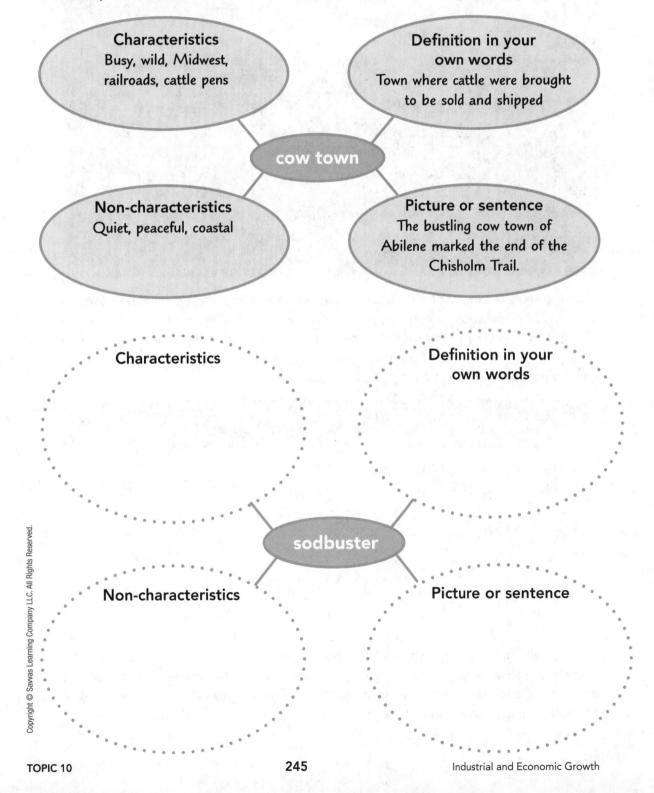

Characteristics
Busy, wild, Midwest, railroads, cattle pens

Definition in your own words
Town where cattle were brought to be sold and shipped

cow town

Non-characteristics
Quiet, peaceful, coastal

Picture or sentence
The bustling cow town of Abilene marked the end of the Chisholm Trail.

Characteristics

Definition in your own words

sodbuster

Non-characteristics

Picture or sentence

Quick Activity Westward Bound!

With a partner or small group, examine this illustration depicting the Oklahoma Land Rush. As you look at the picture, discuss possible reasons why people were so eager to move to Oklahoma. What natural resources might have made Oklahoma a good place to settle?

How did the availability of different natural resources affect westward expansion and patterns of population growth? In your group, brainstorm a list of the natural resources of the West. Be sure to include resources that you read about in this lesson. Then think about the different areas of the West where each resource was most plentiful. Use the chart below to take notes during the brainstorm.

Natural Resource	Locations

Team Challenge! Your group has been put in charge of a campaign to convince people to move West. Select a region, state, or city in the West and create a poster advertising the area's natural resource(s) to potential settlers. Every advertising campaign needs an audience, so share your poster with the rest of the class.

Take Notes

Literacy Skills: Summarize Use what you have read to complete the table. Include at least one detail from the text for each subtopic listed. The first one has been completed for you. Then, use the information you have gathered to create a summary statement that answers the question provided.

Plains Life Before White Settlement	Changes to Plains Indian Life	Plains Conflicts with White Settlers
Lifestyle: Survival depended on agriculture, hunting, and after 1680, horses. Homes were semi-permanent, and tepees were used when following bison herds.	**Decline of Bison:**	**Sand Creek Massacre:**
Social Structure: Women made the homes, gathered, taught, and were caregivers. Some governed and hunted. Men hunted, taught boys, and were warriors. Some governed and were military and spiritual leaders.	**Reservations:**	**Battle of Little Big Horn:**

Summary:

INTERACTIVE

For extra help, review the 21st Century Tutorial: **Summarize**.

Practice Vocabulary

Sentence Builder Finish the sentences below with a key term from this section. You may have to change the form of the words to complete the sentences.

Word Bank

travois	tepee	jerky
corral	reservation	allotment

1. Before horses were brought to the Great Plains, the best way to hunt

   bison was to herd them into a(n) .

2. The Dawes Act called for the of

   reservation land to individual American Indian families.

3. When Plains Indians needed to move their villages to follow the bison,

   they loaded their belongings onto .

4. Bison meat that has been cut up and dried is called

   .

5. According to the terms of the Fort Laramie Treaty of 1868, the Lakotas

   and Arapahos would live on .

6. When Plains Indians were following bison herds, they lived in tents

   called .

Take Notes

Literacy Skills: Cite Evidence Use what you have read to complete the flowchart. Provide at least one detail for each subheading. Then, use the details you have gathered to draw a conclusion about the question provided. The first column has been completed for you.

Andrew Carnegie

Background:

After seeing the Bessemer process at work, he was inspired to borrow money and start a steel mill.

Business Strategy:

He used profits to buy out rivals.

His vertical integration involved buying iron mines, railroads, steam-ships, and warehouses to control all parts of the steel industry.

Philosophy:

Trusts are good and too much competition is harmful.

The rich have a duty to help the poor ("gospel of wealth").

John D. Rockefeller

Background:

Business Strategy:

Philosophy:

Draw a Conclusion: Why were business people like Carnegie and Rockefeller so successful?

 INTERACTIVE

For extra help, review the 21st Century Tutorial: **Support Ideas With Evidence**.

Practice Vocabulary

True or False? Decide whether each statement below is true or false. Circle T or F, and then explain your answer. Be sure to include the underlined vocabulary word in your explanation. The first one is done for you.

1. **T / F** <u>Capitalism</u> is an economic system in which businesses are owned by the government.
False; <u>Capitalism</u> is an economic system in which businesses are owned by private citizens.

2. **T / F** <u>Dividends</u> are shares of a corporation's profit that are paid to stockholders.

3. **T / F** A business that is owned by investors is called a <u>corporation</u>.

4. **T / F** The principle of <u>scarcity</u> is that the economy improves when businesses and customers have few choices.

5. **T / F** A <u>trust</u> is a group of corporations run by a single individual.

6. **T / F** The Standard Oil trust controlled such a significant part of the oil industry that it formed a <u>monopoly</u>.

7. **T / F** <u>Stock</u> is the income that a business earns after it recovers costs.

Take Notes

Literacy Skills: Analyze Text Structure Use what you have read to complete the outline about the labor movement. Be sure to include significant headings, subheadings, and supporting details in your outline. The first section has been completed for you.

I. Changes in Working Conditions

    A. Child Labor

        1. Children worked long hours at dangerous jobs.

        2. Child laborers were often uneducated.

    B. Dangerous Workplaces

        1. Factories, sweatshops, mines, and steel mills paid workers low wages for long hours in dangerous conditions.

        2. The government did not regulate businesses to protect workers.

II.

 INTERACTIVE

For extra help, review the 21st Century Tutorial: **Identify Main Ideas and Details**.

Practice Vocabulary

Sentence Revision Revise each sentence so that the underlined vocabulary word is used logically. Be sure not to change the vocabulary word. The first one is done for you.

---

1. <u>Anarchists</u> are people who support organized government.

   <u>Anarchists</u> are people who are opposed to all forms of organized government.

---

2. <u>Strikebreakers</u> are hired to negotiate with striking workers.

3. In <u>sweatshops</u>, people work long hours in poor conditions to receive overtime pay.

4. A <u>trade union</u> unites workers from many different trades.

5. The <u>Triangle Fire</u> led to a decrease in the number of safety laws protecting factory workers.

6. In <u>collective bargaining</u>, individual workers negotiate through discussions with multiple levels of management.

Take Notes

Literacy Skills: Identify Supporting Details Study the concept web for *transatlantic communication*. Use what you have read to complete the concept web for *telephone*. Then make concept webs of your own for *refrigeration*, *automobile*, and *airplane*.

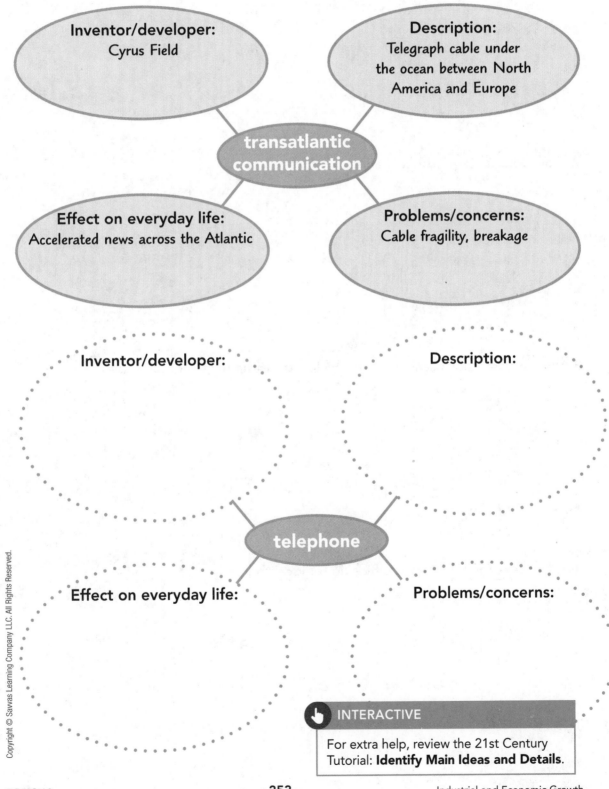

👆 INTERACTIVE

For extra help, review the 21st Century Tutorial: **Identify Main Ideas and Details**.

Practice Vocabulary

Words in Context For each question below, write an answer that shows your understanding of the boldfaced key term.

1. How did Ford's use of the **moving assembly line** affect production industries?

2. How does **mass production** affect product prices?

3. What was the significance of Cyrus Field's **transatlantic** telegraph cable?

4. What does the U.S. **Patent** Office do for inventors?

Quick Activity Inventing for Change

With a partner or small group, examine these photos and brainstorm ways that the invention of the automobile forever changed the United States.

How did automobiles affect businesses and the economy? How did automobiles affect the landscape? What forms of transportation did the automobile replace? How did the automobile change everyday life?

Team Challenge! As a group, select one of the other inventions from the lesson and create an exhibit for a virtual Museum of Invention. Your group's museum exhibit should give information about the inventor, describe the invention, and inform viewers about the significance of the invention. Consider: How did the invention change people's lives in the 1800s? Does it still affect people's lives today? Display your results with the rest of the class, and take a "museum tour" around the classroom!

Writing Workshop Arguments

As you read, build a response to this question: What role should the government play in the development of a nation's infrastructure? The prompts below will help walk you through the process.

Lesson 1 Writing Task: Introduce Claims (See Student Text, page 597)

Write two sentences that summarize your position on the government's role in creating a national infrastructure. This will be the position you defend in the argument you will write at the end of the topic.

Lesson 2 and 4 Writing Task: Support Claims and Use Credible Sources
(See Student Text, pages 609 and 629)

As you read lessons 2 and 4, pay attention to details or concepts that support your claim. In the table below, write three sentences that support your claim and cite trustworthy sources for your information.

Supporting Details and Concepts	Source
1.	1.
2.	2.
3.	3.

Lesson 3 Writing Task: Distinguish Claims from Opposing Claims
(See Student Text, page 619)

A well-constructed argument takes into account the views of the opposing side. In this table, first write a sentence summarizing the opposing claim. On the left, provide reasons and evidence that the opposing side might use to support their claim. On the right, express how your evidence differs.

Opposing Claim:	
Opposing Reasons and Evidence	How My Evidence Differs

Lesson 5 Writing Task: Shape Tone (See Student Text, page 637)

Look back at what you've written so far and analyze your tone. Does the argument make you feel angry or inspired? Does your writing seem emotional or calm? Determine the type of tone you would like your argument to have. Then revise the claim you wrote in lesson 1 so that it reflects the tone you want.

Lesson 6 Writing Task: Write a Conclusion (See Student Text, page 644)

The conclusion of your essay should do more than summarize what you have already said; it should restate your claim in powerful and persuasive ways that your reader will remember. Review all your reasons and evidence. Then, use a separate sheet of paper to write a draft conclusion for your argument using the tone you've identified.

Writing Task (See Student Text, page 647)

Using the outline you have created, write a five-paragraph argument that expresses your position on the question: What role should the government play in the development of a nation's infrastructure?

TOPIC 11

The Progressive Era Preview

Essential Question What can individuals do to affect society?

Before you begin this topic, think about the Essential Question by answering the following question.

List the ways you have made a positive impact on the people you know or your community. Circle the one of which you are most proud.

Timeline Skills

As you read, write and/or draw at least three events from the topic. Draw a line from each event to its correct position on the timeline.

1860	1870	1880

Map Skills

Using maps throughout the topic, color each state based on the percentage of its residents in 1900 who had been born in other countries. Create a key for your map.

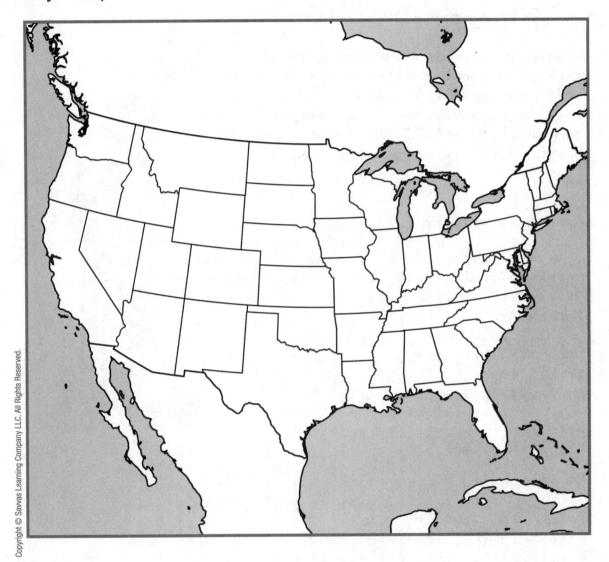

| 1890 | 1900 | 1910 | 1920 |

Quest

Effects of Immigration

On this Quest, you need to find out about the experience of immigrants to the United States around the year 1900 and how immigration during that time affected the United States. You will examine sources about how people viewed immigrants. At the end of the Quest, you will write an essay about the immigrant experience and the perceptions of immigrants.

1 Ask Questions (See Student Text, page 652)

As you begin your Quest, keep in mind the Guiding Question: **How did immigration affect the United States around the year 1900?** and the Essential Question: **What can individuals do to affect society?**

What other questions do you need to ask in order to answer these questions? Consider the following aspects of immigrant life. Two questions are filled in for you. Add at least two questions for each category.

Theme Opportunity

Sample questions:

What push factors encouraged immigrants to come to the United States?

What pull factors encouraged immigrants to come to the United States?

Theme Hardship

Theme Culture

Theme Nativism

Theme My Additional Questions

 INTERACTIVE

For extra help with Step 1, review the 21st Century Tutorial: **Ask Questions**.

Quest CONNECTIONS

② Investigate

As you read about immigration to the United States, collect five connections from your text to help you answer the Guiding Question. Three connections are already chosen for you.

Connect to the Immigrant Experience

Lesson 1 Why Did People Immigrate? (See Student Text, page 654)

Here's a connection! Look at this section in your text. Why did new immigrants take jobs in factories? Why was it so important for a new immigrant to find a job?

Why do you think immigrants described the United States as the land of opportunity?

Connect to Urbanization

Lesson 2 What Was the Settlement House Movement?
(See Student Text, page 667)

Here's another connection! What does this section tell you about the connection between immigration and urbanization? Why did settlement houses offer services to the poor?

What services did volunteers for the Hull House offer people in the slum community?

Connect to Immigration Policies

Lesson 5 The Government Restricts Asian Immigration
(See Student Text, page 695)

What does this connection tell you about the experience of Asian immigrants in the United States? How were they treated?

How did the policy toward Japanese immigration change during this time?

It's Your Turn! **Find two more connections. Fill in the title of your connections, then answer the questions. Connections may be images, primary sources, maps, or text.**

Your Choice | Connect to

Location in text

What is the main idea of this connection?

What does it tell you about immigration in the United States around the year 1900?

Your Choice | Connect to

Location in text

What is the main idea of this connection?

What does it tell you about immigration in the United States around the year 1900?

③ Examine Primary Sources (See Student Text, page 710)

Examine the primary and secondary sources provided online or from your teacher. Fill in the chart to show how these sources provide further information about how immigration affected the United States around the year 1900. The first one is completed for you.

Source	Immigration affected the United States by . . .
Constitution of the Immigration Restriction League	leading some people to form groups that opposed immigration. They wanted to limit or curtail immigration.
The Promised Land	
The Biography of a Chinaman	
The Chinese Exclusion Conference	
Working in a Sweatshop	

INTERACTIVE

For extra help with Step 3, review the 21st Century Tutorial: **Analyze Primary and Secondary Sources**.

Quest FINDINGS

4 Write Your Essay (See Student Text, page 710)

Now it's time to put together all of the information you have gathered and use it to write your essay.

1. **Prepare to Write** You have collected connections and explored primary and secondary sources that show how immigration affected the United States around the year 1900. Look through your notes and decide which facts you would like to include in your essay. Record them here.

Facts about Immigration

2. **Write a Draft** Using evidence from the information in the textbook and the primary and secondary sources you explored, write a draft of your essay. Be sure to write about both the experience immigrants had and what some Americans believed about them. Include details from the evidence in the material you've studied in this Quest.

3. **Share with a Partner** Exchange your draft with a partner. Tell your partner what you like about his or her draft and suggest any improvements.

4. **Finalize Your Essay** Revise your essay. Correct any grammatical or spelling errors.

5. **Reflect on the Quest** Think about your experience completing this topic's Quest. What did you learn about the immigrant experience and reaction to immigration? What questions do you still have about immigration? How will you answer them?

Reflections

INTERACTIVE

For extra help with Step 4, review the 21st Century Tutorial: **Write an Essay**.

Take Notes

Literacy Skills: Summarize Use what you have read to complete the outline, summarizing the main ideas of the lesson. Some parts have been completed for you.

I. Why Did People Immigrate?
    A. Push factors

       scarcity of land, political and religious persecution, political unrest

    B. Pull factors

       industrial jobs in U.S., promise of freedom

II. What Was an Immigrant's Journey Like?
    A.

    B.

III. What was the Immigrant Experience in America?
    A.

    B.

IV. Why Did Nativists Oppose Immigration?
    A.

    B.

 INTERACTIVE

For extra help, review the 21st Century
Tutorial: **Summarize**.

Practice Vocabulary

True or False? Decide whether each statement below is true or false. Circle T or F, and then explain your answer. Be sure to include the underlined vocabulary word in your explanation. The first one is done for you.

1. **T / F** A <u>pogrom</u> was an organized attack on a Jewish village.
   True; <u>The pogroms</u> were supported by the Russian government.

2. **T / F** A <u>push factor</u> is a condition that attracts immigrants to a new area.

3. **T / F** The <u>Chinese Exclusion Act</u> barred Chinese laborers from entering the United States after its passage in 1882.

4. **T / F** The first generation of immigrants to arrive in America went through a process called <u>acculturation</u>.

5. **T / F** A <u>pull factor</u> is a condition that drives people from their homes.

6. **T / F** People who wanted to limit immigration and preserve the country for native-born, white Protestants were called <u>nativists</u>.

7. **T / F** Immigrants could have afforded nice quarters on ships that sailed to America, but they chose to stay in <u>steerage</u> to save money.

Quick Activity Write a Song

Throughout American history, musicians have written songs about immigrants. Use these pictures to get some ideas for writing your own immigration song, or find inspiration by searching the Internet for these songs and reading the lyrics.

◀ Many families sailed to America at the turn of the 20th century looking for a better life.

▲ Immigrant children often worked in factories before laws were passed to forbid this practice.

Team Challenge! After everybody in your class posts their songs around the classroom, read the songs. Discuss with your classmates why they chose to write what they did. You also might want to talk about the melody they will use with their songs. Will it be happy or sad? Why?

Take Notes

Literacy Skills: Identify Cause and Effect Use what you have read to complete the flowcharts. In each lower box, enter an effect that resulted from the cause in the top box. The first one has been partially completed for you.

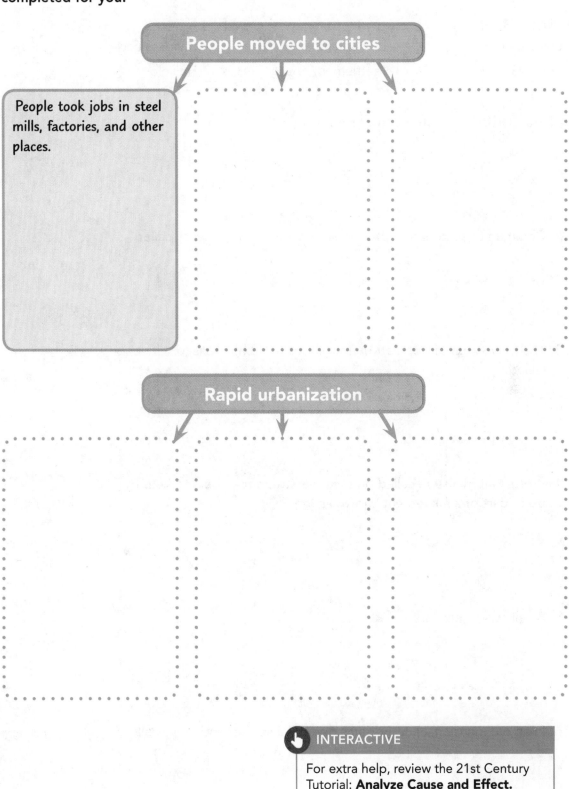

People moved to cities

People took jobs in steel mills, factories, and other places.

Rapid urbanization

INTERACTIVE

For extra help, review the 21st Century Tutorial: **Analyze Cause and Effect.**

Practice Vocabulary

Sentence Builder Finish the sentences below with a key term from this section. You may have to change the form of the words to complete the sentences.

Word Bank

urbanization	tenement	building code
Social Gospel	settlement house	Hull House

1. Standards for construction or safety are called

2. Community centers that offered services to the poor were called

3. The movement of population from farms to urban areas, or cities, is called

4. Protestant ministers called on their well-to-do members to help the poor, part of a movement known as the

5. Small apartments are called

6. In an old mansion, Jane Addams opened a settlement house called

Quick Activity Tracing Urbanization

At the beginning of the 1900s, many people moved to cities. Immigrants and Americans who lived in rural areas moved to cities like Boston and New York. The growth of the cities can be seen by looking at old maps. Compare these two maps of Queens, a borough of New York City, to see how urbanization changed from the first map, showing 1900, to the second map, showing 1930.

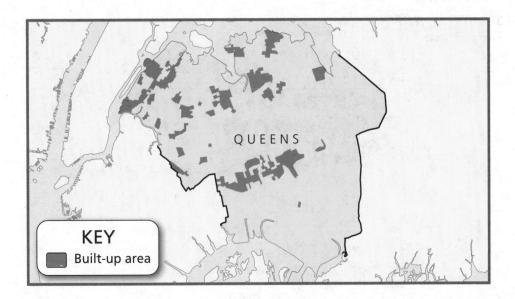

QUEENS

KEY
Built-up area

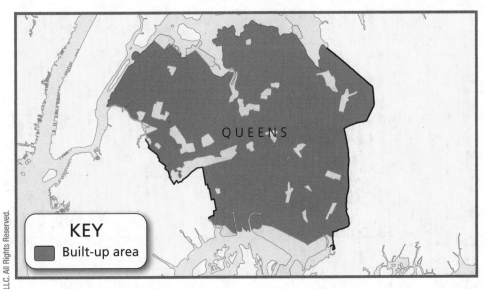

QUEENS

KEY
Built-up area

Team Challenge! Create two maps for a fictional city, one showing the city as it looks today and another showing what the city will look like in thirty years. The future map should show that the city has grown substantially.

Take Notes

Literacy Skills: Identify Supporting Details Use what you have read to complete the graphic organizers. In the outer circles enter details that support the main idea in the center. The first one has been partially completed for you.

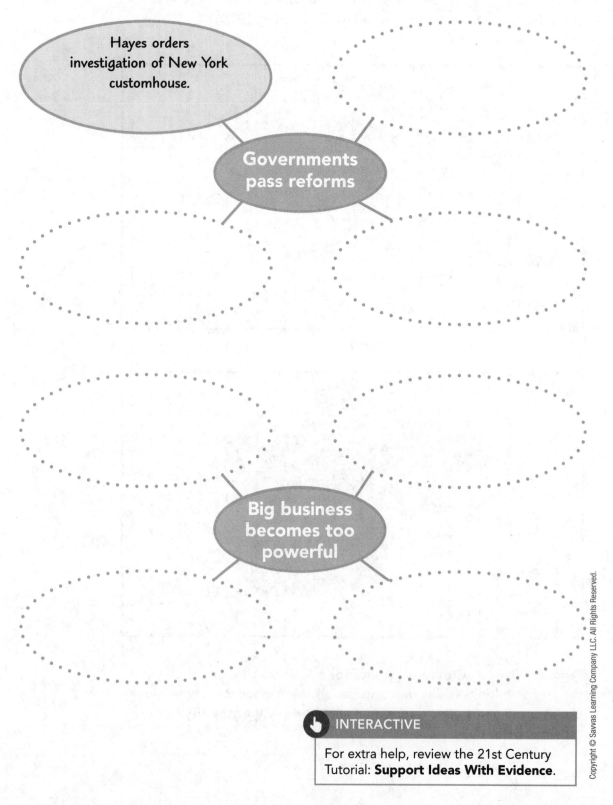

Hayes orders investigation of New York customhouse.

Governments pass reforms

Big business becomes too powerful

👆 **INTERACTIVE**

For extra help, review the 21st Century Tutorial: **Support Ideas With Evidence**.

Practice Vocabulary

Vocabulary Quiz Show Some quiz shows ask a question and expect the contestant to give the answer. In other shows, the contestant is given an answer and must supply the question. If the blank is in the Question column, write the question that would result in the answer in the Answer column. If the question is supplied, write the answer.

Question	Answer
1.	1. Progressives
2.	2. civil service
3. What is an election in which voters choose a political party's candidate for the general election?	3.
4. What allows voters to remove an elected official from office?	4.
5.	5. muckrakers
6.	6. initiative
7. What is it called when elected officials give jobs to political supporters?	7.
8.	8. referendum

Take Notes

Literacy Skills: Classify and Categorize Use what you have read to complete the table. Write the most important Progressive reforms proposed by each President. The first one has been started for you.

Theodore Roosevelt	• regulated and broke up bad trusts
William Howard Taft	
Woodrow Wilson	

INTERACTIVE

For extra help, review the 21st Century Tutorial: **Categorize**.

Practice Vocabulary

True or False? Decide whether each statement below is true or false. Circle T or F, and then explain your answer. Be sure to include the underlined vocabulary word in your explanation. The first one is done for you.

1. **T / F** A <u>trustbuster</u> is a person who wants to control, or regulate, trusts.
   False; **Trustbusters** wanted to destroy all trusts.

2. **T / F** The <u>New Freedom</u> program was designed to increase competition in the American economy.

3. **T / F** The <u>Federal Reserve Act</u> allows the government to investigate companies and order them to stop using unfair practices to destroy competitors.

4. **T / F** Theodore Roosevelt promised to provide a <u>Square Deal</u> because he believed all Americans should have the same opportunity to succeed.

5. **T / F** In 1912, supporters of Theodore Roosevelt became known as the <u>Bull Moose Party</u> because he accepted the nomination of the Progressive Party by saying, "I feel as strong as a bull moose."

6. **T / F** The <u>Federal Trade Commission</u> set up an organization that controls the supply of money to the U.S. financial system and sets interest rates.

7. **T / F** Theodore Roosevelt's commitment to <u>conservation</u> led to the creation of the National Forest Service and the creation of national parks.

Take Notes

Literacy Skills: Determine Central Ideas Use what you have read to complete the flowcharts. In the top box, write the central idea, then complete the lower boxes with missing details. Both organizers have been partially completed for you.

```
┌ ─ ─ ─ ─ ─ ─ ─ ─ ─ ─ ─ ─ ─ ─ ─ ─ ─ ─ ─ ─ ─ ─ ─ ─ ─ ─ ─ ─ ┐

└ ─ ─ ─ ─ ─ ─ ─ ─ ─ ─ ─ ─ ─ ─ ─ ─ ─ ─ ─ ─ ─ ─ ─ ─ ─ ─ ─ ─ ┘
```

| Elizabeth Cady Stanton and Susan B. Anthony create the National Woman Suffrage Association. | Women win the right to vote in western states. | |

```
┌ ─ ─ ─ ─ ─ ─ ─ ─ ─ ─ ─ ─ ─ ─ ─ ─ ─ ─ ─ ─ ─ ─ ─ ─ ─ ─ ─ ─ ┐

└ ─ ─ ─ ─ ─ ─ ─ ─ ─ ─ ─ ─ ─ ─ ─ ─ ─ ─ ─ ─ ─ ─ ─ ─ ─ ─ ─ ─ ┘
```

| The Chinese Exclusion Act is passed. | Japanese immigrants are barred from owning land. | |

INTERACTIVE

For extra help, review the 21st Century Tutorial: **Identify Main Ideas and Details**.

Practice Vocabulary

Matching Logic Using your knowledge of the underlined vocabulary words, draw a line from each sentence in Column 1 to match it with the sentence in Column 2 to which it logically belongs.

Column 1	Column 2
1. More than 1,000 African Americans were <u>lynched</u> in the 1890s.	In 1919, it became illegal to sell alcoholic drinks anywhere in the United States.
2. Mexican Americans and Mexican immigrants formed *mutualistas*.	Members pooled money to buy insurance and pay for legal advice.
3. Women fought very hard for many years for <u>suffrage</u>.	The mobs that murdered African Americans outraged people like Ida B. Wells.
4. Mexicans preserved their language and culture in <u>barrios</u>.	One of its founders, W.E.B. Du Bois, wanted to actively fight discrimination.
5. People in the temperance movement wanted to enact <u>prohibition</u>.	Elizabeth Cady Stanton and Susan B. Anthony fought in the 1800s for a constitutional amendment to give women the right to vote.
6. The National Association for the Advancement of Colored People (<u>NAACP</u>) worked for equal rights for African Americans.	Traditional festivals were celebrated in these neighborhoods.

Take Notes

Literacy Skills: Analyze Text Structure Use what you have read to complete the outline, summarizing the main ideas of the lesson. The first one has been partially completed for you.

I. Changes and Challenges in City Life
   A. Touching the Sky
      1. Skyscrapers were tall buildings with many floors.
      2. First skyscraper was built in Chicago.
      3.
   B. Transportation Innovations
      1. Electric streetcar was developed.
      2.
      3.
   C. Places to Relax
      1. Frederick Law Olmsted planned Central Park in New York City.
      2.
   D. A New Pastime
      1. Departments stores opened, with more goods at cheaper prices.
      2.
II. Why Did Sports Become Popular?
   A.

      1.

      2.

   B.

      1.

      2.

   C.

      1.

      2.

INTERACTIVE

For extra help, review the 21st Century Tutorial: **Summarize**.

Practice Vocabulary

Sentence Revision Revise each sentence so that the underlined vocabulary word is used logically. Be sure not to change the vocabulary word. The first one is done for you.

1. Writers who practiced <u>yellow journalism</u> reported stories that business and government leaders wanted to read.
   Writers who practiced <u>yellow journalism</u> reported stories that covered scandals, crime, and gossip.

2. <u>Ragtime</u> was a form of music with a slow, calming sound.

3. Architects designed <u>skyscrapers</u>, which are buildings with few floors that were made of wood.

4. Writers, like Mark Twain, used <u>local color</u> to make their stories more fantastical.

5. A <u>suburb</u> is a residential area in the center of the city.

6. A group of writers, called <u>realists</u>, depicted an idealized version of life.

7. People went to <u>vaudeville</u> shows to see the opera.

Writing Workshop Research Paper

Write a research paper that answers this question: **What is a significant change in American culture or society that occurred during the Progressive Era?** The prompts below will help walk you through the process.

Lesson 1 Writing Task: Generate Questions to Focus Research
(See Student Text, page 660)

In the box below, write two to four questions about a significant change in American culture or society during the Progressive Era to help focus your research.

Lesson 2 and 3 Writing Task: Find and Use Credible Sources
(See Student Text, pages 668 and 678)

Look for reliable sources. Be aware that a lot of information on the Internet is wrong or misleading. Take notes, recording information that you may use in your paper. Record Web addresses and other source information so you can return to them and cite accurately.

Source	Notes

Lesson 4 Writing Task: Support Ideas with Evidence
(See Student Text, page 686)

Outline your research paper by writing your main ideas. Next to each main idea, write facts and other evidence that support that idea.

Main Idea	Evidence

Lesson 5 Writing Task: Cite Sources (See Student Text, page 698)

Review the sources that you noted. On another piece of paper, write citations for all your sources, following the format your teacher provided. Include the name of the article or text, the author, the publisher, the date of publication, and the Web address (if applicable).

Lesson 6 Writing Task: Use Technology to Produce and Publish
(See Student Text, page 708)

When you are ready to write your paper, use available technology and share it with your classmates online.

Writing Task (See Student Text, page 711)

Using your notes, write a research paper that answers this question: What is a significant change in American culture or society that occurred during the Progressive Era? Explain why this change was so significant and how it made an impact.

Imperialism and World War I Preview

Essential Question **What is America's role in the world?**

Before you begin this topic, think about the Essential Question by completing the following activities.

1. List three words or ideas that you associate with the United States. Do you think a person from another country would perceive the United States the same way? Why or why not?

2. Preview the topic by skimming lesson titles, headings, and graphics. Then place a check mark next to the words that you think will describe the *majority* of the United States' actions and foreign policy from 1853 to 1919.

__imperialist   __neutral   __pacifist

__militaristic   __isolationist   __colonialist

__terrorist   __expansionist   __generous

Timeline Skills

As you read, write and/or draw at least three events from the topic. Draw a line from each event to its correct position on the timeline.

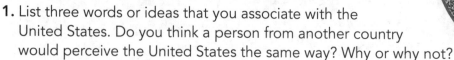

1850   **1875**

Map Skills

Below is a partial list of forts and training camps found throughout the United States in the early 1900s. Using the map in your text, shade in the states where these 12 military bases are located.

Camp Bowie, TX	Fort Lewis, WA	Camp Cody, NM
Fort Dodge, IA	Fort Dix, NJ	Camp Fremont, CA
Fort Lee, VA	Camp Sherman, AL	Fort Devens, MA
Fort Meade, MD	Camp Gordon, GA	Camp Custer, MI

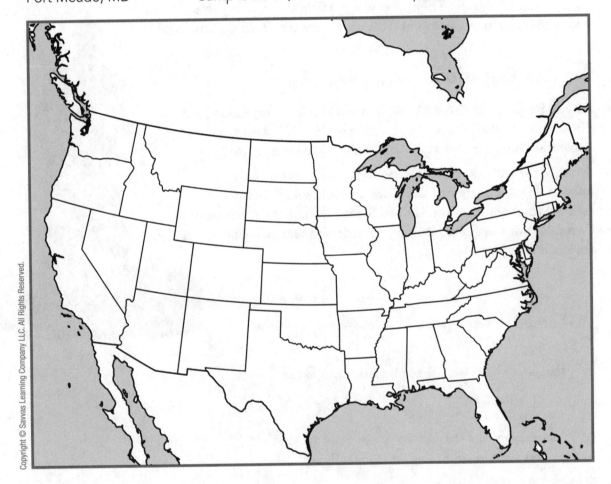

1900

1925

Quest
Civic Discussion Inquiry

Imperialism and Annexation

On this Quest, you will play the role of a U.S. State Department official as you explore sources and gather information about the annexation of Hawaii. Then, you will participate in a civic discussion with other State Department officials about the Guiding Question.

1 Ask Questions (See Student Text, page 716)

As you begin your Quest, keep in mind the Guiding Question: **Should the United States have annexed Hawaii?** and the Essential Question: **What is America's role in the world?**

What other questions do you need to ask in order to answer these questions? Consider the following themes related to changes in the United States during the 19th century. Two questions are filled in for you. Add at least two questions for each category.

Theme Expansionists vs. Anti-Imperialists
Sample questions:

What arguments were made by American expansionists?

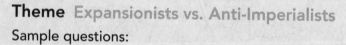

What reasons did the United States have for annexing Samoa and Hawaii? How did the United States act differently with China?

Theme The Spanish-American War

Theme The United States and Latin America

Theme World War I

Theme The Return to Isolationism

Theme My Additional Questions

🖑 INTERACTIVE

For extra help with Step 1, review the
21st Century Tutorial: **Ask Questions**.

Quest CONNECTIONS

② Investigate

As you read about the annexation of Hawaii, collect five connections from your text to help you answer the Guiding Question. Three connections are already chosen for you.

Connect to the Annexation of Hawaii

Lesson 1 The United States Expands in the Pacific (See Student Text, page 725)

Here's a connection! Read this text selection about the annexation of Hawaii. What reasons supported annexation?

Why did President Cleveland oppose annexation?

Connect to Relations with Cuba and the Philippines

Lesson 2 The United States Becomes a Colonial Power
(See Student Text, page 733)

Here's another connection! Read this section of the text. How did
U.S. treatment of Cuba and the Philippines compare to U.S. treatment
of Hawaii?

What were the arguments for and against the 1898 peace treaty
with Spain?

Connect to the Fourteen Points

Primary Source Woodrow Wilson, The Fourteen Points
(See Student Text, page 775)

What does this connection tell you about President Wilson's views
toward expansionism?

The introduction to the primary source states that Wilson's views did
not match those of many Europeans. What do you think were the views
of those Europeans?

It's Your Turn! **Find two more connections. Fill in the title of your connections, then answer the questions. Connections may be images, primary sources, maps, or text.**

Your Choice | Connect to

Location in text

What is the main idea of this connection?

What does it tell you about whether the United States should have annexed Hawaii?

Your Choice | Connect to

Location in text

What is the main idea of this connection?

What does it tell you about whether the United States should have annexed Hawaii?

③ Examine Primary Sources (See Student Text, page 776)

Examine the primary and secondary sources provided online or from your teacher. Fill in the chart to show how these sources provide further information about the differing opinions on the annexation of Hawaii.

Should the United States Have Annexed Hawaii?	
Source	**Yes or No? Why?**
Transmitting a Treaty to Annex the Hawaiian Islands	
Joint Resolution	
"First Annual Message"	
"Royal Hawaii"	

👆 INTERACTIVE

For extra help with Step 3, review the 21st Century Tutorials: **Analyze Primary and Secondary Sources** and **Compare Viewpoints**.

Quest FINDINGS

4 Discuss! (See Student Text, page 776)

Now that you have collected clues and explored documents about imperialism in the late 1800s, you are ready to discuss with your fellow State Department officials the Guiding Question: **Should the United States have annexed Hawaii?** Follow the steps below, using the spaces provided to prepare for your discussion.

1. **Prepare Your Arguments** You will be assigned a position on the question, either YES or NO.

My position:

Work with your partner to review your notes from the Quest Connections and Quest Sources.

- If you were assigned YES, choose the strongest arguments from President Harrison and the 1898 U.S. Congress Joint Resolution in favor of annexing Hawaii.

- If you were assigned NO, choose what you think were the strongest arguments from President Cleveland and Jeff Phillips opposed to annexing Hawaii.

2. **Present Your Position** Those assigned YES will present their arguments and evidence first. As you listen, ask clarifying questions to gain information and understanding.

What Is a Clarifying Question?	
These types of questions do not judge the person talking. They are only for the listener to be clear on what he or she is hearing.	
Example: Can you tell me more about that?	Example: You said [x]. Am I getting that right?

While the opposite side speaks, take notes on what you hear in the space below.

3. **Switch!** Now NO and YES will switch sides. If you argued YES before, now you will argue NO. Work with the same partner and use your notes. Add any arguments and evidence from the clues and sources. Those *now* arguing YES go first.

When both sides have finished, answer the following:

Before I started this discussion with my fellow State Department officials, my opinion was that America	*After* this discussion with my fellow State Department officials, my opinion is that America
____should have annexed Hawaii.	____should have annexed Hawaii.
____should not have annexed Hawaii.	____should not have annexed Hawaii.

4. **Point of View** Do you all agree on the answer to the Guiding Question?

- ____Yes

- ____No

If not, on what points do you all agree?

INTERACTIVE

For extra help with Step 4, review the 21st Century Tutorial: **Participate in a Discussion or Debate.**

Take Notes

Literacy Skills: Summarize Use what you have read to complete the chart. Add key details about U.S. interactions with the country during the late 1800s. The first one has been completed for you. Then use the information you have gathered to write a summary sentence answering the question provided.

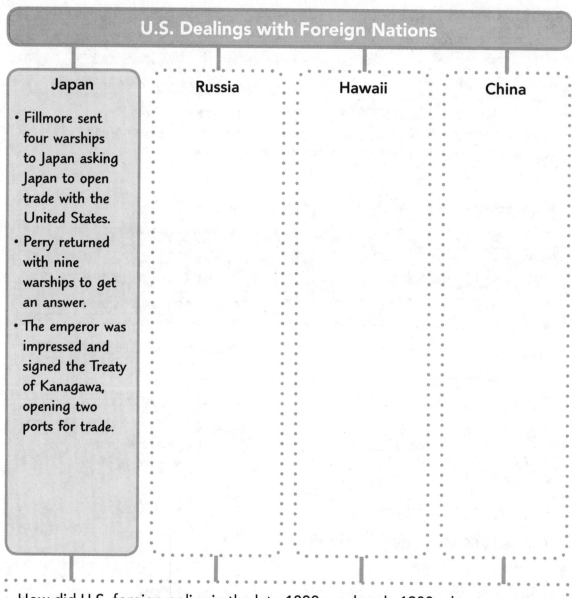

U.S. Dealings with Foreign Nations

Japan

- Fillmore sent four warships to Japan asking Japan to open trade with the United States.
- Perry returned with nine warships to get an answer.
- The emperor was impressed and signed the Treaty of Kanagawa, opening two ports for trade.

Russia

Hawaii

China

How did U.S. foreign policy in the late 1800s and early 1900s demonstrate imperialist goals?

 INTERACTIVE

For extra help, review the 21st Century Tutorial: **Summarize.**

Practice Vocabulary

Use a Word Bank Choose one word from the word bank to fill in each blank. When you have finished, you will have a short summary of important ideas from the section.

Word Bank

Great White Fleet   Open Door Policy   imperialism

isolationism   Treaty of Kanagawa

The U.S. dealings with Japan in the late 1800s demonstrated a shift

from the previous U.S. policy of .... In the

1850s, Commodore Matthew Perry took steam-powered warships

to Japan to demonstrate America's strength. The display convinced

the Japanese emperor to sign the ....

and open ports to trade with the United States. Later, the U.S.

Navy's modern steam-powered ships would become known as the

....

The United States also took an interest in China during the Age of

.... Russia, Japan, and several European

nations all had spheres of influence in China. Because the United States

did not want to be cut out of trade with China, Secretary of State John

Hay sent letters to the countries with spheres of influence and convinced

them to accept the .... The United States

also took an active role in ending the Boxer Rebellion and promoting

respect of Chinese independence.

Take Notes

Literacy Skills: Identify Main Ideas Use what you have read to complete the table. In each space write the main idea that is supported by the corresponding details. The first one has been completed for you.

Main Idea	Details
Yellow journalism helped lead the United States into war with Spain.	• Newspapers published by Hearst and Pulitzer printed graphic stories about Spanish atrocities. • Yellow journalism was often exaggerated or completely untrue, but the newspaper owners knew a war would boost sales. • When the USS *Maine* exploded in Cuba, the newspapers blamed it on Spain even though the cause of the explosion was unclear.
	• As soon as war was declared on Spain, the Pacific fleet went to the Spanish-controlled Philippines and defeated the Spanish fleet. • American soldiers won a decisive battle at San Juan Hill in Cuba, where the U.S. fleet also defeated the Spanish fleet. The United States suffered few battle casualties, and the war ended quickly.
	• The United States gained control of Puerto Rico and Guam and purchased the Philippines. • Cuba was given independence, but the United States made Cuba accept the Platt Amendment, which would allow the United States to continue to intervene in Cuban affairs. • The Foraker Act of 1900 made Puerto Ricans U.S. citizens and set up a new government that Puerto Ricans did not have much control over.
	• Puerto Ricans and Filipinos wanted their independence. • Emilio Aguinaldo led a Filipino revolt, which became the Philippine-American War. • The Philippine-American War was more expensive and deadly on both sides than the Spanish-American War had been.

🖑 **INTERACTIVE**

For extra help, review the 21st Century Tutorial: **Identify Main Idea and Details**.

Practice Vocabulary

Sentence Revision Revise each sentence so that the underlined vocabulary word(s) is used logically. Be sure not to change the vocabulary word(s). The first one is done for you.

1. The <u>Spanish-American War</u> lasted for many years, and 4,000 American soldiers died in battle.

   The <u>Spanish-American War</u> lasted for 4 months, and 379 American soldiers died in battle.

2. Under the <u>Foraker Act</u> of 1900, the United States set up a new government in the Philippines that gave Filipinos complete control over their own affairs.

3. <u>Yellow journalism</u> was a style of reporting that exaggerated war crimes to scare Americans out of supporting a war against Spain.

4. The <u>Platt Amendment</u> gave Cuba complete freedom from Spain and all other imperial powers.

5. The press refused to print stories about Spanish <u>atrocities</u> because they did not want to stir up support for a war with Spain.

6. Because Cuba was an American <u>protectorate</u>, it had complete independence.

Take Notes

Literacy Skills: Use Evidence Use what you have read to complete the chart. Add details about actions taken by U.S. presidents toward Latin America. The first one has been completed for you. Then use the information you have gathered to draw a conclusion that answers the question provided.

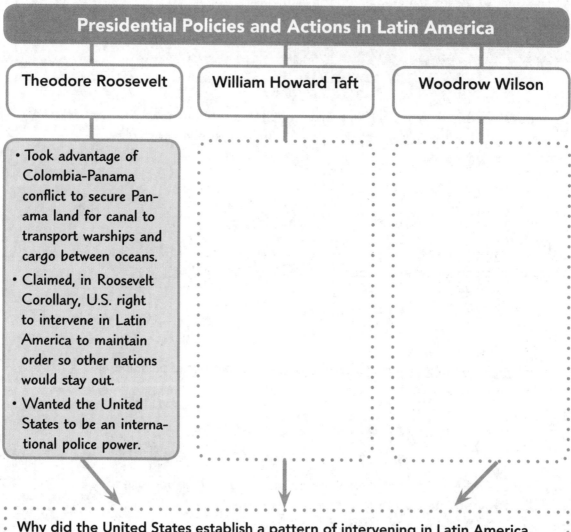

Presidential Policies and Actions in Latin America

Theodore Roosevelt

- Took advantage of Colombia-Panama conflict to secure Panama land for canal to transport warships and cargo between oceans.
- Claimed, in Roosevelt Corollary, U.S. right to intervene in Latin America to maintain order so other nations would stay out.
- Wanted the United States to be an international police power.

William Howard Taft

Woodrow Wilson

Why did the United States establish a pattern of intervening in Latin America, and what were the results?

🖐 INTERACTIVE

For extra help, review the 21st Century Tutorial: **Identify Evidence**.

Practice Vocabulary

Words in Context For each question below, write an answer that shows your understanding of the boldfaced key term.

1. How did Woodrow Wilson's **moral diplomacy** differ in theory from the diplomacy of previous presidents?

2. Why was the **isthmus** of Panama a good location for a canal?

3. What were the positive and negative effects of **dollar diplomacy**?

4. What message did the **Roosevelt Corollary** send to the rest of the world?

Quick Activity Building the Panama Canal

With a partner or small group, examine this photo of workers
building the Panama Canal.

Did you notice the mountainous terrain on either side of the area
where the men are working? Blasting through mountains was just
one challenge that workers had to face. With your partner or group,
brainstorm other challenges faced by the builders of the Panama Canal
and list them in the space below. Then discuss which one you think
would have been the most difficult and circle it.

Team Challenge! With your group, create a cartoon, poster, or
graphic novel page illustrating what you think was the most difficult
part of building the Panama Canal. Display your artwork so that
other teams can see it. Walk around the classroom and observe the
challenges others picked. How many of the challenges appeared on
your brainstorming list? Did any groups pick a challenge that was not
on your list?

Take Notes

Literacy Skills: Sequence Use what you have read to complete the chart with the sequence of events that engulfed the major European powers in war. For each event, provide the specific date or date range and a brief description. You may need to infer the date from the information in the text. The first and last events in the sequence have been completed for you.

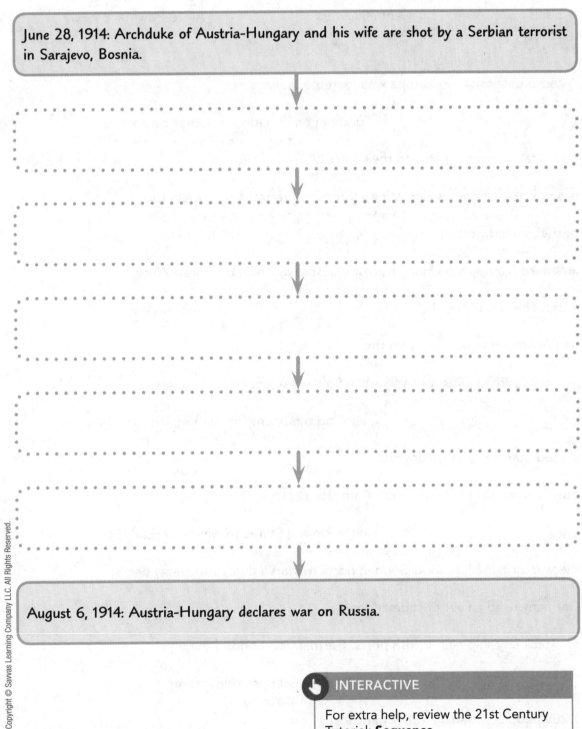

June 28, 1914: Archduke of Austria-Hungary and his wife are shot by a Serbian terrorist in Sarajevo, Bosnia.

August 6, 1914: Austria-Hungary declares war on Russia.

INTERACTIVE

For extra help, review the 21st Century Tutorial: **Sequence**.

Practice Vocabulary

Use a Word Bank Choose one word from the word bank to fill in each blank. When you have finished, you will have a short summary of important ideas from the section.

Word Bank

Lusitania	militarism	nationalism
neutral	propaganda	trench warfare
U-boats	Central Powers	Allied Powers
terrorist		

A cause of tensions in Europe was extreme feelings of

...., pride in one's nation. Another cause was

European nations expanding their forces. ....

is a policy of strengthening armed forces to prepare for war. On top

of that, an individual .... attacked an

archduke from Austria-Hungary visiting Bosnia, which triggered World

War I. The war pitted the ....—Germany

and Austria-Hungary—against the ....

—France, Britain, Russia, and Serbia. Soldiers engaged in long-term

...., shelling the enemy in ditches. The

United States officially adopted a ....

position, refusing to take a side. Both sides spread

.... in the United States to win favor. Early in

the war, Britain blockaded German ports to starve them into surrender, so

Germany used a fleet of submarines, ...,

to attack any ship near British ports. Germany torpedoed the

...., a British passenger ship, killing

1,200 people, including 128 Americans.

Quick Activity Life in the Trenches

With a partner, examine this artist's rendering of a World War I trench.

With your partner, discuss what it would have been like to be a soldier in the trenches during World War I. What dangers would you have faced? What sights, sounds, and smells would you have encountered? In your opinion, what would have been the most difficult part of living in the trenches? As you discuss, take brief notes about your thoughts in the space below.

Team Challenge! With a partner, imagine that you are a World War I soldier. Write a journal entry or a letter home describing your life in the trenches. Be sure to include details about at least one of the challenges that you identified in the discussion with your partner.

Take Notes

Literacy Skills: Summarize Use what you have read to complete the chart. Add details from the text to support each subtopic. The first subtopic has been completed for you. Then write a summary statement that answers the question provided.

U.S. Moves Toward War	Changes at Home
Diplomacy with Germany In response to Britain's blockade, Germany attacked any ship around Britain's ports, including ships from neutral nations and a passenger ship, so President Wilson threatened to break off diplomatic relations.	**Strengthening the Military**
Zimmerman Telegram	**Increasing Production and Funding**
The Russian Revolution	**Effects on People**

What changes did entering World War I bring to the United States, and what were some lasting results?

 INTERACTIVE

For extra help, review the 21st Century Tutorial: **Summarize**.

Practice Vocabulary

Use a Word Bank Choose one word from the word bank to fill in each blank. You may need to change the form of a word. When you have finished, you will have a short summary of important ideas from the section.

Word Bank

warmonger   Zimmermann telegram   Selective Service Act

illiterate   bureaucracy   Liberty Bond

pacifist   socialism

In 1916, Wilson ran for reelection against Republican Hughes,

who favored neutrality but was portrayed by Democrats as

a ...., one who provokes war.

American anti-German feelings soared after the discovery of the

........................., which urged Mexico to attack the

United States if it declared war on Germany. Americans prepared for

war. The .... required all men ages 21 to

30 to register for the military draft. About 25 percent of recruits were

........................., unable to read or write. The government

created a huge .... to manage the war effort,

reorganizing the economy to produce arms and other goods needed to

fight the war. American citizens bought ....,

lending money to the government to pay for the war. Some Americans

opposed the war. ...., believing that all war is

wrong, refused to participate. ...., people

who wanted public ownership of the means of production, such as

factories, argued that the war benefited factory owners but not workers.

Take Notes

Literacy Skills: Analyze Text Structure Use what you have read to complete the outline. Be sure to include important headings, subheadings, and details in your outline. The first heading has been completed for you.

I. Allied Setbacks
   A. Russia's Withdrawal from the War
      1. Lenin, leader of the Bolsheviks, believed the war was benefiting the ruling classes and wanted to withdraw to focus on a Communist revolution.
      2. The Treaty of Brest-Litovsk (1918) between Russia and Germany put Russia out of the war and gave Germany land and resources.
   B. German Offensive
      1. Germany organized an all-out attack near Amiens in France to try to push through the Allied lines and end the war.
      2. The attack on Amiens was ultimately unsuccessful, but Germany succeeded at pushing through the Allied lines elsewhere and got close to Paris.

II.
   A.
      1.

      2.

   B
      1.

      2.

III.
   A.
      1.

      2.

   B
      1.

      2.

IV.

 INTERACTIVE

For extra help, review the 21st Century Tutorial: **Summarize**.

Practice Vocabulary

Vocabulary Quiz Show Some quiz shows ask a question and expect the contestant to give the answer. In other shows, the contestant is given an answer and must supply the question. If the blank is in the Question column, write the question that would result in the answer in the Answer column. If the question is supplied, write the answer.

Question	Answer
1.	1. Battle of Belleau Wood
2. What was the name of the group of American troops led by General John J. Pershing?	2.
3. What is an agreement to stop armed battle?	3.
4.	4. epidemic
5.	5. Battle of the Argonne Forest

Take Notes

Literacy Skills: Use Evidence Use what you have read to complete the chart. In each column write details about the topic given. The first one has been completed for you. Then, use the information you have gathered to write a conclusion about the question provided.

Wilson's Fourteen Points	Treaty of Versailles	American Opposition to the Treaty
• Wilson designed the Fourteen Points, a peace plan to prevent international crises from causing another war. • The Fourteen Points called for an end to secret agreements and encouraged freedom of the seas, free trade, and limits on armaments. • Wilson supported self-determination for national groups and peaceful settlement of colonial disputes. • The 14th point called for the creation of a League of Nations, a forum where nations would be able to discuss future problems and protect the independence of all nations.		

Why was Wilson's plan for peace rejected by Americans and Europeans?

 INTERACTIVE

For extra help, review the 21st Century Tutorial: **Identify Evidence**.

Practice Vocabulary

True or False? Decide whether each statement below is true or false. Circle T or F, and then explain your answer. Be sure to include the underlined vocabulary word(s) in your explanation. The first one is done for you.

1. **T / F** The peace plan outlined by the Big Four was known as the <u>Fourteen Points</u>.
False. The peace plan outlined by Woodrow Wilson was known as the <u>Fourteen Points</u>.

2. **T / F** Britain and France were given <u>mandates</u> to govern territory in Czechoslovakia and Yugoslavia.

3. **T / F** Under the <u>Treaty of Versailles</u>, Germany was forced to accept full responsibility for the war.

4. **T / F** Henry Cabot Lodge wanted to change the <u>League of Nations</u> because it could compel the United States to join future European wars.

5. **T / F** The <u>reparations</u> paid to Germany by the Allies totaled more than $300 billion.

6. **T / F** Wilson was opposed to the principle of national <u>self-determination</u>, the right of nations to colonize other nations.

Writing Workshop Informative Essay

As you read, build a response to this prompt: **Describe U.S. expansion and intervention during the late 1800s and early 1900s.** The prompts below will help walk you through the process.

Lesson 1 Writing Task: Consider Your Purpose (See Student Text, page 726)

At the end of this workshop, you will be asked to write an informative essay about the prompt above. Write a sentence describing what you must do to meet the requirements of the writing task.

Lesson 2 Writing Task: Develop a Clear Thesis (See Student Text, page 735)

Write a thesis statement, summarizing the main idea of your essay.

Thesis

Lesson 3 Writing Task: Pick an Organizing Strategy (See Student Text, page 743)

For your five-paragraph essay, you will have an introduction paragraph, three body paragraphs, and a concluding paragraph. The body paragraphs should be organized in a way that is logical and intentional. Describe how you will organize the information in your essay.

Lesson 4 Writing Task: Write an Introduction (See Student Text, page 751)

Write an introductory paragraph for your essay. Be sure to include your thesis statement.

Lesson 5 Writing Task: Support Thesis with Details
(See Student Text, page 760)

Identify details that you will include in your essay to support your thesis statement.

Lesson 6 Writing Task: Draft Your Essay (See Student Text, page 767)

Draft your essay. Use your introduction, including your thesis statement, to familiarize your reader with your topic. Each paragraph should begin with a main idea and continue with supporting details.

Lesson 7 Writing Task: Write a Conclusion (See Student Text, page 774)

Write a concluding paragraph for your essay. Be sure to summarize your main ideas, using transition words to tie them together.

Writing Task (See Student Text, page 777)

Using the outline and the draft you created, respond to the following prompt in a five-paragraph informative essay: Describe U.S. expansion and intervention during the late 1800s and early 1900s.

Essential Question What should governments do?

Before you begin this topic, think about the Essential Question by completing the following activities.

1. Write a list of five ways that government affects your life. Then write two more things you think the government should do but doesn't.

2. Preview the topic by skimming lesson titles, headings, and graphics. Then place a check mark next to the ways you think the government might have helped people during the Great Depression.

__Government opened soup kitchens.   __Public works projects were enacted.

__Hoovervilles were built.   __Square Deal was passed.

__Industries were deregulated.   __Farms were subsidized.

Timeline Skills

As you read, write and/or draw at least three events from the topic. Draw a line from each event to its correct position on the timeline.

| 1915 | 1919 | 1924 |

Map Skills

Using the map in your text, color each region based on the amount of increase in vehicle registrations between 1920 and 1928. Create a key for your map.

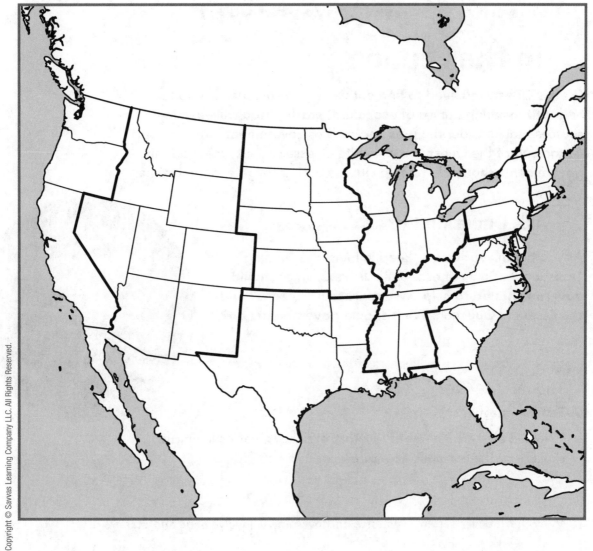

1929   1934   1939

Document-Based Writing Inquiry

The Role of Government in the Economy

On this Quest, you need to find out what governments can do to help citizens during times of economic hardship. You will examine sources that consider the pros and cons of government intervention. At the end of the Quest you will write an essay about what you think governments should do to help citizens during tough economic times.

1 Ask Questions (See Student Text, page 782)

As you begin your Quest, keep in mind the Guiding Question: **In times of economic distress, what should governments do to help or support their citizens?** and the Essential Question: **What should governments do?**

Theme The Free Market

Sample questions:

Why did Herbert Hoover believe that businesses, not government, should end the economic downturn?

Why did Hoover soften his stance on government involvement and start public works projects?

Theme Banking

Theme Jobs

Theme Regulation

Theme Economic Reform

Theme My Additional Questions

 INTERACTIVE

For extra help with Step 1, review the
21st Century Tutorial: **Ask Questions**.

2 Investigate

As you read about the Great Depression, collect five connections from your text to help you answer the Guiding Question. Three connections are already chosen for you.

Connect to Farmers' Struggles

Lesson 4 The Downside of the 1920s (See Student Text, page 812)

Here's a connection! Read this section in your text. Why were farmers unable to pay their debts in the 1920s? How could government have helped them?

What problems could occur if the government gets involved in farming?

Connect to the Hoover Dam

Lesson 5 How Did the President Respond? (See Student Text, page 820)

Here's another connection! Why did Herbert Hoover call for the construction of the Hoover Dam? How was this decision a change from Hoover's belief that the government should not get directly involved in ending the economic downturn?

The Hoover Dam is still in operation today and provides water and hydroelectric power to the Las Vegas area. How does this support the idea that it was a good investment?

Connect to the Emergency Banking Relief Act

Primary Source Franklin Roosevelt, Fireside Chat on Banking
(See Student Text, page 833)

What does this connection tell you about President Roosevelt's point of view on how involved the government should be in the country's financial affairs? What steps did the government take, under Roosevelt's leadership, to secure the banking industry during the Great Depression?

Why was it so important for President Roosevelt to reassure the American people that the banks would be stable with the government's support?

It's Your Turn! **Find two more connections. Fill in the title of your connections, then answer the questions. Connections may be images, primary sources, maps, or text.**

Your Choice | Connect to

Location in text

What is the main idea of this connection?

What does it tell you about government in the 1930s?

Your Choice | Connect to

Location in text

What is the main idea of this connection?

What does it tell you about government in the 1930s?

3 **Examine Primary Sources** (See Student Text, page 842)

Examine the primary and secondary sources provided online or from your teacher. Fill in the chart to show how these sources provide further information about how the government helped citizens in the 1930s. The first one is completed for you.

Source	Government helped citizens by
Dear Mrs. Roosevelt	providing part-time work to youth and young adults from poor families
The Civilian Conservation Corps	
Relief Efforts	
Government Intervention in the Economy	
Philosophy of Production: Restoration by Private Enterprise	

INTERACTIVE

For extra help with Step 3, review the 21st Century Tutorial: **Analyze Primary and Secondary Sources**.

Quest FINDINGS

4 Write Your Essay (See Student Text, page 842)

Now it's time to put together all of the information you have gathered and use it to write your essay.

1. **Prepare to Write** You have collected connections and explored primary and secondary sources that show how the United States government helped its citizens during the Great Depression. Look through your notes and decide which facts you would like to include in your essay. Record them here.

Facts about Government Help in the 1930s

2. **Write a Draft** Using evidence from the information in the textbook and the documents you explored, write a draft of your essay. Be sure to write about the different ways the government helped citizens during the Great Depression. Include details from the evidence in the documents you've studied in this Quest.

3. **Share with a Partner** Exchange your draft with a partner. Tell your partner what you like about his or her draft and suggest any improvements.

4. **Finalize Your Essay** Revise your essay. Correct any grammatical or spelling errors.

5. **Reflect on the Quest** Think about your experience completing this topic's Quest. What did you learn about the way the U.S. government helped people during the 1930s? What questions do you still have about the government's response to the Great Depression? How will you answer them?

Reflections

INTERACTIVE

For extra help with Step 4, review the 21st Century Tutorial: **Write an Essay**.

Take Notes

Literacy Skills: Summarize Use what you have read to complete the graphic organizers. In the column titled "Important Details," enter two of the most important details from the section. The first one has been started for you.

Republicans Regain the White House	Important Details
A Landslide Victory	• Warren Harding swamps opponent. • Harding picks Mellon and Hoover for his cabinet.
The Ohio Gang	
Coolidge Becomes President	

Why Did the United States Return to Isolationism?	Important Details
Latin American Investments	
The First Communist State	
Pursuing Peace	

👆 **INTERACTIVE**

For extra help, review the 21st Century Tutorial: **Summarize**.

Practice Vocabulary

Use a Word Bank Choose one word from the word bank to fill in each blank. When you have finished, you will have a short summary of important ideas from the section.

Word Bank

communism	interest	disarmament
installment buying	recession	stock
margin	bull market	

There were not enough jobs for returning soldiers. This resulted

in a ...., or economic slump. People

wanted to buy things they could not afford, so businesses

allowed ...., or buying on credit.

Buyers made monthly payments until they paid the full price, plus

......................, a percentage charged as a fee for

the loan. Consumer debt and the stock market jumped. Corporations

sold ...., or shares of ownership, to

investors. More people invested in the stock market than ever before.

A period of increased stock trading and rising stock prices is known as a

.... People bought stock for a down payment,

or ...., held the stock until the price

rose, and then sold it at a profit. Meanwhile, the Soviet Union

adopted .... The government owned

all wealth and property. Europe and the United States began

......................, the reduction of armed forces and

weapons of war.

Take Notes

Literacy Skills: Draw Conclusions Use what you have read to complete the graphic organizers. In the bottom box, draw at least two conclusions from the event in the top box. The first one has been started for you.

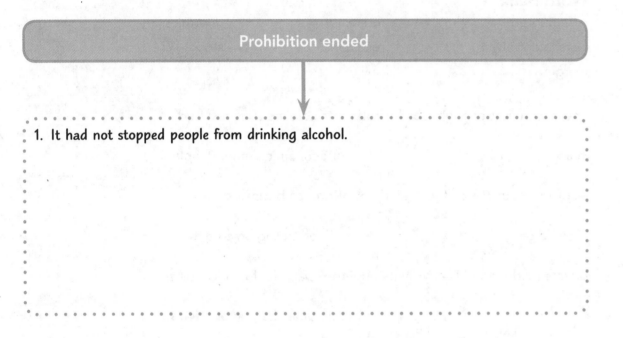

Prohibition ended

1. It had not stopped people from drinking alcohol.

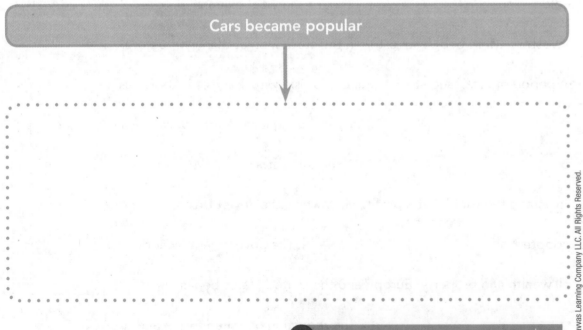

Cars became popular

INTERACTIVE

For extra help, review the 21st Century Tutorial: **Draw Conclusions**.

Practice Vocabulary

Matching Logic **Using your knowledge of the underlined vocabulary words, draw a line from each sentence in Column 1 to match it with the sentence in Column 2 to which it logically belongs.**

Column 1	Column 2
1. Prohibition led to an increase in <u>organized crime</u>.	Many Americans watched Charlie Chaplin on the big screen.
2. The <u>Equal Rights Amendment</u> was proposed to protect everybody's rights, regardless of gender.	Alice Paul spent her whole life trying to get it ratified.
3. <u>Prohibition</u> on the sale of alcohol went into effect in 1920.	Gangsters supplied alcohol to speakeasies.
4. <u>Mass culture</u> grew because people watched the same movies and heard the same news reports.	The 21st Amendment made alcohol legal again.
5. By the end of the 1920s, people were calling for the <u>repeal</u> of Prohibition.	Federal agents traveled around the country to try to enforce the ban.
6. <u>Bootleggers</u> smuggled liquor into the country.	Some people found ways to get around Prohibition.

Take Notes

Literacy Skills: Summarize Use what you have read to complete the tables. In the column titled "Important Details," enter a few of the most important details from the section. The first one has been completed for you.

Main Trends of the 1920s	Important Details
Fun Fads	Flagpole sitting Marathon dancing and the Charleston Games like crossword puzzles and mah-jongg
Flapper Fashion	
Rise of Jazz Music	
Athletic Heroes	
Lucky Lindy	

New American Writers Emerge	Important Details
Hemingway and Fitzgerald	
Other Important Contributions	

👆 **INTERACTIVE**

For extra help, review the 21st Century Tutorial: **Summarize**.

Practice Vocabulary

Use a Word Bank Choose one word from the word bank to fill in each blank. When you have finished, you will have a short summary of important ideas from the section.

Word Bank

expatriates   flappers

fads   jazz

Many different .... became popular in the 1920s. Some young people took up flagpole sitting, others danced in dance marathons, and a game called mah-jongg became popular. Young women called .... pursued these trends. They wore their hair short and also wore short dresses. They shocked some people by wearing bright red lipstick. A new form of music called .... was born in New Orleans during this decade, and people continue to listen to it today. Some of the best writers in American history wrote books in the 1920s. Some were .... who had lived overseas.

Quick Activity Changing Fashions

Along with other cultural changes experienced during the 1920s, Americans also saw changes in the ways that men and women dressed. With a partner or small group, examine these two pictures.

▲ Women's fashion was conservative around the turn of the 20th century.

▲ In the 1920s, women's fashion changed dramatically.

Team Challenge! Write a list of the ways women's fashion changed at the beginning of the 20th century, noting the differences. Also list similarities. When your list is finished, take part in a classroom discussion about the changes in fashion and why they might have happened.

Take Notes

Literacy Skills: Identify Cause and Effect Use what you have read to complete the graphic organizers. In the top boxes, enter three causes. The first one has been started for you.

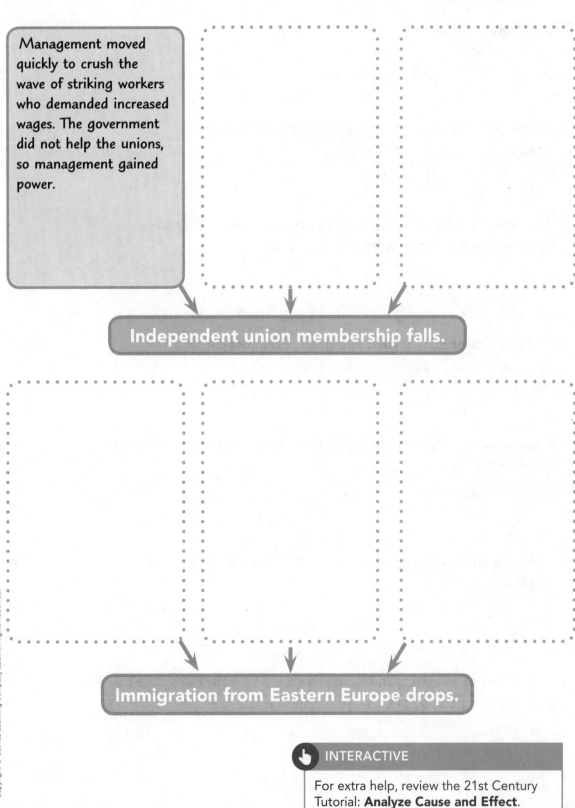

Management moved quickly to crush the wave of striking workers who demanded increased wages. The government did not help the unions, so management gained power.

Independent union membership falls.

Immigration from Eastern Europe drops.

INTERACTIVE

For extra help, review the 21st Century Tutorial: **Analyze Cause and Effect**.

Practice Vocabulary

Sentence Builder **Finish the sentences below with a key term from this section. You may have to change the form of the words to complete the sentences.**

Word Bank

Great Migration	deport	company union
sabotage	quota system	anarchist

1. People who oppose organized government are called

2. Americans became more fearful of foreigners because they were concerned about enemy spies and

3. As a result of hostility toward foreigners, Congress set up a

4. A large number of African Americans moved to northern and western cities during the

5. Membership in independent unions declined by 1.6 million after employers created

6. The actions of anarchists and Communists led to many foreigners being

Take Notes

Literacy Skills: Sequence Use what you have read to complete the graphic organizers. Enter the events in the sequence in which they happened. The first one has been started for you.

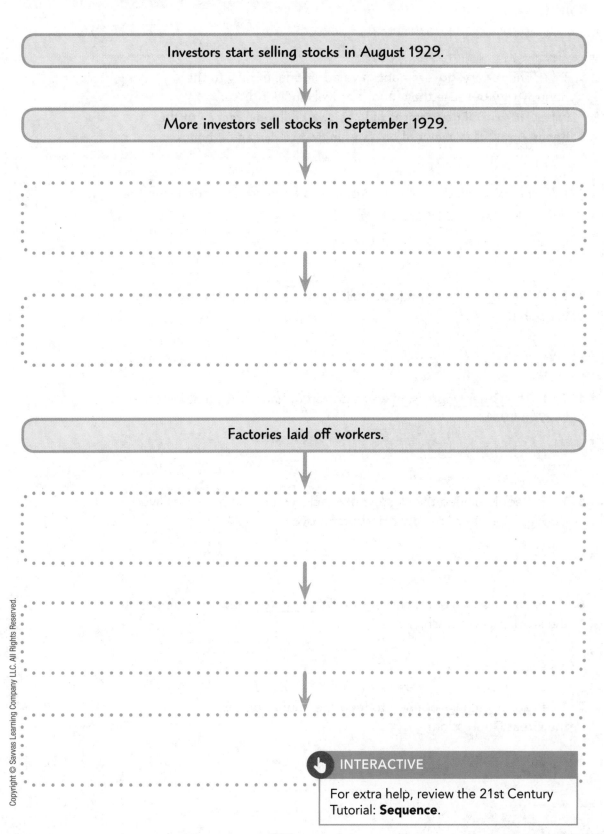

Investors start selling stocks in August 1929.

More investors sell stocks in September 1929.

Factories laid off workers.

INTERACTIVE

For extra help, review the 21st Century Tutorial: **Sequence**.

Practice Vocabulary

True or False? Decide whether each statement below is true or false. Circle T or F, and then explain your answer. Be sure to include the underlined vocabulary word in your explanation. The first one is done for you.

1. **T / F** The federal government gave additional money to the <u>Bonus Army</u> because they fought bravely in World War I.
   False; The federal government did not give additional money to the <u>Bonus Army</u>. They marched on Washington to demand a bonus.

2. **T / F** People who did not own businesses were not affected when the businesses went <u>bankrupt</u>.

3. **T / F** <u>Public works</u> are projects built by the private sector for use by the public.

4. **T / F** The <u>Great Depression</u> was a period of hard times that lasted from 1929 to 1941.

5. **T / F** People named the clusters of shacks where the homeless lived <u>Hoovervilles</u> after President Herbert Hoover.

6. **T / F** The practice of purchasing stocks <u>on margin</u> had little impact on the stock market crash.

7. **T / F** <u>Soup kitchens</u> opened to feed the hungry during the Great Depression.

Take Notes

Literacy Skills: Analyze Text Structure Use what you have read to complete the graphic organizer. Complete the outline to summarize the main ideas of the lesson. The first one has been partially completed for you.

I. How Did FDR Fight the Depression?

   A. Strengthened Banks

      1. Declared a bank holiday

      2.

      3.

   B. Laws for Recovery

      1.

      2.

      3.

   C. Early Relief Programs

      1.

      2.

      3.

   D. The Works Progress Administration

      1.

      2.

      3.

 INTERACTIVE

For extra help, review the 21st Century Tutorial: **Organize Your Ideas**.

Practice Vocabulary

Use a Word Bank Choose one word from the word bank to fill in each blank. When you have finished, you will have a short summary of important ideas from the section.

Word Bank

collective bargaining	pension	Social Security Act
bank holiday	fireside chats	deficit spending
national debt	Hundred Days	New Deal

To assist with the country's economic recovery, Roosevelt declared

a ...., closing all banks for four days.

Congress mandated that only banks with enough funds to meet

depositors' demands could reopen. Roosevelt gave 30 radio talks

known as .... In his first days in office,

Congress passed a record 15 major new laws. This period was

called the .... These laws made up

the ...., which had three main goals:

relief for the jobless, plans for economic recovery, and reforms to

prevent another Depression. Congress passed the Wagner Act, which

guaranteed workers the right to .... They

also passed the ...., which created an

old-age .... program. Critics expressed

alarm because the government was spending more than it took in.

This practice of .... hugely increased

the ...., the total amount of money the

government owes.

Take Notes

Literacy Skills: Summarize Use what you have read to complete the tables. In the column titled "Important Details," enter a few of the most important details from the section. The first one has been started for you.

The Dust Bowl	Important Details
Causes	• Years of overgrazing and plowing destroyed grass that held soil in place.
Effects	

How the Depression Affected Women	Important Details
Working Women	
The First Lady Takes a Stand	

INTERACTIVE

For extra help, review the 21st Century Tutorial: **Summarize**.

Practice Vocabulary

Sentence Builder Finish the sentences below with key terms from this section. You may have to change the form of the words to complete the sentences.

Word Bank

civil rights	migrant worker	Indian New Deal
Dust Bowl	Black Cabinet	

1. African Americans, such as Robert C. Weaver and Mary McLeod Bethune, who advised Franklin D. Roosevelt were called the

2. Rights due to all citizens are

3. The area where a severe drought caused soil to blow in wind storms was called the

4. A series of laws that gave American Indians greater control over their own affairs has been called the

5. Okies who packed their belongings into cars and went to the West Coast looking for jobs were called

Quick Activity Great Depression Timeline

Explore these important events, and then write a journal entry about one of the events from the perspective of someone who lived through it.

Year	Event
1929	Stock market crashes in October, causing it to lose $30 billion in value by November.
1931	Bank of the United States in New York collapses, causing the loss of $200 million in deposits.
1932	Franklin Roosevelt defeats Herbert Hoover by a landslide in the presidential election.
1933	The Civilian Conservation Corps, Federal Relief Administration, and the Civilian Works Administration are established to help suffering Americans. Unemployment peaks at 25.6 percent.
1935	The Social Security Act is put into law, providing retired Americans a pension.
1937	After four years of job gains, unemployment rises again.
1938	Congress passes a spending package to stimulate the economy. Unemployment begins to fall.
1941	The United States enters World War II, effectively ending the Great Depression.

Team Challenge! With a partner, choose one of the events from the chart above and write a journal entry from the perspective of a young person who lived through it. Consider how a person living in that time might have felt. Would he or she have been hopeful or worried? After you've written your journal entry, post it in your classroom. Take a walk around the classroom to read some of your classmates' journal entries.

Writing Workshop Research Paper

Select a specific aspect of the New Deal and write a research paper that answers this question: **What impact did this aspect of the New Deal have on Americans?** The prompts below will help walk you through the process.

Lesson 1 Writing Task: Generate Questions to Focus Research
(See Student Text, page 788)

Write two to four questions about the New Deal and its impact on Americans. Start with this one: What was the New Deal? Use the rest of your questions to help you focus on one aspect of the New Deal that you want to research further. Circle the question that pinpoints your research choice. This will be the main point of your thesis statement.

Lessons 2, 3, and 6 Writing Task: Find and Use Credible Sources
(See Student Text, pages 796, 803, and 832)

Find reliable sources. Information on the Internet is often inaccurate. Note information that you may use in your essay. Follow the citation format that your teacher provides.

Citation	Notes

Lessons 4 and 5 Writing Task: Support Ideas with Evidence
(See Student Text, pages 812 and 820)

Outline your research essay with a thesis, main ideas, and evidence. Under each main idea, write two pieces of evidence that support that idea.

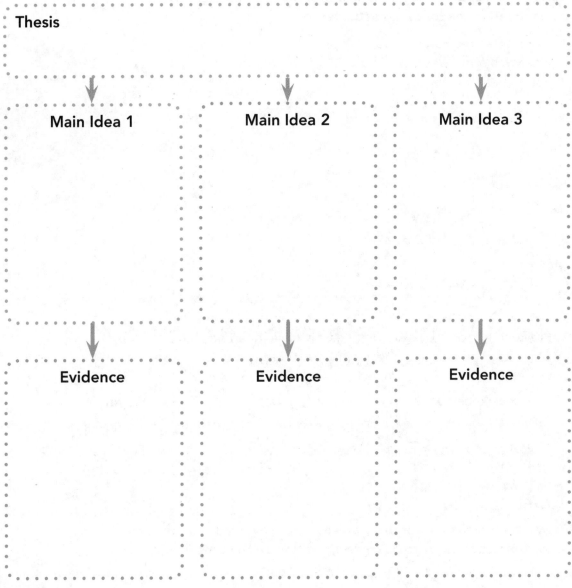

Thesis

Main Idea 1   Main Idea 2   Main Idea 3

Evidence   Evidence   Evidence

Lesson 7 Writing Task: Use Technology to Produce and Publish
(See Student Text, page 841)

When you are ready to write your essay, use a word-processing program. When you are finished revising, use technology to publish your essay by sharing it online with your classmates.

Writing Task (See Student Text, page 843)

Using your notes, write a research paper about the specific aspect of the New Deal that you researched. Explain how it made a big impact on Americans.

Essential Question **When is war justified?**

Before you begin the topic, think about the Essential Question by completing the following activities.

1. Think of a time you defended yourself or stood up for what was right. Describe why you did this and how you felt afterward.

2. Preview the topic by skimming lesson titles, headings, and graphics. Then place a check mark next to items that you predict will most influence the United States to join World War II.

__appeasement __atomic bombs __discrimination

__isolationism __Japan __Latin America

__Nazi Germany __Neutrality Acts __totalitarianism

Timeline Skills

As you read, write and/or draw at least three events from the topic. Draw a line from each event to its correct position on the timeline.

1930   **1935**

Map Skills

Using the map in your text, label the outline map with the nuclear facilities listed. Use a symbol to indicate nuclear facility locations, and create a key that explains the symbol. Label Washington, D.C., and all states shown, using correct postal abbreviations.

Metallurgical Laboratory, Chicago, Illinois

Los Alamos, New Mexico

Hanford, Washington

Oak Ridge, Tennessee

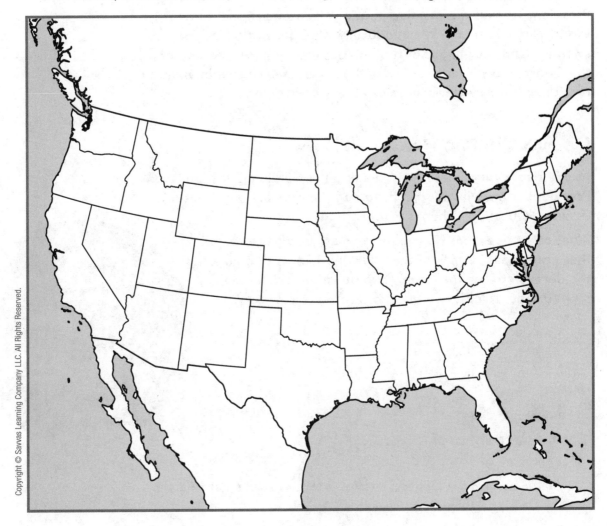

1940

1945

1950

Quest
Document-Based Writing Inquiry

Dropping the Atomic Bomb

On this Quest, you will build an informed opinion about whether President Truman was justified in using the atomic bomb during World War II. You will examine documents from world leaders and scientists and see images of the bomb's aftermath. At the end of the Quest, you will write an essay that expresses your opinion about President Truman's decision to use the atomic bomb.

1 Ask Questions (See Student Text, page 848)

As you begin your Quest, keep in mind the Guiding Question: **Was President Truman justified in dropping the atomic bomb?** and the Essential Question: **When is war justified?**

What other questions do you need to ask in order to answer these questions? Consider the following factors that affected the decision to use the bomb. Two questions are filled in for you. Add at least two questions for each category.

Theme The War in the Pacific and the Potsdam Declaration

Sample questions:

What was the Potsdam Declaration?

What action did the United States plan to take against Japan if the Potsdam Declaration went unheeded?

Theme The Position Taken by Scientists

Theme The Bombing of Hiroshima

Theme The Japanese Response

Theme President Truman's Rationale

Theme My Additional Questions

 INTERACTIVE

For extra help with Step 1, review the
21st Century Tutorial: **Ask Questions**.

2 Investigate

As you read about World War II, collect five connections from your text to help you answer the Guiding Question. Three connections are already chosen for you.

Connect to Japanese Motives

Lesson 2 The United States Enters the War (See Student Text, page 863)

Here's a connection! Read about the events that led up to the attack on Pearl Harbor. What reasons did Japan have for going to war? What role did the United States play in Japan's aggression?

Describe relations between the United States and Japan by November 1941.

Connect to Roosevelt's Reaction

Primary Source Franklin D. Roosevelt, "Day of Infamy" Speech
(See Student Text, page 865)

Here's another connection! What insight does this primary source give you into the political relationship between the United States and Japan? According to President Roosevelt, what action was the appropriate response to the Japanese attack?

How do you think President Roosevelt might have viewed President Truman's decision to use the atomic bomb?

Connect to the End of the War in the Pacific

Lesson 4 Japan Surrenders (See Student Text, page 882)

Look at the images in your text of Hiroshima before and after the dropping of the atomic bomb. How do you think seeing the devastation of the first atomic bomb might have affected President Truman's decision to use a second atomic bomb on Nagasaki?

What does the decision to use a second bomb tell you about President Truman's goals?

It's Your Turn! Find two more connections. Fill in the titles of your connections and then answer the questions. Connections may be images, primary sources, maps, or text.

Your Choice | Connect to

Location in text

What is the main idea of this connection?

What does it tell you about President Truman's decision to use the atomic bomb?

Your Choice | Connect to

Location in text

What is the main idea of this connection?

What does it tell you about President Truman's decision to use the atomic bomb?

③ Examine Primary Sources (See Student Text, page 886)

Examine the primary sources provided online or from your teacher. Fill in the chart to show how these sources provide further information about President Truman's decision to use the atomic bomb. The first one is completed for you.

Source	What this source tells me about the decision to use the atomic bomb
The Potsdam Declaration	• The Allies gave Japan the option of a peaceful surrender that would involve punishment only for war criminals. • The Allies warned Japan that failure to surrender would result in destruction.
"A Petition to the President of the United States"	
Photographic Record of the Bombing of Hiroshima	
Secret History of the Greater Asian War	
Letter to James L. Cate	

👆 INTERACTIVE

For extra help with Step 3, review the 21st Century Tutorial: **Analyze Primary and Secondary Sources**.

4 Write Your Opinion Essay (See Student Text, page 886)

Now it's time to put together all of the information you have gathered and use it to write an opinion essay.

1. **Prepare to Write** You have collected connections and explored primary sources about President Truman's decision to use the atomic bomb. Look through your notes and decide your answer to the question: **Was President Truman justified in dropping the atomic bomb?** Record the key points of your response here.

In my opinion . . .

2. **Write a Draft** Using information from the text and the sources you explored, write a draft of your essay. Be sure to include an introduction that states your opinion, body paragraphs with supporting evidence, and a conclusion that sums up your main ideas.

3. **Share with a Partner** Exchange your draft with a partner. Tell your partner what you like about his or her draft and suggest any improvements.

4. **Finalize Your Essay** Revise your essay, using suggestions made by your partner when appropriate. Correct any grammatical or spelling errors.

5. **Reflect on the Quest** Think about your experience completing this topic's Quest. What did you learn about President Truman's decision? How did what you learned inform or possibly change your understanding of the events of World War II? How does reflecting on the difficult decision Truman faced affect your understanding of difficult decisions faced by presidents and other leaders today?

Reflections

INTERACTIVE

For extra help with Step 4, review the 21st Century Tutorial: **Support Ideas with Evidence**.

Take Notes

Literacy Skills: Summarize Use what you have read to complete the outline. Pay attention to headings, subheadings, and key terms. The outline has been started for you.

I. Dictators Take Power in Italy and Germany

   A. Fascism

      1. Philosophy based on militarism, extreme nationalism, and loyalty to state

      2. Supported by business leaders and landowners

   B. Fascist Italy

      1.

      2.

   C. Nazi Germany

      1.

      2.

II. Strong Leaders in the Soviet Union and Japan

   A. Soviet Union

      1. Stalin rises to power in 1924 and creates a totalitarian state.

      2.

      3.

   B. Japan

      1.

      2.

III. U.S. Remains Isolated

   A. The Neutrality Acts

      1.

      2.

   B. Latin America

      1.

      2.

   C. Soviet Union

      1.

      2.

 INTERACTIVE

For extra help, review the 21st Century Tutorial: **Summarize.**

Practice Vocabulary

Word Map Study the word map for the word *fascism*. Characteristics are words or phrases that relate to the word in the center of the word map. Non-characteristics are words and phrases not associated with the word. Use the blank word map to explore the meaning of the word *aggression*. Then make word maps of your own for these words: *Nazi, scapegoat, concentration camp, totalitarian state, Neutrality Acts,* and *Good Neighbor Policy.*

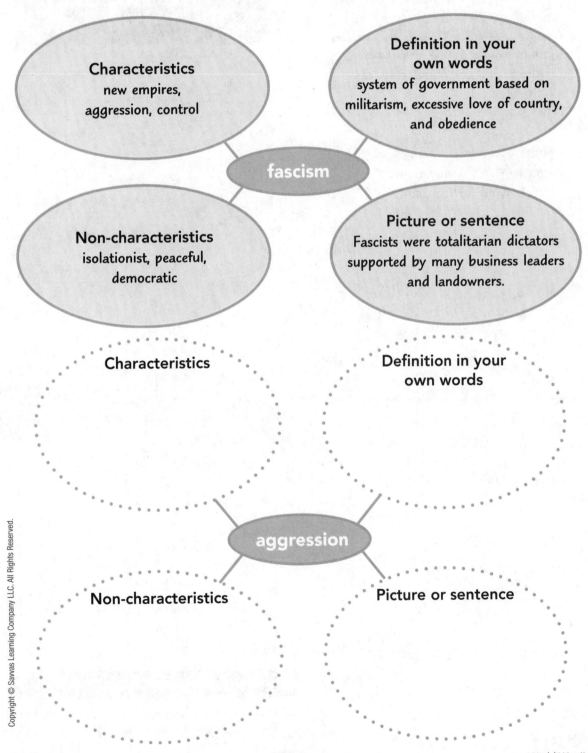

Characteristics
new empires, aggression, control

Definition in your own words
system of government based on militarism, excessive love of country, and obedience

fascism

Non-characteristics
isolationist, peaceful, democratic

Picture or sentence
Fascists were totalitarian dictators supported by many business leaders and landowners.

Characteristics

Definition in your own words

aggression

Non-characteristics

Picture or sentence

Take Notes

Literacy Skills: Identify Cause and Effect Use what you have read to complete the flowchart. In each space, write details about the events that eventually led the United States to enter World War II. The chart has been started for you.

Aggression Leads to War Between the Axis and Allied Powers

- Japan invades China, massacres civilians, and commandeers areas with resources.

- Hitler occupies the Rhineland, annexes Austria, and claims the Sudetenland for Germany.

United States Aids the Allies

United States Enters the War

 INTERACTIVE

For extra help, review the 21st Century Tutorial: **Analyze Cause and Effect**.

Practice Vocabulary

Use a Word Bank Choose one word from the word bank to fill in each blank. When you have finished, you will have a short summary of important ideas from the section. Some words in the bank may not be used.

Word Bank

Munich Conference	appeasement	Nazi-Soviet Pact
blitzkrieg	Axis	Allies
Battle of Britain	Lend-Lease Act	Atlantic Charter

World War II was fought between the .... — the United States, the United Kingdom, France, and the Soviet Union— and the .... powers—Germany, Italy, and Japan. At first, the United States tried to stay out of the conflict, but Congress did pass the ...., in which the United States agreed to sell or loan war materials to the Allies.

Many people hoped that war could be avoided by following a policy of .... toward Hitler. However, when Hitler violated the promises he made at the .... by launching a .... against Poland, Britain and France declared war on Germany. Less than a year later, France fell to Axis powers. The British, however, were able to turn back the Germans during the .... The United States still stayed out of the war, but President Roosevelt and British Prime Minister Winston Churchill met in 1941 to set goals for the postwar world. Their agreement was called the ....

Take Notes

Literacy Skills: Classify and Categorize Use what you have read to complete the flowchart. In each column, record details about the changes that World War II brought for certain groups of Americans on the home front. The first one has been completed for you.

Effect of World War II on . . .

Women	Japanese Americans	African Americans
• About 5 million women entered the work force. • Rosie the Riveter symbolized American women working to support the war. • Women's pay and benefits improved but were still not the same as men's. • Women wore pants and overalls because they were more practical for work. • About 400,000 women joined the armed services but were not sent into combat.		

INTERACTIVE

For extra help, review the 21st Century Tutorial: **Categorize**.

Practice Vocabulary

Use a Word Bank Choose one word from the word bank to fill in each blank. When you have finished, you will have a short summary of important ideas from the section.

Word Bank

Tuskegee Airmen	Bracero Program	War Production Board
Rosie the Riveter	"Double V" campaign	victory gardens
rationing	internment	

The .... shifted factories from consumer

goods to war materials. Raw materials for war production were ensured

through .... , government limits on certain

goods people could buy. Americans combatted food shortages

by planting more than 20 million .... ,

producing 40 percent of U.S.-grown vegetables. Responding to urgent

demands for labor, almost 5 million women entered the work force.

.... symbolized women's contributions to the

war effort. Under the U.S.-Mexico .... , many

Mexicans moved north to work on farms and railroads. Many African

Americans joined the cause and pursued a .... ,

victory over the enemy abroad and victory over discrimination at home.

The .... were a group of African American

fighter pilots who destroyed or damaged about 400 enemy aircraft.

Thousands of Japanese American men fought in Europe in segregated

units. In 1988, Congress apologized and compensated Japanese

Americans who suffered .... , or temporary

imprisonment, during the war.

Quick Activity In This Together

With a partner or small group, examine this poster that was used to encourage people to buy war bonds.

▲ Let's ALL fight! Buy War Bonds.

Discuss how the poster grabs the viewer's attention. What emotions is it supposed to make the viewer feel? What images does it use to get its point across? Write a few sentences to answer these questions. Then study the image below. How are these two images different?

▲ I've found the job where I fit best! Find your war job in industry, agriculture, or business.

Team Challenge! As a group, create a poster that could have been used during World War II to encourage people to support the war in some way. Display your poster so that other groups can view it. Take a few minutes to visit other groups' posters on display.

Take Notes

Literacy Skills: Sequence Use what you have read to complete the flowchart. In each space, record a key event related to the "beat Hitler first" strategy that turned the tide of the war and led to Germany's surrender. Be sure to record the events in the order in which they occurred, indicating a specific date or time span when possible. The first one has been completed for you.

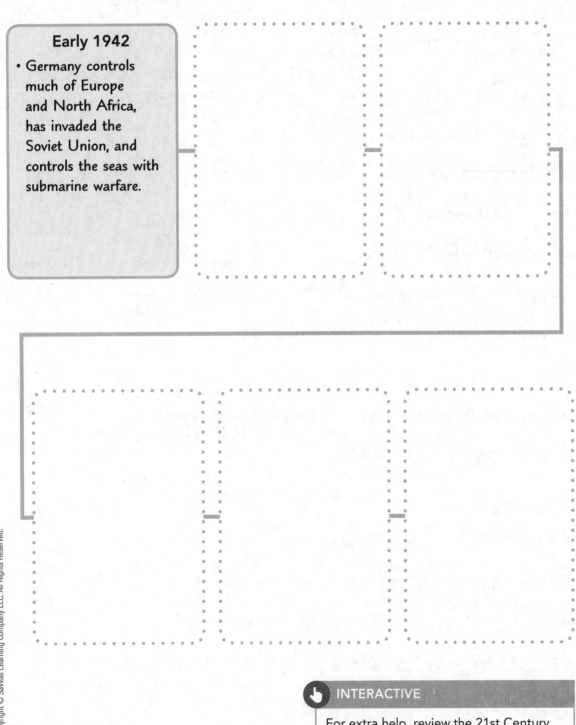

Early 1942

- Germany controls much of Europe and North Africa, has invaded the Soviet Union, and controls the seas with submarine warfare.

INTERACTIVE

For extra help, review the 21st Century Tutorial: **Sequence**.

Practice Vocabulary

Use a Word Bank Choose one word from the word bank to fill in each blank. When you have finished, you will have a short summary of important ideas from the section. Some words in the word bank may not be used.

Word Bank

Battle of the Bulge	Battle of Midway	concentration camp
death camp	Holocaust	island-hopping
Nuremberg Trials	Operation Overlord	

In 1942, two turning points in the war were the United States Navy

winning a major victory at the ....

in the Pacific, sinking four Japanese aircraft carriers, and D-Day,

when the Allies landed on France's Normandy beaches. This sea,

air, and land invasion was part of .... ,

the code name for the Allied invasion of Europe. The invasion force

moved east toward Germany. The Germans mounted a counter-

attack in the .... but were unable to

push the Allied forces back. Meanwhile, the United States fought

to take control of the Pacific from Japan. Through a campaign

of .... , American forces captured islands

closer to Japan.

World War II was the deadliest war in human history. Especially

horrifying was the .... , the slaughter

of Europe's Jews by the Nazis. After the truth of the Holocaust

was revealed, some Nazi leaders were charged with war crimes. At

the .... , 12 were sentenced to death.

Quick Activity Turning the Tide of War

With a partner or small group, examine the infographic about the Pacific Theater of World War II.

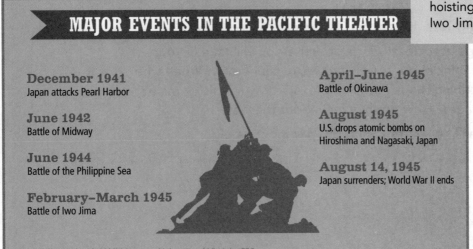

MAJOR EVENTS IN THE PACIFIC THEATER

December 1941
Japan attacks Pearl Harbor

June 1942
Battle of Midway

June 1944
Battle of the Philippine Sea

February–March 1945
Battle of Iwo Jima

April–June 1945
Battle of Okinawa

August 1945
U.S. drops atomic bombs on Hiroshima and Nagasaki, Japan

August 14, 1945
Japan surrenders; World War II ends

Sources: The National WWII Museum; University of Virginia; PBS

Discuss how each event listed impacted the course of the war. In the space below, list other important events that happened between the summer of 1941 and the war's end.

Team Challenge! As a group, select at least ten events that occurred in the war between 1941 and 1945. You may choose events from the infographic, your list, or both. Then create an illustrated timeline of World War II for the events you selected. Tape sheets of paper together to make them large enough for your timeline. Present your work to the class.

Writing Workshop Narrative Essay

As you read, think about what it was like to live through World War II. You will write a narrative from the perspective of an American soldier or an American on the home front. The prompts below will help walk you through the process.

Lesson 1 Writing Task: Introduce Characters (See Student Text, page 854)

You are in charge! Decide which perspective you will take in your narrative. Then think about the characters in your story. Write three sentences describing them. For example, are they female or male? What are their ages? How do they feel about the war?

My narrative will be written from the perspective of

Lesson 2 Writing Task: Establish Setting (See Student Text, page 864)

The setting is where and when your story takes place. It helps set the mood. It will depend partly on the perspective you chose. You may have more than one setting. Write a few sentences describing the setting.

Lesson 3 Writing Task: Organize Sequence of Events
(See Student Text, page 872)

Use the flowchart below to organize events in your story. Briefly describe six things that will happen, placing them in the order in which they will occur.

[Flowchart with six empty boxes connected by downward arrows]

Lesson 4 Writing Task: Use Narrative Techniques (See Student Text, page 885)

You are ready to begin writing! Draft the first part of your narrative. Use techniques such as dialogue, description, and similes (comparisons, like "as old as the hills").

Writing Task (See Student Text, page 887)

Using your outline and partial draft, write a narrative from the perspective of an American soldier during World War II or an American on the home front. As you write, think about ways to incorporate facts or specific historical events you learned about in this topic. Be creative! Come up with a dramatic ending for your story.

Essential Question What is America's role in the world?

Before you begin this topic, think about the Essential Question by completing the following activities.

1. List two positive aspects and two negative aspects of postwar America.

2. Preview the topic by skimming lesson titles, headings, and graphics. Then place a check mark next to the issues you think will be important during this era.

__racial discrimination   __Internet   __communism

__women's right to vote   __President Kennedy's   __Industrial Revolution

__Cold War   assassination   __conservation

                                            __boycotts

Timeline Skills

As you read, write and/or draw at least three events from the topic. Draw a line from each event to its correct position on the timeline.

1940	1950

Map Skills

Using the map in your text, label the outline map with the places listed. Then color in the states that experienced a population growth of over 100% between 1950 and 1970.

Alaska   Nevada   California   Colorado

Florida   Maryland   North Dakota   Delaware

Arizona   New York   Louisiana   Michigan

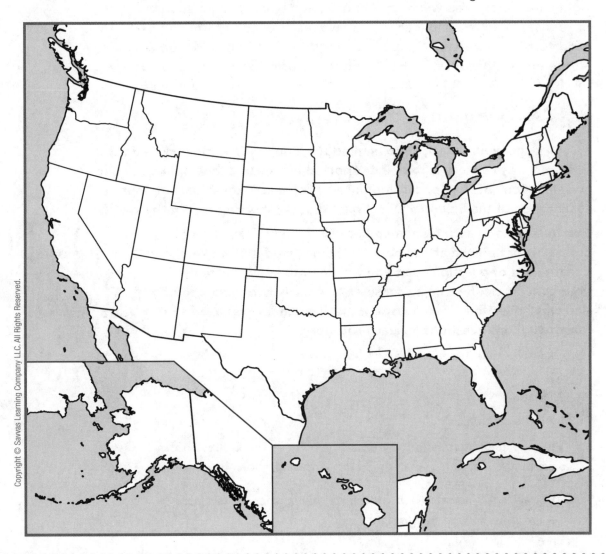

1960   1970   1980

Quest

Project-Based Learning Inquiry

Reporting the Facts

On this Quest, you are a journalist working with a team to create a civil rights newsletter. You will gather information by examining sources in your text and by conducting your own research to determine how reporters influenced public opinion about the Civil Rights Movement. At the end of the Quest, you will write an article about your findings.

1 Ask Questions (See Student Text, page 892)

As you begin your Quest, keep in mind the Guiding Question: **How do the different ways a story is told and reported influence public opinion about social movements?** Also, consider international opinion as part of your exploration of the Essential Question: **What is America's role in the world?**

For your project, each team member will collect information to create his or her own article about a theme listed in this exercise. Create a list of questions that you will need to know to create your own article. Be sure to consider "who, what, where, when, and why" questions. Two questions are filled in for you. Add at least two more questions for each category.

Theme Segregation

Sample questions:

What did photographs in the media prove about the United States concerning equal rights after the Fourteenth and Fifteenth amendments?

What evidence indicates that growing public awareness escalated legal progress toward integration?

Theme Legal Integration

Theme Civil Disobedience

Theme Leadership

Theme Nonviolence

Theme Riots

Theme My Additional Questions

INTERACTIVE

For extra help with Step 1, review the
21st Century Skills Tutorial: **Ask Questions.**

Quest CONNECTIONS

2 Investigate

As you read about the Civil Rights Movement, collect five connections from your text to help you answer the Guiding Question. Three connections are already chosen for you.

Connect to Desegregation

Lesson 4 The Legal Struggle for Equality (See Student Text, page 919)

Here's a connection! Read about Central High School in your text and look at the accompanying photograph. How did the national press cover it?

How did the Little Rock newspaper cover it?

Connect to the 1963 March on Washington

Primary Source Martin Luther King, Jr., "I Have a Dream"
(See Student Text, page 928)

How did reporters cover the 1963 March on Washington? Did they focus on the crowd's reaction, the success of the march, or King's speech?

How does the media focus affect current public opinion about the march, the speech, and the movement?

Connect to More Equal Rights Movements

Lesson 5 The Women's and Gay Rights Movements
(See Student Text, page 933)

Was the Strike for Equality Parade widely covered in newspapers and on TV? What did these sources say?

How did the coverage influence what people thought in the United States and internationally?

It's Your Turn! **Find two more connections. Fill in the title of your connections, then answer the questions. Connections may be images, primary sources, maps, or text.**

Connect to | Your Choice

Location in text

How did media coverage influence U.S. public opinion?

What effect might media coverage have had on international public opinion?

Connect to | Your Choice

Location in text

How did media coverage influence U.S. public opinion?

What effect might media coverage have had on international public opinion?

3 Conduct Research (See Student Text, page 956)

Form teams based on your teacher's instructions. Meet to decide who will create each segment. In the chart below, record team member's theme assignments and article citations. Your teacher will provide preferences for formal citation details.

You will only research the theme that you are responsible for, but you may also have layout responsibilities. The team should agree on a workflow process and a plan for enhancing the newsletter with visuals.

Team Member	Theme	Citation
	Segregation	
	Legal Integration	
	Boycotts	
	Civil Disobedience	
	Leadership	
	Nonviolence	
	Riots	

INTERACTIVE

For extra help, review the 21st Century Skills Tutorials: **Work in Teams**, **Search for Information on the Internet**, and **Avoid Plagiarism**.

Quest FINDINGS

4 Create Your Newsletter (See Student Text, page 956)

Now it's time to put together all of the information you have gathered and write your article.

1. Prepare to Write Review the research you've collected, and make sure the information you've gathered really supports the main point of your article.

The main point of your piece:

Key information to support that point:

Sources to cite:

Possible visual/visuals to support your main point:

2. **Write a Draft** The article should be about five paragraphs long. Similar to an essay, you should develop an opening paragraph, followed by three paragraphs to support the claims you make in the opening paragraph. The final paragraph should be your conclusion.

3. **Share With a Partner** Once you have finished your draft, ask one of your team members to read your draft, or listen to you read, and provide comments on the clarity and flow of the information. Revise the article based on his or her comments, and comment on his or her segment, if possible.

4. **Create a Visual** Now that you have the text for your article, find or create visuals to support your key points. This will help your viewers have something to look at while you are delivering your segment. Write captions!

5. **Put Together Your Newsletter** Once all the team members have written and revised their articles, it's time to put them together. You can do this in a couple of ways: 1) by printing, cutting, and pasting pieces into page layouts; or 2) by using a computer program and a newsletter template to create page layouts. Organize and style your text and insert the images and captions near the appropriate text. Use design elements, such as boldface and different fonts and colors, to draw attention to headlines, captions, and other points of interest. Don't forget to give your newsletter a title!

6. **Share Your Newsletter** Trade your newsletter with other groups. Read what each person has written and, using another sheet of paper, take notes on the information he or she has shared. Pay close attention to how the information is presented.

7. **Reflect** After you have read the other newsletters, discuss your thoughts on your group's newsletter and the newsletters written by others. Reflect on how each person presented the information in their story. Consider how various articles and images published during the civil rights movement may have swayed public opinion about particular events or about the movement as a whole.

Reflections

 INTERACTIVE

For extra help, review the 21st Century Skills Tutorials: **Give an Effective Presentation** and **Work in Teams.**

Lesson 1 The Beginning of the Cold War

Take Notes

Literacy Skills: Summarize Use what you have read to complete the table. List supporting details under each main idea heading, then write a summary statement based on those details. The first detail has been filled in for you.

Europe's State After World War II	Postwar Alliances	Causes of the Cold War
NATO forms to contain Soviet influence		

Summary Statement

 INTERACTIVE

For extra help, review the 21st Century Tutorial: **Summarize**.

Practice Vocabulary

Use a Word Bank Choose one word from the word bank to fill in each blank. When you have finished, you will have a short summary of important ideas from the section.

Word Bank

Cold War	iron curtain	containment
Marshall Plan	United Nations	Berlin Wall
North Atlantic Treaty Organization	Warsaw Pact	Berlin Airlift

Europe faced many problems during the ....

To stop Soviet control over West Berlin, President Truman approved the

..........................., which brought much-needed supplies to West

Berlin. This was part of his .... policy. Although the

United States helped West Germany rebuild, the ....

was built to separate West Berlin from East Germany. This was part of the

..........................., a boundary that cut off Soviet-run Eastern

Europe from the democratic governments of the West. In June 1947, the

.... was proposed to help Europe rebuild and to reduce

the threat of Communist revolutions. As part of a larger postwar effort to contain

Soviet influences, the United States joined the ....

with many Western European countries, agreeing to defend each other

against any attack. The Soviet Union formed its own military alliance,

..........................., forcing allied neighbors to follow its policies.

The ...., a new world organization was formed,

with member nations agreeing to bring disputes before the body for

peaceful settlement.

Take Notes

Literacy Skills: Use Evidence Use what you have read to complete the table.
In the Evidence column, record evidence that supports the Statement.
The first one has been completed for you.

Statement	Evidence
President Truman was opposed to Communist aggression in Korea.	• He asked the United Nations to send a military force to Korea. • The Soviet Union moved into North Korea, so the United States entered South Korea. • The United States backed a non-Communist government in South Korea.
General MacArthur undermined attempts for peace in Korea.	
Americans feared communism.	
Local crises in Africa turned into international conflicts.	

INTERACTIVE

For extra help, review the 21st Century Tutorial: **Identify Main Ideas and Details**.

Practice Vocabulary

Vocabulary Quiz Show Some quiz shows ask a question and expect the contestant to give the answer. In other shows, the contestant is given an answer and must supply the question. If the blank is in the Question column, write the question that would result in the answer in the Answer column. If the question is supplied, write the answer.

Question

1. What is the term for lying under oath?

2. What is the name of the area in Korea where no military forces were allowed?

3.

4.

5. In 1954, what did the Senate pass a resolution to do about Senator Joseph McCarthy?

Answer

1.

2.

3. the 38th parallel

4. McCarthyism

5.

Take Notes

Literacy Skills: Classify and Categorize Use what you have read to complete the table. Under each heading, record details that illustrate these three important aspects of American Society After World War II. The first one has been started for you.

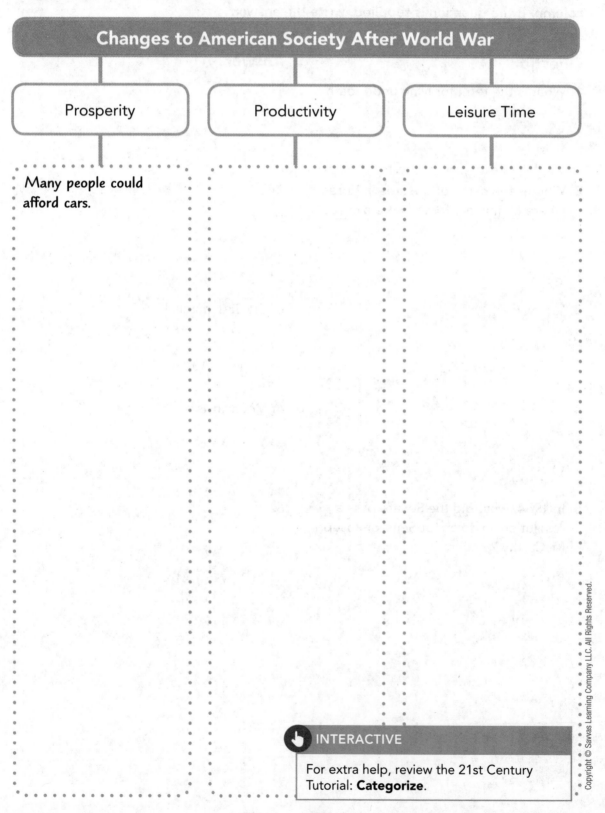

Changes to American Society After World War

Prosperity	Productivity	Leisure Time
Many people could afford cars.		

👆 INTERACTIVE

For extra help, review the 21st Century Tutorial: **Categorize**.

Practice Vocabulary

Word Map Study the word map for the phrase *Fair Deal*. Characteristics are words or phrases that relate to the word in the center of the word map. Non-characteristics are words and phrases not associated with the word. Use the blank word map to explore the meaning of the phrase *standard of living*. Then make word maps of your own for these words and phrases: *GI Bill of Rights, inflation, baby boom, productivity, suburb, Sunbelt,* and *beatnik.*

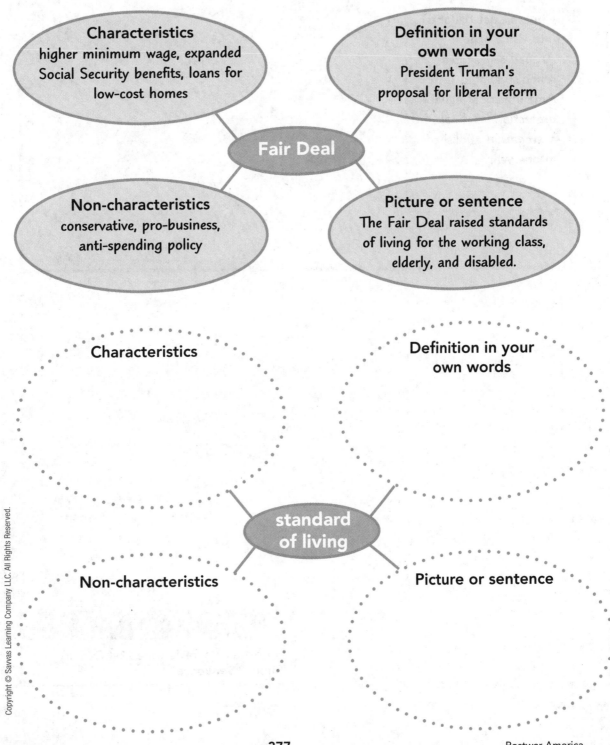

Characteristics
higher minimum wage, expanded Social Security benefits, loans for low-cost homes

Definition in your own words
President Truman's proposal for liberal reform

Fair Deal

Non-characteristics
conservative, pro-business, anti-spending policy

Picture or sentence
The Fair Deal raised standards of living for the working class, elderly, and disabled.

Characteristics

Definition in your own words

standard of living

Non-characteristics

Picture or sentence

Take Notes

Literacy Skills: Sequence Use what you have read to complete the diagram. In each space, name and describe a court case with an outcome that contributed to the defeat of segregation. Organize them in the order in which they occurred and record the year. The first one has been completed for you.

1954: *Brown v. Board of Education*

- Couldn't get daughter into white school. Argued segregated schools violated 14th Amendment's "equal protection." School segregation abolished in one year.

INTERACTIVE

For extra help, review the 21st Century Tutorial: **Sequence**.

Practice Vocabulary

True or False? Decide whether each statement below is true or false. Circle T or F, and then explain your answer. Be sure to include the underlined vocabulary word in your explanation. The first one is done for you.

1. **T / F** <u>Segregation</u> occurs when people are separated, such as according to race.
   True; Racial <u>segregation</u> has occurred in many public places, such as schools, theaters, and restaurants.

2. **T / F** <u>Affirmative action</u> programs seek to hire and promote those who have been discriminated against.

3. **T / F** During <u>civil disobedience</u>, people use violent methods to fight against unjust laws.

4. **T / F** During the <u>Civil Rights Movement</u>, African Americans strongly fought for equal treatment.

5. **T / F** During a <u>boycott</u>, people promote the use of particular goods or services.

6. **T / F** <u>Integration</u> is the mixing of racial groups.

7. **T / F** During a <u>sit-in</u>, people sit in racially segregated areas.

Quick Activity Civil Rights Movement Timeline

With a partner or small group, fill in this timeline with some important events that occurred during the Civil Rights Movement.

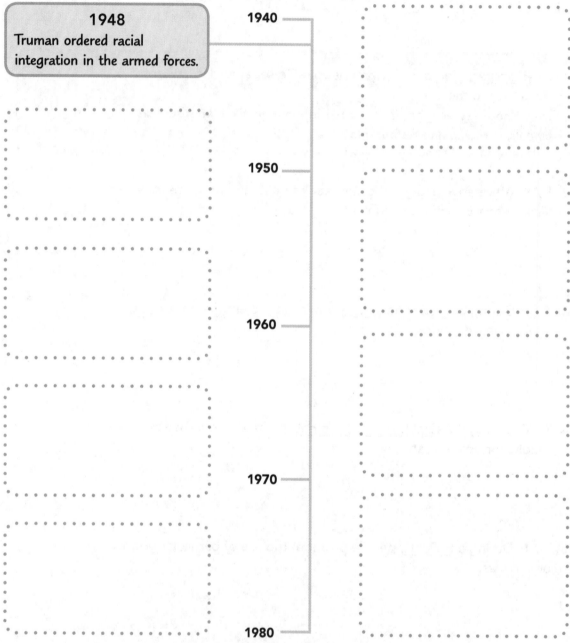

1948
Truman ordered racial integration in the armed forces.

1940

1950

1960

1970

1980

Team Challenge! Expand, illustrate, and refine your Civil Rights Movement timeline on a poster. Include important dates, people, and events. Draw pictures or print photographs from the Internet, attaching them to the correct locations on the timeline. All teams should hang their posters in their classroom. Take a gallery walk to view everyone's ideas, comparing how the selections portray the Civil Rights Movement in different ways.

Take Notes

Literacy Skills: Classify and Categorize Use what you have read to complete the table. In each cell, describe a societal issue that the movement focused on improving. The first one has been started for you.

Discrimination Leads to Action

Women's Rights Movement

- Men were not hiring qualified women for certain jobs.

Gay and Lesbian Rights Movement

INTERACTIVE

For extra help, review the 21st Century Tutorial: **Categorize**.

Practice Vocabulary

Sentence Builder Finish the sentences below with a key term from this section. You may have to change the form of the words to complete the sentences.

Word Bank

migrant worker	bilingual
Equal Pay Act	Civil Rights Act

1. In 1963, women gained the right to earn equal pay for equal work under the

2. People who can speak two languages are known as

3. People who travel from farm to farm for seasonal work are called

4. Hiring based on gender and race became illegal under the

Take Notes

Literacy Skills: Analyze Text Structure Use what you have read to complete the outline. Add details to explain the significance of President Kennedy's and President Johnson's administrations. Some entries are completed for you.

I. Kennedy and National Public Opinion

    A. Victory aided by first televised presidential debates

    B. Nation inspired by his youth, idealism, and call for service

II. Kennedy, Communism, and Cuba

    A. Supported Cuban exiles' Bay of Pigs Invasion to oppose Soviet communism in the Americas

    B.

III.

    A.

    B.

    C.

IV. Johnson's Great Society

    A. Kennedy assassination landed him in power

    B.

    C.

V.

    A. Vietcong becoming Communist seen as a threat in context of domino theory

    B. Gulf of Tonkin Resolution allowed Johnson to bomb and send troops

    C.

VI.

    A.

    B.

INTERACTIVE

For extra help, review the 21st Century Tutorial: **Identify Main Ideas and Details**.

Practice Vocabulary

Use a Word Bank Choose one word from the word bank to fill in each blank. When you have finished, you will have a short summary of important ideas from the section.

Word Bank

counterculture movement	Great Society	domino theory
Peace Corps	Tet Offensive	Bay of Pigs invasion
superpowers	Gulf of Tonkin Resolution	Cuban missile crisis
Organization of American States		

Rivalry between _____, nations with worldwide influence, led to clashes.

To combat communism, Kennedy approved the _____ of Cuba. This led

to the _____ when the Soviet Union gave Cuba more weapons. Kennedy

set up the _____ so American volunteers could serve in developing

countries. The United States became a leader of the _____, promoting

economic progress in the Americas. President Johnson created the _____,

declaring war on U.S. poverty. The _____ led the U.S. to believe that

if South Vietnam became Communist, other regional countries would follow. North

Vietnam attacked an American ship, so Congress passed the _____,

allowing bombing of North Vietnam. The Vietcong launched the _____,

attacking an American embassy. Many Americans protested the war as part of a

larger _____.

Quick Activity You're the Newscaster!

With a partner or small group, assign a moderator to conduct your group discussion and ask questions. Discuss what you learned about the Vietnam War and the protests throughout the United States. What do you think are the most striking or interesting details about the war and the protests that resulted? Do you believe the actions of President Johnson were correct? Do you think the protesters should have behaved as they did? Was the draft fair or unfair?

Discussion Notes

Team Challenge! Create a mock newscast about the Vietnam War. Include information about the progress of the war and the protests at home. Conduct research on the Internet if you need more information. Write scripts to mimic the style of news reports that you have watched on television and the Internet. Have each person in the group read one of the scripts in front of the class. Compare the details used in the scripts to see how different groups handled the topics.

Take Notes

Literacy Skills: Determine Central Ideas Use what you have read to complete the concept map. Fill in details that help explain the central idea. The first one has been completed for you.

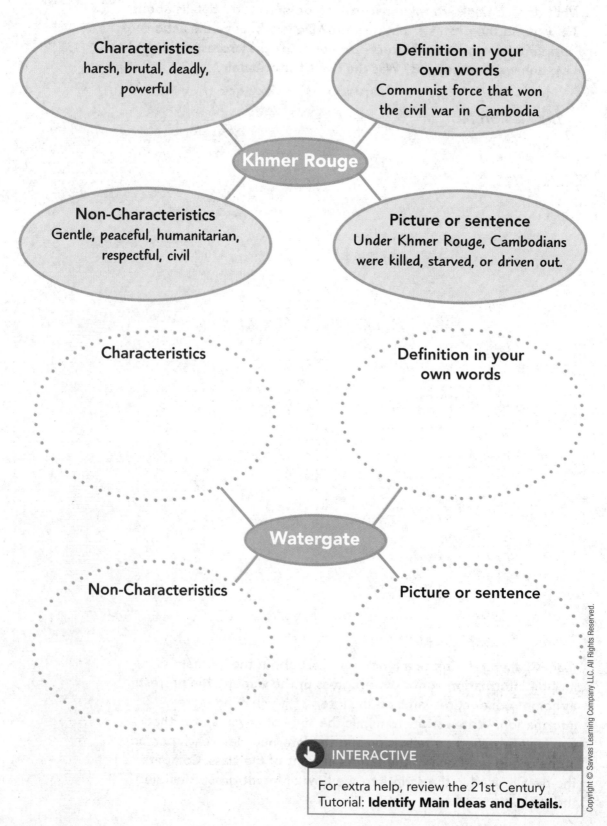

Characteristics
harsh, brutal, deadly, powerful

Definition in your own words
Communist force that won the civil war in Cambodia

Khmer Rouge

Non-Characteristics
Gentle, peaceful, humanitarian, respectful, civil

Picture or sentence
Under Khmer Rouge, Cambodians were killed, starved, or driven out.

Characteristics

Definition in your own words

Watergate

Non-Characteristics

Picture or sentence

👍 INTERACTIVE

For extra help, review the 21st Century Tutorial: **Identify Main Ideas and Details.**

Practice Vocabulary

Matching Logic Using your knowledge of the underlined vocabulary words, draw a line from each sentence in Column 1 to match it with the sentence in Column 2 to which it logically belongs.

Column 1	Column 2
1. Nixon said he wanted to help the <u>silent majority</u>.	By establishing more trade and other contacts between the superpowers, Cold War tensions eased.
2. The United States economy suffered from <u>stagflation</u> during the Nixon administration.	The burglars aimed to spy on Democrats by taking secret documents and wiretapping.
3. Nixon engaged in a <u>détente</u> policy with the Soviet Union.	To halt inflation and stimulate economic growth, Nixon froze wages and prices and increased federal spending.
4. The initial <u>SALT Agreement</u> was signed in 1972.	They escaped Vietnam, but often died before reaching safety.
5. The <u>Watergate</u> scandal shocked American voters.	True to his campaign promise, he began a "law-and-order" program.
6. The Cambodian civil war was won by the <u>Khmer Rouge</u>.	The number of nuclear warheads and missiles that the superpowers can possess is limited.
7. Eventually, many <u>boat people</u> from Vietnam and Cambodia were allowed to settle in the United States.	They imposed a brutal reign of terror on their own people.

Writing Workshop Informative Essay

As you read, build a response to this question: **How did the United States change after World War II?** The prompts below will help walk you through the process.

Lesson 1 Writing Task: Consider Your Purpose and Audience
(See Student Text, page 898)

Who are your readers? What do you want your readers to gain from your essay?

Lesson 2 Writing Task: Develop a Clear Thesis (See Student Text, page 906)

Express in one sentence which American postwar changes are most significant to you. This will be your thesis statement for the informative essay you will write at the end of the topic.

Lesson 3 Writing Task: Support Thesis with Details (See Student Text, page 913)

Begin to gather details that support your thesis. How can these details inform your readers and convey information? Only include details that support your thesis, and explain how or why they serve this purpose.

Lesson 4 Writing Task: Organize Your Essay (See Student Text, page 927)

Create an outline for your essay. Start with an introductory paragraph, followed by three body paragraphs that explain the most significant ways that the United States changed during the postwar years. End with a concluding paragraph.

Lesson 5 Writing Task: Write an Introduction (See Student Text, page 935)

Write an introduction to your informative essay.

Lesson 6 Writing Task: Draft Your Essay (See Student Text, page 947)

Use your outline to draft your essay. Be sure to use your thesis in your introduction paragraph and revisit it in your conclusion paragraph. With your conclusion, aim to inspire your reader. Consider how you can use formatting and graphics to develop your ideas more fully. For example, you might use old photographs of entertainers, activists, or political leaders.

Writing Task (See Student Text, page 957)

Using your draft and any feedback you may have gathered, refine your essay answering the following question in a five-paragraph explanatory essay: How did the United States change after World War II? To link ideas, use transition words such as *in addition, also, for example, specifically, consequently, therefore,* and *as a result.* Correct any spelling or grammar errors.

16 A Global Superpower Facing Change Preview

Essential Question **How should we handle conflict?**

Before you begin this topic, think about the Essential Question by completing the following activities.

1. List four ways of dealing with conflict. Circle the method that you feel is most effective, and draw a line through the method you feel is least effective.

2. Preview the topic by skimming lesson titles, headings, and graphics. Then, place a check mark next to the factors that you predict will increase conflict for the United States from 1975–2000.

__Iranian Revolution   __national budget   __NAFTA

__Mikhail Gorbachev   __disarmament   __apartheid

__fall of the Berlin Wall   __Bosnian civil war   __Moral Majority

Timeline Skills

As you read, write and/or draw at least three events from the topic. Draw a line from each event to its correct position on the timeline.

1970	1980

Map Skills

Using the map in your text, label the outline map with the places listed. Then, shade in the U.S.S.R. and any areas of water. Create a key that describes the shading.

Armenia	Azerbaijan	Belarus	Estonia
Georgia	Kazakhstan	Kyrgyzstan	Latvia
Lithuania	Moldova	Tajikistan	Turkmenistan
Ukraine	U.S.S.R.	Uzbekistan	

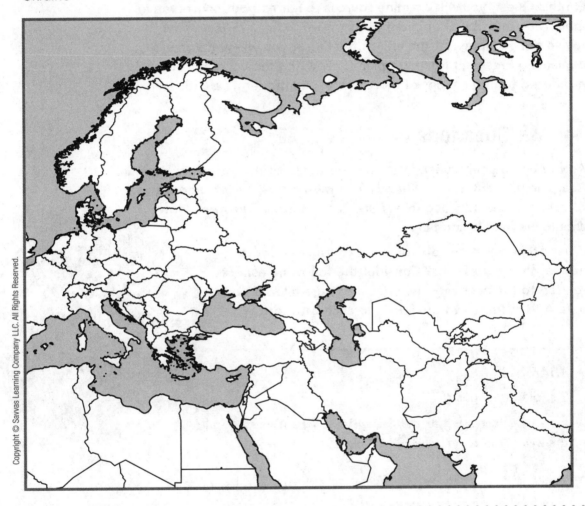

1990   2000

Quest

Analyzing the Reagan Conservative Movement

On this Quest, you will examine sources to learn about conservative, moderate, and liberal opinions put forward in the 1980s on how to revive the economy. At the end of the Quest you will write an essay explaining President Reagan's plan for reviving the economy and how it differed from the plans of more liberal and moderate politicians.

① Ask Questions (See Student Text, page 962)

As you begin your Quest, keep in mind the Guiding Question: **How did Reaganomics differ from liberals' and moderates' beliefs about how to achieve a healthy economy?** and the Essential Question: **How should we handle conflict?**

What other questions do you need to ask in order to answer these questions? Consider the following aspects related to the economy. Two questions are filled in for you. Add at least two questions to each category.

Theme Taxes

Sample questions:

How does increasing or decreasing taxes for businesses and the wealthy impact the whole country?

When is it necessary for the federal government to raise taxes?

Theme National Budget

Theme Roles of Federal and State Governments

Theme Government-Funded Social Programs

Theme My Additional Questions

👆 INTERACTIVE

For extra help with Step 1, review the
21st Century Tutorial: **Ask Questions**.

2 Investigate

As you read about the Conservative Revolution, collect five connections from your text to help you answer the Guiding Question. Three connections are already chosen for you.

Connect to the Presidency of Jimmy Carter

Lesson 1 President Carter's Administration (See Student Text, page 965)

Here's a connection! What was the key problem with the economy during Carter's administration, and how did he try to fix the problem?

Were President Carter's attempts successful? Why or why not?

Connect to the Conservative Movement

Lesson 1 Graphic Organizer The Conservative Movement

(See Student Text, page 967)

Here's another connection! What does this graphic organizer tell you about the goals of conservatives in the 1980s?

Which of the goals relate to improving the economy?

Connect to the Presidency of George H. W. Bush

Lesson 1 The Reagan and Bush Presidencies (See Student Text, page 969)

Here's another connection! Read the section Bush's Economic Troubles. How did economic policies pursued by President Bush contribute to a worsening of the economy?

What does this connection tell you about the difference between economic goals and realities?

It's Your Turn! Find two more connections. Fill in the title of your connections, then answer the questions. Connections may be images, primary sources, maps, or text.

Your Choice | Connect to

Location in text

What is the main idea of this connection?

What does it tell you about Reaganomics and/or more moderate and liberal ideas about the economy?

Your Choice | Connect to

Location in text

What is the main idea of this connection?

What does it tell you about Reaganomics and/or more moderate and liberal ideas about the economy?

3 Examine Primary Sources (See Student Text, page 994)

Examine the primary sources provided online or by your teacher. Fill in the chart to show how these sources provide further information on Reaganomics and how it differed from moderate and liberal plans for the economy. The first one is completed for you.

Source	Ideas About the Economy
Debate Between Republican Presidential Candidates George H. W. Bush and Ronald Reagan	Bush: Reagan's plan of major tax cuts would not work to increase revenues and halt inflation. Smaller supply-side tax cuts, a balanced budget, and reduced government spending were needed to fix the economy. Reagan: Large, across-the-board tax cuts and incentive taxes to stimulate productivity would increase federal revenues and enable the government to balance the budget while still increasing defense spending.
State of the Union Address	
Address to the Nation on the Economy	
Remarks on Signing the Economic Recovery Tax Act of 1981	
Mondale's Acceptance Speech	

INTERACTIVE

For extra help with Step 3, review the 21st Century Tutorial: **Analyze Primary and Secondary Sources**.

④ Write Your Essay (See Student Text, page 994)

Now it's time to put together all of the information you have gathered and use it to write your essay.

1. **Prepare to Write** You have collected connections and explored primary sources that show the differences between Reaganomics and more moderate and liberal ideas about the economy. Look through your notes and decide which differences you want to highlight in your essay. Record them here.

Differences

2. Write a Draft Using evidence from the connections you found and the documents you explored, write a draft of your essay. Introduce the subject of your essay with a thesis statement. Then, be sure to support your thesis using evidence from the documents you've studied in this Quest.

3. Share with a Partner Exchange your draft with a partner. Tell your partner what you like about his or her draft and suggest any improvements.

4. Finalize Your Essay Revise your essay. Correct any grammatical or spelling errors. Finally, write a final copy of your essay.

5. Reflect on the Quest Think about your experience completing this topic's Quest. What did you learn about Reaganomics and the American economy? What questions do you still have about the impact of economic policies of the 1980s and 1990s? How will you answer them?

Reflections

👆 **INTERACTIVE**

For extra help with Step 4, review the 21st Century Tutorial: **Write an Essay**.

Take Notes

Literacy Skills: Classify and Categorize Use what you have read to complete the chart. In each space write key details about the Presidents and their administrations. The first one has been completed for you.

Presidents of the Late 20th Century	
Jimmy Carter	• Democrat, elected 1976 • Washington outsider and strong defender of human rights • Unable to fix high inflation and poor economy • Supported the Shah during the Iranian Revolution of 1979, which resulted in the Iran Hostage Crisis • Iranian Revolution and Hostage Crisis led to disruption of U.S. oil supply and energy crisis
Ronald Reagan	
George H. W. Bush	
Bill Clinton	

INTERACTIVE

For extra help, review the 21st Century Tutorial: **Categorize**.

Practice Vocabulary

Vocabulary Quiz Show Some quiz shows ask a question and expect the contestant to give the answer. In other shows, the contestant is given an answer and must supply the question. If the blank is in the Question column, write the question that would result in the answer in the Answer column. If the question is supplied, write the answer.

Question

1. What agreement opened the markets of Canada, the United States, and Mexico to trade and investment across borders?

2.

3.

4. What group founded by Jerry Falwell supported political candidates who favored conservative religious goals?

5.

6. What was the economic program enacted by President Reagan that called for lowering taxes, decreasing the size of the federal government, and deregulating businesses?

7.

Answer

1.

2. balanced budget

3. downsizing

4.

5. "Contract With America"

6.

7. deregulation

Take Notes

Literacy Skills: Sequence Use what you have read to complete the chart. In each space, write one event that led up to and/or contributed to the breakup of the Soviet Union and the end of the Cold War. The first one has been completed for you.

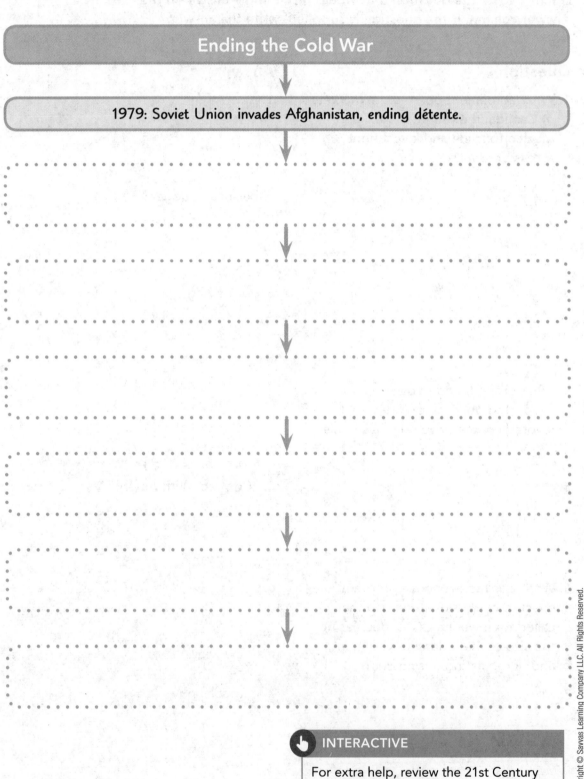

Ending the Cold War

1979: Soviet Union invades Afghanistan, ending détente.

INTERACTIVE

For extra help, review the 21st Century Tutorial: **Sequence**.

Practice Vocabulary

Words in Context For each question below, write an answer that shows your understanding of the boldfaced key term.

1. Why did the United States oppose the Polish government's use of **martial law**?

2. Why did President Reagan and Mikhail Gorbachev hold a series of **summit meetings**?

3. What was the purpose of the **Star Wars** program?

4. What was the significance of the Polish group **Solidarity**?

5. Why did Mikhail Gorbachev promote *glasnost*?

Quick Activity Who Am I?

With a partner or small group, examine the quotes below. Which single historical figure would most likely have made all of these statements?

- "The United States must be able to defend itself in the event of a missile strike by the Soviet Union."

- "The Soviet Union is the ultimate evil in today's world, and we must oppose it in every way possible."

- "I believe in trusting people, but if they have nothing to hide then they shouldn't mind if I double check on them!"

- "Martial law violates basic human rights."

- "If the Soviet Union adopts a policy of openness, then I may be more willing to negotiate with its leaders."

Who Am I?

Team Challenge! Pick another individual from this lesson. Using what you learned from the text, come up with four or five "quotes" that would help others identify the individual you picked. Create your own "Who Am I?" puzzle and exchange puzzles with another group. Solve the other group's puzzle.

Take Notes

Literacy Skills: Summarize Use what you have read to complete the table. In each space write details about the United States' interventions in foreign countries. The first one has been completed for you.

Diplomacy and Mediation	Economic Involvement	Use of Military Force
• Bush and Clinton pursued open communication with China instead of firmly standing against Chinese communism. • United States supported Russia's transition to a free market economy under Boris Yeltsin. • United States hosted peace talks in Dayton, Ohio, for the Bosnian Civil War. • Senator George Mitchell was sent to aid in Northern Ireland peace talks between Catholics and Protestants. • Carter hosted peace talks between the Egyptian president and the Israeli prime minister that led to the Camp David Accords of 1978 and a peace treaty in 1979. • United States hosted and mediated peace talks between Israel and the PLO in 1993.		

👆 INTERACTIVE

For extra help, review the 21st Century Tutorial: **Summarize**.

Practice Vocabulary

Sentence Revision Revise each sentence so that the underlined vocabulary word is used logically. Be sure not to change the vocabulary word. The first one is done for you.

---

1. The United States used economic sanctions against Cuba to end that country's strict policy of <u>apartheid</u>.

   The United States used economic sanctions against South Africa to end that country's strict policy of <u>apartheid</u>.

---

2. In the <u>Camp David Accords</u>, Palestinian Arabs agreed to recognize Israel and Israel agreed to limited Palestinian self-rule.

3. During the Bosnian civil war in the 1990s, the United States acted as a <u>mediator</u> by sending troops to enforce peace agreements.

4. To retaliate against the United States for supporting Israel in the 1973 war, <u>OPEC</u> enacted a complete trade embargo between the United States and the nations of the Middle East.

5. The <u>Strategic Arms Reduction Treaty</u> of 1991 was a treaty signed by the United States, Israel, India, and Pakistan designed to reduce stockpiles of nuclear weapons.

6. One stated goal of the <u>PLO</u>, or Palestinian Liberation Organization, was to strengthen Israel.

7. President Clinton called for economic <u>sanctions</u> supporting India and Pakistan to show his approval of their advancements in weapons technology.

Quick Activity Building a Timeline

With a partner or small group, examine this photo from the Bosnian civil war of the 1990s. Discuss the possible impact of photos like this on U.S. involvement in regional conflicts.

Select at least four regional conflicts mentioned in this lesson that took place following the end of the Cold War. Find an appropriate image from the text, or from your own research, to represent each conflict. Use the graphic organizer below to organize your notes about the conflicts and the images you selected.

Regional Conflict: Date and Location	Image Notes

Team Challenge! Using your notes and the images you found, create a timeline of post–Cold War regional conflicts. Your timeline can be either physical (e.g., drawing, collage, poster) or digital (e.g., digital drawing, web page, slide show). Use a combination of images and text. Present your timeline to the class. Be ready to explain why your group chose a specific image to represent a particular conflict.

Writing Workshop Explanatory Essay

As you read, pay special attention to information about **the Cold War and the collapse of the Soviet Union**. The prompts below will help walk you through the process of writing an explanatory essay.

Lesson 1 Writing Task: Develop a Clear Thesis (See Student Text, page 972)

After reading Lesson 1 and conducting preliminary research, identify the thesis, or central message, of your explanatory essay about the Cold War and collapse of the Soviet Union. Write your thesis in one or two sentences below.

Lesson 2 Writing Task: Support Thesis with Details (See Student Text, page 979)

Perform further research, using reliable sources, to find details that support your thesis. As you research, use the graphic organizer below to track your sources and the supporting details they contain. Remember, your textbook counts as a reliable source!

Source	Details from this source that support my thesis

Lesson 3 Writing Task: Write an Introduction and Conclusion
(See Student Text, page 991)

In your opening paragraph, introduce the subject you are writing about and include the thesis, or central message, of your essay. Draft your introduction in the space below.

In the closing paragraph of your essay, restate your thesis and explain how the details you provided in your body paragraphs support that thesis. Draft your conclusion in the space below.

Writing Task (See Student Text, page 995)

Using the notes you took and the paragraphs you drafted, write a five-paragraph explanatory essay on the Cold War and the collapse of the Soviet Union.

17 Meeting New Challenges Preview

Essential Question What can individuals do to affect society?

Before you begin this topic, think about the Essential Question by completing the following activities.

1. List five ways you have affected society. Your list can include both minor, everyday actions and more significant contributions. Then write two things you would like to do in the future to affect society.

Timeline Skills

As you read, write and/or draw at least three events from the topic. Draw a line from each event to its correct position on the timeline.

| 1990 | 2000 |

Map Skills

Using the map in your text, color each country based on its trade per capita. Create a key for your map.

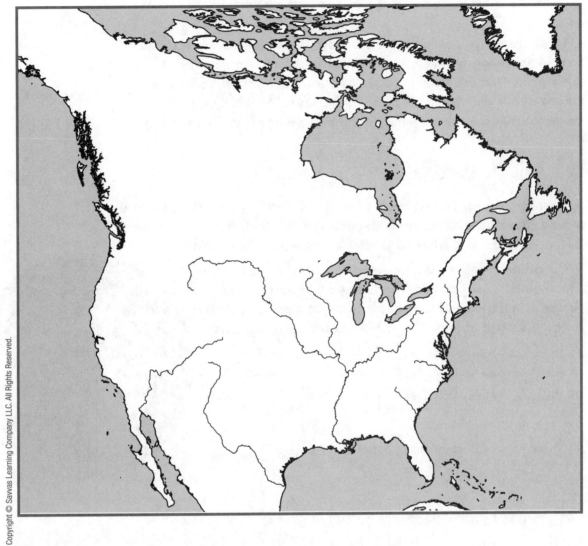

2010   2020

Quest

Document-Based Writing Inquiry

Look Into the Future

On this Quest, you will explore the ways technological innovations and social changes have created challenges and opportunities for Americans. You will examine sources about how this will affect the future of our country. At the end of the Quest you will write an explanatory essay about what young people envision for the future.

1 Ask Questions (See Student Text, page 1000)

As you begin your Quest, keep in mind the Guiding Question: **What do young Americans envision for themselves and their future?** and the Essential Question: **What can individuals do to affect society?**

What other questions do you need to ask in order to answer these questions? Consider the following aspects of the future in America and the world. Two questions are filled in for you. Add at least two questions for each category.

Theme Volunteering

Sample questions:

What types of volunteering opportunities exist?

How does volunteering benefit society?

Theme War and Peace

Theme Technology

Theme Diversity

Theme My Additional Questions

 INTERACTIVE

For extra help with Step 1, review the
21st Century Tutorial: **Ask Questions**.

Quest CONNECTIONS

2 Investigate

As you read about the United States' future, collect five connections from your text to help you answer the Guiding Question. Three connections are already chosen for you.

Connect to War and Peace

Lesson 1 What Has Been Done to Stop the Spread of Nuclear Weapons? (See Student Text, page 1008)

Here's a connection! Look at this section in your text. How have deals to limit the spread of nuclear weapons made the world a safer place?

How does a safer world make our futures brighter?

Connect to Technology

Lesson 3 What Are Some Advances in Biology and Medicine?
(See Student Text, page 1028)

Here's another connection! What do the advances in biotechnology mean for people's health?

What advantages does a well-nourished, healthy person have?

Connect to Opportunities

Lesson 4 America's Promise (See Student Text, page 1040)

What does this connection tell you about the impact of new opportunities for minorities and women?

Have new opportunities for women and minority groups benefited everybody?

Your Choice | Connect to

Location in text

What is the main idea of this connection?

What does it tell you about the future in America and the world?

Your Choice | Connect to

Location in text

What is the main idea of this connection?

What does it tell you about the future in America and the world?

③ Examine Primary Sources (See Student Text, page 1044)

Examine the primary and secondary sources provided online or from your teacher. Fill in the chart to show how these sources provide further information about the future in America and the world. The first one has been started for you.

Source	In the future, people in America and the world will . . .
"We Are the Next Generation"	need to take responsibility and care for the environment.
"Young Adults: Can You Picture Your Retirement?"	
"A Brief History of Forever"	
"Learning to Fail"	

INTERACTIVE

For extra help with Step 3, review the 21st Century Tutorial: **Analyze Primary and Secondary Sources**.

4 Write Your Essay (See Student Text, page 1044)

Now it's time to put together all of the information you have gathered and use it to write your essay.

1. **Prepare to Write** You have collected connections and explored primary and secondary sources about future challenges and opportunities. Look through your notes and decide which facts you would like to include in your essay. Record them here.

Facts

2. Write a Draft Using evidence from the information in the textbook and the primary and secondary sources you explored, write a draft of your essay. Be sure to write both about the opportunities and challenges that the United States and Americans will face. Include details from the evidence in the material you've studied in this Quest.

3. Share with a Partner Exchange your draft with a partner. Tell your partner what you like about his or her draft and suggest any improvements.

4. Finalize Your Essay Revise your essay. Correct any grammatical or spelling errors.

5. Reflect on the Quest Think about your experience completing this topic's Quest. What did you learn about the United States, Americans, their challenges, and their opportunities? What questions do you still have about the future? How will you answer them?

Reflections

 INTERACTIVE

For extra help with Step 4, review the 21st Century Tutorial: **Write an Essay**.

Take Notes

Literacy Skills: Use Evidence Use what you have read to complete
the graphic organizers. In the outer circles, enter evidence that helps
support the idea in the center. The first one has been started for you.

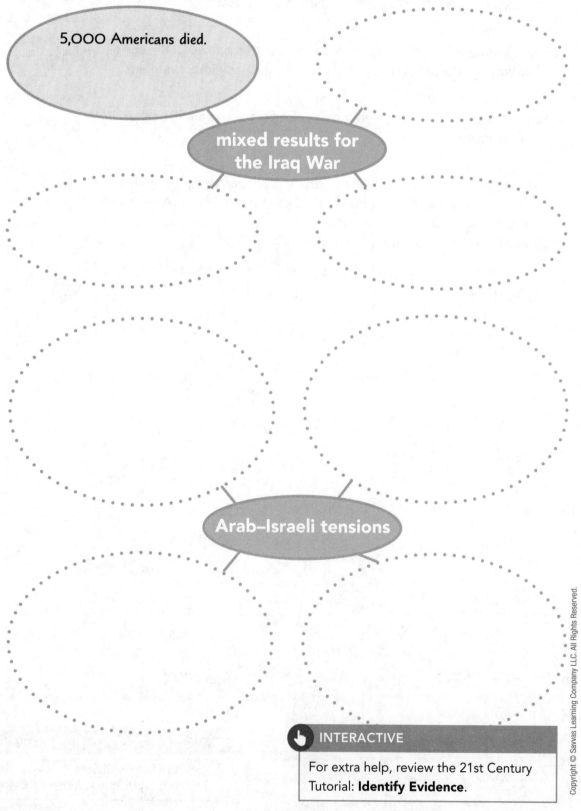

5,000 Americans died.

mixed results for
the Iraq War

Arab–Israeli tensions

👆 **INTERACTIVE**

For extra help, review the 21st Century
Tutorial: **Identify Evidence**.

Practice Vocabulary

Use a Word Bank Choose one word from the word bank to fill in each blank. When you have finished, you will have a short summary of important ideas from the section.

Word Bank

jihadism	Arab Spring	Islamic fundamentalist
Nuclear Non-Proliferation Treaty	North Atlantic Treaty Organization	weapons of mass destruction
terrorism	insurgency	

.... is a movement that supports

violence in the struggle against those seen as enemies of Islam.

The .... who support this movement

believe Islamic religious texts should be taken literally. One

group in this movement, Al Qaeda, has pursued a strategy of

.... The United States attacked Iraq in 2003

because U.S. officials said it had .... In the

years following the invasion of Iraq, ... rose

against American soldiers and the Iraqi government.

To stop the spread of nuclear weapons, most countries signed the

.... by the early 2000s. In early 2010,

protestors in Tunisia and other Arab countries marched for democracy

in the .... The United States, as a member

of the .... , has supported the addition of

Eastern European countries to the alliance.

Take Notes

Literacy Skills: Sequence Use what you have read to complete the graphic organizers. Enter events in the sequence they occurred. The first one has been partially completed for you.

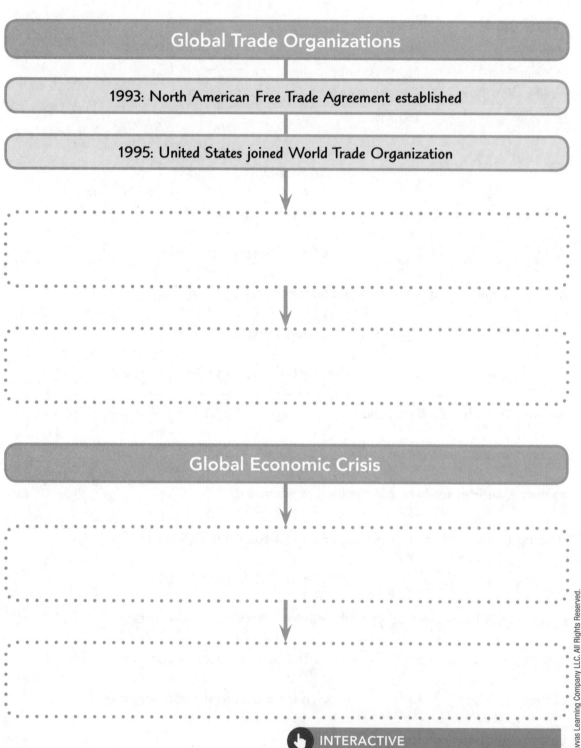

Global Trade Organizations

1993: North American Free Trade Agreement established

1995: United States joined World Trade Organization

Global Economic Crisis

 INTERACTIVE

For extra help, review the 21st Century Tutorial: **Sequence**.

Practice Vocabulary

True or False? Decide whether each statement below is true or false. Circle T or F, then explain your answer. Be sure to include the underlined vocabulary word in your explanation. The first one is done for you.

1. **T / F** <u>Globalization</u> has created a strong global economy without causing problems for anybody.
   False; Although some people and businesses have benefited from <u>globalization</u>, it has also caused problems for workers whose jobs have moved overseas.

2. **T / F** President Obama signed the <u>American Recovery and Reinvestment Act</u> into law to stimulate the economy and reduce unemployment.

3. **T / F** Republicans in Congress would not raise the <u>debt ceiling</u> unless President Obama agreed to reduce the federal government's spending.

4. **T / F** <u>Subprime mortgages</u> were offered to people whom banks considered to be a safe bet.

5. **T / F** High demand for dot-com stocks created a stock market <u>bubble</u> in the 1990s.

6. **T / F** People were not concerned about <u>default</u> during the debt ceiling crises in 2011 and 2013.

7. **T / F** Low interest rates made <u>mortgages</u> less affordable, which eventually led to falling home prices.

Quick Activity Create an Illustrated Timeline

Many people have been affected by economic development and changes in the economy since the 1990s. Create an illustrated timeline, drawing images that show different ways the economy has changed since the 1990s.

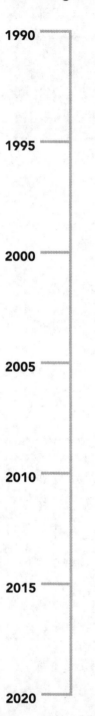

1990

1995

2000

2005

2010

2015

2020

Team Challenge! After you've completed your timeline, post it on your classroom wall. After looking at your classmates' timelines, take part in a classroom discussion about the changes in the economy and how you think these have affected Americans.

Take Notes

Literacy Skills: Analyze Text Structure Use what you have read to complete the outlines. Fill in each outline to summarize the main ideas of the lesson. The first one has been partially completed for you.

I. Responding to Environmental Challenges
    A. What Is the Environmental Movement?
        1. Movement begins with publication of *Silent Spring*.
        2. Use of DDT is restricted.

        3.

        4.

    B. The Issue of Climate Change
        1. Climate change is measurable long-term change in climate.
        2. Temperature rises 1.4 degrees in 1900s.

        3.

        4.

        5.

    C. Progress on Cleaner Energy
        1. Government encourages use of renewable energy.
        2. Nuclear power, solar, wind, and biofuels are renewable sources.
II. Advances in Biology and Medicine
    A. The Biotech Revolution

        1.

        2.

        3.

        4.

    B. Fighting Disease

        1.

        2.

        3.

INTERACTIVE

For extra help, review the 21st Century Tutorial: **Summarize**.

Practice Vocabulary

Use a Word Bank Choose one word from the word bank to fill in each blank. When you have finished, you will have a short summary of important ideas from the section.

Word Bank

Environmental Protection Agency	AIDS	pollution
droughts	biotechnology	emissions
fossil fuels	smart phones	climate change
Internet		

In the early 2000s, ... provided most of

the energy used to create economic growth. They include coal, oil,

and natural gas, which cause .... when

burned. Greenhouse gas .... have helped

cause .... Scientists are concerned that

this has led to more frequent .... The

.... has encouraged energy conservation and

the development of cleaner energy.

Researchers have used .... to make drugs

to treat diseases. Globalization has increased the reach of infectious

diseases, including ...., which is caused

by HIV.

The .... links computers worldwide. People

use computers and .... to access the

information found on this network.

Quick Activity Forecasting the Future

There have been impressive advances in science and technology over the past 30 years. The next 30 will surely have many more. Brainstorm three possible advances in science and technology you imagine will happen in the future.

Team Challenge! After you've brainstormed your ideas, form small groups with your classmates and discuss them. Work together to gather the best ideas and give a short presentation to the class.

Take Notes

Literacy Skills: Summarize Use what you have read to complete the
graphic organizers. The first one has been started for you.

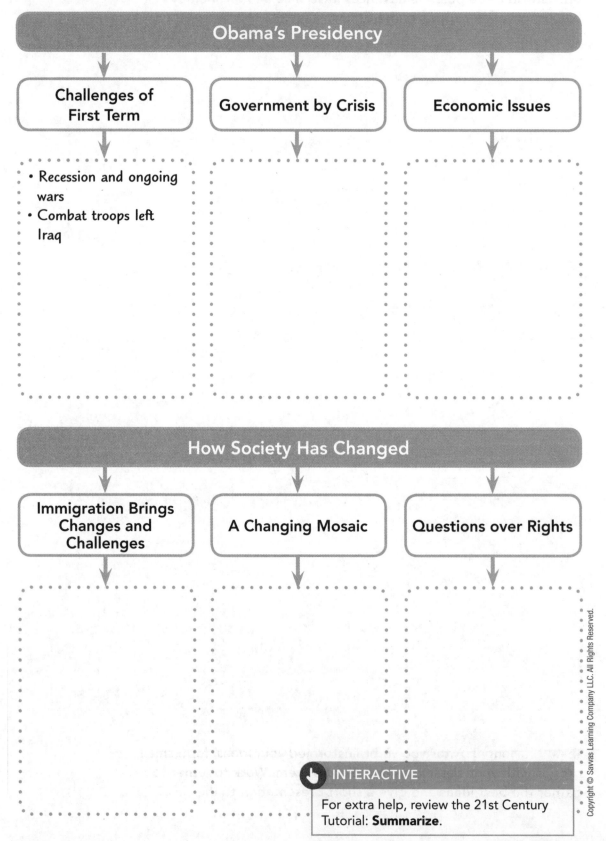

Obama's Presidency

Challenges of First Term

- Recession and ongoing wars
- Combat troops left Iraq

Government by Crisis

Economic Issues

How Society Has Changed

Immigration Brings Changes and Challenges

A Changing Mosaic

Questions over Rights

👆 INTERACTIVE

For extra help, review the 21st Century
Tutorial: **Summarize**.

Practice Vocabulary

Sentence Builder Finish the sentences below with a key term from this section. You may have to change the form of the words to complete the sentences.

Word Bank

affirmative action   temperament   Affordable Care Act

deficit   populist

1. All Americans must have private health insurance under the

2. The usual attitude, mood, or behavior of a person is his or her

3. The amount of spending that is greater than income is called the

4. A person who claims to represent the common people is called a

5. The preference for hiring members of groups that have faced discrimination is called

Writing Workshop Research Paper

Choose a significant invention or societal change that you learned about in this topic and write a research paper that answers this question: **What impact has a significant invention or change had on society?** The prompts below will help walk you through the process.

Lesson 1 Writing Task: Generate Questions to Focus Research
(See Student Text, page 1012)

Write three to four questions about societal changes in the United States following the attacks of September 11, 2001. Start with this one: How did the American people respond to the new threat of terrorism? Use the rest of your questions to help you focus your research on the topic of technological innovations and societal changes. Circle the question that pinpoints your research choice. This will be the main point of your thesis statement.

Lessons 2 Writing Task: Support Ideas with Evidence
(See Student Text, page 1022)

On a separate piece of paper, outline your research essay by identifying the main ideas. Under each main idea, list two key facts or other evidence that supports that idea. As you work, keep track of the sources you reviewed and page numbers with important details so you can find the information again.

Lesson 3 Writing Task: Cite Sources (See Student Text, page 1032)

Review the sources that you noted. Write citations for all the sources from which you decide to use evidence, following the citation format that your teacher provides. You may be required to include the name of the article or text, the author, the publisher, the date of publication, and, for Internet resources, the URL.

Source	Citation

Lesson 4 Writing Task: Develop a Clear Thesis (See Student Text, page 1042)

Using the information you've collected, form a clear thesis that will be the basis for your research paper.

Writing Task (See Student Text, page 1045)

When you are ready to write your essay, use a word processing program. When you are finished revising, use technology to publish your essay by sharing it as directed by your teacher.

Acknowledgments

Photography

COVER:

CVR Shaunl/E+/Getty Images

002 Mireille Vautier/Art Resource, NY; **004** Bjorn Landstrom/ National Geographic/Getty Images; **005** Art Directors & TRIP/ Alamy Stock Photo; **006** Mansa Kankan Musa I, 14th century king of the Mali empire (gouache on paper), McBride, Angus (1931–2007)/Private Collection/Look and Learn/Bridgeman Art Library; **007** Mikael Utterström/Alamy Stock Photo; **009** Greg Balfour Evans/Alamy Stock Photo; **010** Colport/Alamy Stock Photo; **011** PhotoStock-Israel/Alamy Stock; **024** North Wind Picture Archives/Alamy Stock Photo; **026** North Wind Picture Archives/Alamy Stock Photo; **028** Anonymous Person/ AKG Images; **029** Courthouse, Philadelphia (oil on canvas), Smith, Russell William Thompson (1812–98)/Philadelphia History Museum at the Atwater Kent/Courtesy of Historical Society of Pennsylvania Collection/Bridgeman Art Library; **031** Marka/UIG/Getty Images; **033** Niday Picture Library/ Alamy Stock Photo; **056** Archive Images/Alamy Stock Photo; **057** Digital Image Library/Alamy Stock Photo; **060** Vlad G/ Shutterstock; **066** Archive Images/Alamy Stock Photo; **076** World History Archive/Alamy Stock Photo; **079** Culture Club/Getty Images; **080** Albert Knapp/Alamy Stock Photo; **081** Orhan Cam/Shutterstock; **083** Ken Cedeno/Corbis/Getty Images; **090** Hulton Archive/MPI/Getty Images; **099** Cartoonist Group; **104** North Wind Picture Archives/Alamy Stock Photo; **106** Orhan Cam/Shutterstock; **107** Carol M Highsmith/Library of Congress Prints and Photographs Division Washington [LC-DIG-highsm-09904]; **108** Science Source; **109** GL Archive/ Alamy Stock Photo; **111** Lanmas/Alamy Stock Photo; **112** The Metropolitan Museum of Art/Art Resource, NY; **118** Library of Congress Prints and Photographs Division Washington [LC-DIG-ppmsca-31832]; **130** W H Jackson/MPI/Getty Images; **132T** Prisma Archivo/Alamy Stock Photo; **132B** Underwood Archives/Getty Images; **134** Carol M. Highsmith/ Library of Congress Prints and Photographs Division [LC-DIG-highsm-27900]; **135** World History Archive/Alamy Stock Photo; **137** World History Archive/Alamy Stock Photo; **142** Heritage Image Partnership Ltd/Alamy Stock Photo; **155** Hulton Archive/ Getty Images; **158** Niday Picture Library/Alamy Stock Photo; **160** UIG/Underwood Archives/Akg-images; **161** North Wind Picture Archives/Alamy Stock Photo; **162** Courtesy of the New York Public Library; **163** North Wind Picture Archives/ Alamy Stock Photo; **165** Hulton Archive/Getty Images; **166** Picture History/Newscom; **167** American Anti-Slavery Society/Library of Congress Rare Book and Special Collections Division Washington [LC-USZC4-5321]; **176** Photo12/UIG/ Getty Images; **184** John Parrot/Stocktrek Images/Alamy Stock Photo; **186** Katherine Frey/The Washington Post/Getty Images; **187** Everett Collection Inc/Alamy Stock Photo; **188** Abraham Lincoln (1809–65) in public debate with Stephen A. Douglas (1813–61) in Illinois, 1858 (colour litho), American School, (19th century)/Private Collection/Peter Newark American Pictures/Bridgeman Art Library; **189** The New York Historical Society/Getty Images; **191** H.Armstrong Roberts/ClassicStock/ Alamy Stock Photo; **192** Abraham Lincoln with Allan Pinkerton and Major General John A. McClernand, 1862 (b/w photo), Gardner, Alexander (1821–82)/Collection of the New-York Historical Society, USA/Bridgeman Art Library; **193** Lawcain/ Fotolia; **198** Jerry Pinkney/National Geographic Creative/ Alamy Stock Photo; **210** LOC Photo/Alamy Stock Photo; **213** Charles Sumner (1811–74), US Senator; photo by George Warren, Boston (albumen print), American Photographer, (19th century)/American Antiquarian Society, Worcester, Massachusetts, USA/Bridgeman Art Library; **214** Lightfoot/ Getty Images; **215** Universal Images Group North America LLC/Encyclopaedia Britannica, Inc./Library of Congress/Alamy Stock Photo; **217** MPI/Getty Images; **219** Artokoloro Quint Lox Limited/Alamy Stock Photo; **232** AKG Images; **235** Glasshouse Images/JT Vintage/Alamy Stock Photo; **236** Topham/The Image Works; **237** The Stampede, 1912 (oil on canvas), Leigh, William Robinson (1866–1955)/Private Collection/Peter Newark Western Americana/Bridgeman Art Library; **239** Andrey Yurlov/ Shutterstock; **246** MPI/Archive Photos/Getty Images; **255T** CSU Archives/Everett Collection/Alamy Stock Photo; **255B** SSPL/ Getty Images; **258** Topical Press Agency/Hulton Archive/ Getty Images; **260** Josef Hanus/Shutterstock; **261** Library of Congress Prints and Photographs Division Washington [LC-DIG-highsm-25215]; **262** Keystone-France/Gamma-Keystone/Getty Images; **263** North Wind Picture Archives/ Alamy Stock Photo; **266** Photo Researchers, Inc/Alamy Stock Photo; **267** Bettmann/Getty Images; **270T** FPG/Archive Photos/ Getty Images; **270B** Sausage department at Armour and Company's meatpacking factory, Chicago, Illinois, USA. Men and boys stuffing sausage skins. Photograph c1893./Universal History Archive/UIG/Bridgeman Art Library; **284** PF-(usna)/ Alamy Stock Photo; **286** Rolf Richardson/Alamy Stock Photo; **287** Library of Congress Prints and Photographs Division Washington [LC-USZC4-10232]; **288** Library of Congress Prints and Photographs Division Washington [LC-USZ62-108295]; **289** Everett Historical/Shutterstock; **291** US Japan Fleet, Commodore Perry carrying 'The Gospel of God' to the Heathen, 1853 (oil on canvas), Evans, James Guy (19th Century)/Chicago History Museum, USA/Bridgeman Art Library; **300** Everett Historical/Shutterstock; **312** Heritage Image Partnership Ltd/ Stapleton Historical Collection/Alamy Stock Photo; **314** UbjsP/ Shutterstock; **315** Library of Congress Prints and Photographs Division Washington [LC-DIG-ppmsca-23061]; **316** Library of Congress Prints and Photographs Division Washington [LC-DIG-fsa-8b29516]; **317** Keystone Pictures USA/Alamy Stock Photo; **319** Library of Congress Prints and Photographs Division Washington [LC-USZ62-68542]; **320** Everett Collection/CSU Archives/Newscom; **328T** INTERFOTO/Alamy Stock Photo; **328B** H. Armstrong Roberts/ClassicStock/Alamy Stock Photo; **340** PhotoQuest/Getty Images; **342** National Archives and Records Administration; **343** Lordprice Collection/Alamy Stock Photo; **345** INTERFOTO/Alamy Stock Photo; **347** Department of Defense. Department of the Navy. Naval Photographic Center/National Archives and Records Administration; **348** MasPix/Alamy Stock Photo; **349** U.S. Navy/The LIFE Picture Collection/Getty Images; **356T** John Parrot/Stocktrek Images/Getty Images; **356B** Buyenlarge/Archive Photos/Getty Images; **362** Universal History Archive/UIG/Getty images; **364** Bettmann/Getty Images; **366** Everett Collection Historical/ Alamy Stock Photo; **367** AP Images; **370** CSU Archives/ Everett Collection/Alamy Stock Photo; **390** Peter De Jong/AP Images; **392** Robert R. McElroy/Archive Photos/Getty Images; **393** Tom McHugh/Science Source; **394** Wally McNamee/ Corbis historical/Getty Images; **395** Fotosearch/Archive Photos/Getty Images; **397** Ira Schwartz/AP Images; **399** WDC Photos/Alamy Stock Photo; **407** Michael Stravato/AP Images; **410** Triff/Shutterstock; **412** Charles O. Cecil/Alamy Stock Photo; **413** WDG Photo/Shutterstock; **414** Kyodo/AP Images; **415** Bokehart/Shutterstock; **417** RosaIreneBetancourt 1/Alamy Stock Photo; **418** Hemis/Alamy Stock Photo.